W9-BYH-693

W9-BYH-693

The
CIVIL WAR
CATALOG

The CIVIL WAR CATALOG

EDITED BY ANTONY SHAW

COURAGE BOOKS

AN IMPRINT OF RUNNING PRESS
PHILADELPHIA • LONDON

© 2003 Salamander Books Ltd
64 Brewery Road
London N7 9NY
England

A member of **Chrysalis** Books plc

This edition published in the United States by Courage Books, an imprint of
Running Press Book Publishers
125 South Twenty-second Street
Philadelphia, Pennsylvania 19103-4399

All rights reserved under the Pan-American and International Copyright Conventions.
Printed in China

This book may not be reproduced in whole or in part, in any form or by any means, electronic
or mechanical, including photocopying, recording, or by any information storage and retrieval
system or hereafter invented, without written permission from the publisher.

9 8 7 6 5 4 3 2 1

ISBN 0-7624-1625-4

CREDITS

Editor: Antony Shaw
Consultant: Paul Brewer
Designer: John Heritage
Indexer: Alan Rutter
Production: Ian Hughes
Color Production: Anorax Imaging Ltd

This book may be ordered by mail from the publisher.
But try your bookstore first!

Visit us on the web!
www.runningpress.com

ADDITIONAL CAPTIONS
Page 1: 8th Texas Cavalry, "Terry's Texas Rangers", of the Confederate States' Army.
Page 2: A group of Union general officers photographed by Mathew Brady.
Page 3: Regulation drums from New York, Vermont, and Massachusetts regiments.
Page 5: A Cook and Brother musketoon, with ramrod.

CONTENTS

INTRODUCTION

THE AMERICAN CIVIL WAR REMAINS THE COUNTRY'S central national epic, having changed the fledgling "Union" into the "United States". The wounds of that devastating internecine conflict of a century and a half ago have largely healed over, but there remains a seemingly insatiable desire to learn more of the circumstances and the detail of the war.

There were 2,000 battles of varying sizes, from small skirmishes between a handful of troops, to full-scale battles involving up to 200,000 soldiers and more, the greatest military clashes every witnessed on this side of the equator. Around 5,085 separate regiments, battalions, companies, legions, and batteries served in the American Civil War.

The Industrial Revolution gave a new and bloody dimension to the war. Weaponry capable of new levels of destructiveness appeared. Mass production techniques and the railroad ensured the mass armies of North and South could be issued with these deadly weapons and be supplied with the necessary ordnance to sustain their rapid rates of fire.

Above: *A Union Army powder flask.*

Right: *Congressional Medal of Honor holder Sergeant Major Christian Fleetwood, 5th Colored Troops, 3rd Division, 18th Army Corps. He received the medal for bravery at Chaffin's Farm, near Richmond, in 1864.*

Below: *An Illinois battery at Chattanooga with their wives.*

Right: *Troops of Joseph Hooker's army (Brook's division of John Sedgwick's Sixth Corps) entrenched along the banks of the Rappanannock River in May 1863, during the Chancellorsville campaign. Frequently, however, this image is mistakenly captioned as an 1864 view of men under fire in the trenches about Petersburg.*

The war involved great feats of engineering—some of which had actually been completed before the outbreak of hostilities. These included amazing bridges and formidable fortifications. Transport was crucial to the movement of men and supplies. Railroads were a vital strategic consideration for both sides. Rivers and canals were also crucial transport arteries. Horses and mules remained the basic form of land transportation. Most traffic, however, was made up of columns of marching soldiers. Communications were also maintained by the telegraph which played a key part in the conflict.

Many of the men who rushed to enlist after the outbreak of the conflict anticipated a short and glorious conflict to defeat the opposing side. In reality, the war became a protracted struggle absorbing 3 million men and leaving a trail of devastation across large parts of the country. Almost every area would become involved, either as a battlefield, military supply center, training ground, naval base, or besieged township. While the war was fought by Johnny Reb and Billy Yank their communities and families would often become embroiled in the conflict.

The bold photographers who went into the theaters of war brought details fo the conflict home with their vivid images of the dead. These men carried their cameras onto the battlefield and into the camps. They recorded the great commanders, the ordinary enlisted men, the weapons, the death and devastation. Their photographs caused a sensation. For the first time the ordinary Americans far away from the front line were able to see images of the carnage and suffering of war.

This book explores this momentous period in American history, beginning with an account of the war and then examining the personalities, forces, and weaponry of the era. Of particular interest are the chapters dealing with the naval forces who served on the steamy rivers and coastal seas. Their experience—albeit sometimes uneventful—are often overlooked. The sizable collection of historic photographs and drawing, modern artworks and views of the battlefields, plus a fine collection of artifact shots, provide a wonderful visual catalog of the conflict that shook the nation.

ANTONY SHAW

A NATION DIVIDED 1861–65

THE CIVIL WAR WAS THE CULMINATION OF YEARS of division and political conflict between the largely agrarian South and the industrialized North. After almost a century of agitation, over issues that went back practically to the very foundation of the original colonies, it seemed inevitable that the descendants of those colonies, the states, should come to blows. It was a war that would employ the very latest in military technology to wreak death and destruction on the combatants.

Above: Union Light Artillery shako, with stamped metal insignia.

Right: The winter quarters of William T. Sherman's troops during their March to the Sea following the capture of Atlanta in the Fall of 1864. In the course of this march, Sherman cut himself off from his source of supplies, planning for his troops to live off the land as they cut a path through Georgia.

A LARGE COUNTRY WITH VAST territories yet untamed, a nation with sections that differed in climate, economy and attitudes about government, and a nation of fiercely independent people: that was the United States in the 19th century. Clash was inevitable—predestined—as this young country in the international arena emerged from a New World wilderness to a new world power. In the North, there was rapid industrialization. In the South, an agricultural economy based largely on cotton, with a plantation system and slave labor, remained dominant.

There were divisions even within the chief geographical areas of North and South.

In the Northeast, principally New York, Pennsylvania and in the New England states, were the intellectual and moralist leaders—the "very civilized" as it were, the philosophers of the day. And there "too were the cultural and chief financial centers of the young country. Money talked. West of the Allegheny Mountains and the Ohio River were the northern tier of states carved from the wilderness: Ohio, Indiana, Illinois, Wisconsin, Michigan, part of Minnesota. They were not among

the original 13 colonies, and because these states were the offspring of the great American experiment in democracy, people of this region were particularly prideful of and loyal to the Union of states.

Below the Mason-Dixon Line—the generally accepted boundary between North and South—the heavy cotton-producing states of the Deep South differed in attitude and outlook from states of the Upper South, where slavery was not as predominant. The population of the Upper South was less than 30 per-

cent slaves, while in the Deep South slaves accounted for almost half the population (47 percent), and over half in the States of Mississippi (55 percent) and South Carolina (57 percent). Diverse interests, diverse attitudes. The situation was volatile as the mid-19th century approached.

As new states entered the Union the question was: slave or free? From this controversy came Fugitive Slave Laws, the Compromise of 1850, the Kansas-Nebraska Act (which gave rise to the violent era known as "Bleeding Kansas"),

the Dred Scott Decision, and a host of other legislative and judicial measures designed to quell growing sectional unrest over slavery, but that generally led to more bitterness. Tossed into the mix of debate was the question of state rights versus a strong central government, and even whether the western railroad expansion should be from Northern or Southern cities.

Two events of the late 1850s helped force matters from the political arena to the battlefield. In October 1859, the militant abolitionist, John Brown, came

east from Kansas and attempted to create a guerrilla army of runaway slaves in Appaliachia by seizing the Federal armory at Harpers Ferry. He failed miserably, for

Below left: *President Lincoln was known as "Father Abraham". Like the patriarch of the Old Testament, he was perceived as leading a people to freedom.*

Below: *African-American slaves in the South. The issue of slavery split the nation and led to the formation of the Confederate States of America in February 1861.*

many reasons, not the least of which was that there were few slaves in northwestern Virginia. United States troops under Colonel Robert E. Lee took Brown into custody. He was tried and sentenced to hang by a Virginia court. Among the crowd that gathered to watch the execution, which gave the abolitionist movement a martyr, was a young actor named Booth, who this day wore a borrowed uniform of the Virginia militia, but who would one day don the cloak of an assassin.

The second development that brought the nation closer to war was the rise of the Republican party, which began life as a ragbag of anti-slavery Democrats and Nativists, and northern Whigs. The election of Abraham Lincoln, the Republican candidate, in November 1860, was considered by the Deep South to be a victory for abolition and Northern financial interests. As a result, on December 20, the State of South Carolina declared its ties with the Union dissolved. Compromise had failed. A nation moved toward war.

The first quarter of the year was one of great uncertainty, apprehension, and political double-crossing. It became a test of wills early on as the State of South Carolina plucked its star from the flag of the United States and declared itself an independent nation, demanding that the Federal government relinquish all claims to military facilities in the state. The focus was on on Fort Sumter in the middle of Charleston Harbor, where Major Robert Anderson and his small Federal garrison were pawns in a political chess game of impending civil war. Anderson and his men, not more than 120 in number,

including 34 civilian workmen, had been holed up in the fort since the day after Christmas, after moving from nearby Fort Moultrie on Sullivan's Island, which had been deemed too vulnerable to assault from the mainland. The garrison had not been supplied or reinforced, and its capacity to wage war, even to defend itself, dwindled with each passing day, while the "enemy's" grew, as the Carolinians ringed the harbor with guns and fortifications.

If the hapless Sumter garrison looked to Washington for help, the men soon realized that the lame duck occupant of the White House, James Buchanan, wanted nothing more than for the final days of his term to slip away rapidly and without incident. Let the president-elect sort out the mess, Buchanan reasoned. After all, was it not the election of Abraham Lincoln that had sparked the whole crisis of secession? If Buchanan attempted to supply and reinforce Fort Sumter, the "Fire-eaters" (radical secessionist) in South Carolina could claim an act of war. General Winfield Scott, 73 years old, and chief of all United States' forces, cautioned against resupplying the Fort Sumpter under armed escort. Send a merchant vessel, a very fast one, Winfield Scott advised. It was not as threatening. Tensions mounted everywhere. In Georgia,

Below left: *The Confederate National Flag, First Pattern, was adopted by the Provisional Congress of Confederate States on March 4, 1861. It was never authorized by law.*

Below right: *The flag of the 8th Regiment Virginia Volunteer Infantry was presented to the unit by General Beauregard for valiant service at Ball's Bluff (Leesburg) in October 1861.*

militia troops took over the high-walled, moated Fort Pulaski, which guarded the sea route to the waterfront of old Savannah. Also, the nation's capital, nestled squarely in the lap of secessionist sympathy, was said to be in peril of invasion by marauders. Federal arsenals at Mount Vernon, Alabama, and Apalachicola, Florida, were declared properties of those respective states, though both were still in the Union. Then, on January 9, Mississippi seceded, followed over the next two days by Florida and Alabama, then Georgia on the

19th, Louisiana on the 26th, and Texas on February 1. These were the states of the Deep South, where King Cotton ruled, and where the Federal threat to the region's economy and way of life loomed greatest.

Meanwhile, President Buchanan was plagued by double-dealing in his own cabinet. The fast merchant vessel recommended by General Scott, *Star of the West*, had left New York for Fort Sumter on January 5. News of its departure and mission reached South Carolina through the offices of Jacob Thompson, a Mississippian who was also Secretary of

the Interior in Buchanan's shaky cabinet. Thompson telegraphed Charleston that *Star of the West* was on its way with troops and supplies for Fort Sumter, then he resigned his cabinet post and headed south. This incident followed close on the heels of the resignation of Secretary of War John B. Floyd, a Virginian by birth and alumnus of South Carolina College. He had apparently attempted to aid the Southern Cause by stockpiling ordnance in Southern-based installations which, presumably, would soon be seized by the secessionists. Floyd resigned his powerful

cabinet position on December 29. Five days later the War Department cancelled one of Floyd's orders to ship guns south from a Pittsburgh arsenal. The country was falling apart.

When *Star of the West* steamed into Charleston Harbor on the morning of January 9, a battery on Morris Island let loose with a salvo. The message was all too clear. It didn't matter whether supplies came by warship or merchant vessel or rowboat. Any attempt to assist the Fort Sumter garrison, according to South Carolina Governor Francis Pickens, would

be considered an act of war.

On February 4, a convention of the seven seceded states met at the Alabama state capitol in Montgomery and organized a provisional government called the Confederate States of America. After five days of debate, Jefferson Davis, a former U.S. Senator from Mississippi and one-time Secretary of War (who neither sought nor relished a post in the fledgling government of the South), became provisional president. Georgia's Alexander H. "Little Aleck" Stephens (he reputedly weighed a scant 90 pounds) was selected

as vice president. Neither man was considered a radical secessionist, or "Fire-eater," so choosing them to head the Southern government seemed to be

Below left: *Pierre Gustave Toutant Beauregard, the Confederate officer whose batteries opened fire on Fort Sumter in April 1861. This marked the start of the Civil War.*

Below: *Joseph E. Johnston was the Confederate officer who joined forces with Beauregard to defeat the Federals at the Battle of First Manassas in July 1861.*

intended to appeal to the Upper South states, still sitting on the secession fence. It was still a game of politics. No one had been killed yet.

Abraham Lincoln, after avoiding alleged plots to kill him in Baltimore, while en route to Washington from his Illinois home, was inaugurated as the 16th President of the United States on March 4. Lincoln pledged in his inaugural address not to interfere with slavery where it existed. Furthermore, he declared the secession ordinances of the seven departed states null and void, because it was uncon-

stitutional to attempt the dissolution of the Union. And he challenged his "dissatisfied fellow countrymen" in the South that the onus of civil war, should it come, would be upon their shoulders, not the new administration's. Reaction from the South was quick and sharp. Every word of Lincoln's address was construed as nothing short of a declaration of war.

War was not long in coming. On March 29, Lincoln pledged to save Fort Sumter, as well as pledging aid for threatened Fort Pickens at Pensacola, Florida. Three warships and a revenue cutter prepared to

sail. On April 6, official notification of the relief expedition was made to Governor Pickens, who now shared the leadership limelight at Charleston with General Pierre Gustave Toutant Beauregard, the recently appointed commander of all Confederate military forces in the area. All of Charleston and its harbor environs were placed on military alert.

On the 11th a formal demand for the surrender of Fort Sumter was made to Major Anderson by three emissaries under a white flag of truce. He attempted to skirt the surrender issue by stating he'd soon be

starved out, so why resort to armed aggression? The three Confederates weren't prepared for this sort of response, so they rowed back to the mainland to confer with higher officials. By eleven o'clock that night they were back at Fort Sumter, asking Anderson just how long it would be before he was starved out. His answer: the 15th—he'd evacuate the fort at noon on the 15th of April. That was totally unacceptable. Everyone knew a relief expedition was on its way and would surely arrive before the 15th. The emissaries put Anderson on notice that

guns would open on him in one hour. At 4:30 a.m., April 12, 1861, the guns fired, and the American Civil War began.

After a 34-hour bombardment, Major Anderson, on the afternoon of April 13, ran up a white surrender flag. Meanwhile, the relief expedition had arrived at the harbor mouth, but dared go no further. The ships watched helplessly as Fort Sumter was pounded, then they steamed away with all the supplies. Anderson formally surrendered on the 14th, which cost the life of one soldier when a salute gun exploded. He was the only casualty of

the opening engagement of the war.

On April 15, President Lincoln called for 75,000 volunteers to put down the insurrection. States in the Upper South

Below left: *Troops under canvas at Blackburn's Ford, Bull Run. The First Battle of Bull Run in 1861 was a Confederate victory. The Union was again beaten on the battlefield in 1862.*

Below: *A Union Navy flotilla bombards Fort Henry on the Tennessee River in 1862. This was the first major naval engagement of the American Civil War.*

thought his actions were too rash and uncalculated in the circumstances. Talk of secession conventions became rampant, and before the month was out Virginia—the Old Dominion—had cast its lot with the new Confederacy, followed in May by Arkansas and North Carolina, and Tennessee in June. Young men answered the call of their states, North and South, and fields, shops and factories emptied as military ranks swelled with youthful bravado, everyone eager for fighting and glory. Many predicted it would all be over soon—one big battle would settle it—and no one wanted to miss out.

Washington was in turmoil. It seemed as if no worse place could have been found for the nation's capital. Across the Potomac River was Virginia, just seceded from the Union. Surrounding the capital on its other sides was Maryland, a state seething with secessionist sympathies to the point that a firefight had broken out between armed citizens and Massachusetts troops who were marching through Baltimore on their way to Washington. About a dozen people lost their lives in the Baltimore Riot of April 19, which was finally quelled by force of arms.

General Scott had complained on numerous occasions of the inadequate Regular Army of the United States, with hardly enough men in uniform (fewer than 20,000) for peacetime necessities. His opinion was justified as Lincoln looked upon his legions of green warriors. But sufficient time was not at hand to allow these boys proper training.

Rebel forces (just as untrained) under Generals Joseph E. Johnston and Beauregard, posed a real threat in Virginia. Johnston was in the strategic

Shenandoah Valley, a perfect invasion corridor aimed at Washington that would become a constant battleground of the war, while Beauregard's force was at Manassas, near the Federal capital city.

Union General Irvin McDowell was prodded to deal with the threat. Exasperated by meddling politicians and the urgency of public opinion, he finally set his army in motion long before it was properly trained and organized. They met the Rebels along Bull Run, near Manassas, on July 21. McDowell's plan was well thought out: defeat Beauregard before he could join forces with Johnston. But luck was against McDowell, for Johnston's men arrived in time to turn the tide of battle. It was a very confused clash, often characterized as a battle between two mobs, as the inexperience of both armies was all too evident. To make matters worse, some Confederate units wore blue uniforms, and some Federal units wore gray, and the two sides had flags so similar in color and features that after the battle the Confederates designed a new, more distinctive one. The Confederates won this first significant engagement, and one commander, Thomas J. Jackson, earned the nickname "Stonewall," ironically for a defensive stand his men had made, when Jackson's forte would prove to be

Below: *Fort Donelson, on the Cumberland River, was captured by the troops of Ulysses S. Grant on the afternoon of February 16, 1862. Fort Henry on the Tennessee River was captured the same month. This gave Grant access to both waterways, providing paths straight into the Confederacy's heartland. The foe had no choice but to abandon all of Kentucky and almost all of central and west Tennessee.*

lightning marches and audacious attacks. The Yankees were swept from the field in an embarrassing retreat.

After the Battle of Manassas, or Bull Run as it was called in the North, both sides settled into a period of fortifying, training and stockpiling supplies, as the realization dawned on everyone that this would not be a quick, one-battle war. The Confederates, heartened by their recent victory, moved as close to Washington as Centreville, but still a respectful distance away. Southern spirits further in August when news arrived of a victory at Wilson's Creek in Missouri, in which the Union General Nathaniel Lyon, was killed.

The North, stinging from defeat and humiliation, nevertheless was stronger in its commitment to avenge the losses. General Scott was quietly shelved as an old soldier well past his prime.

He was replaced by the swaggering, 34-year-old General George B. McClellan, recent victor in a sideshow campaign in northwestern Virginia. George McClellan, known as "Little Mac" or, as time went by, the "Young Napoleon," set about drilling and refitting his command, which was called the Army of the Potomac, and generally bragging himself into an inflated status, one that he would prove incapable of fulfiling.

West of the Alleghenies, Confederates under General Leonidas Polk violated Kentucky's self-proclaimed neutrality in early September by marching into Columbus and erecting a stronghold overlooking the Mississippi River. A few miles upriver, at Cairo, Illinois, where the Ohio River met the Mississippi, General Ulysses S. Grant commanded a small Federal force. In response to Polk's

occupation of Columbus, Grant, on September 6, seized Paducah, Kentucky, at the confluence of the Tennessee and Ohio rivers.

The following November, Grant dropped down the Mississippi with his men on steamboats to test the Columbus defenses. The result was the Battle of Belmont, Missouri, fought opposite the Columbus fortifications. The battle was a learning experience for the men and officers of both sides. Grant never forgot this early battlefield escapade, when his men lost control and nearly met disaster.

In command of Confederate forces in the West was General Albert Sidney Johnston. He had the unenviable task of holding a vast expanse of territory with inadequate numbers of troops. Johnston attempted to set up a defense in Kentucky, with Tennessee to his back. His line consisted of various forts and installations stretching from the Mississippi River "Gibraltar" at Columbus, through Bowling Green on the Barren River in south-central Kentucky, thence eastward to Cumberland Gap in the mountains on the border with Virginia. Two rivers cut

through Kentucky as potential invasion routes into Tennessee, so to defend these waterways the Confederacy built Fort Henry on the Tennessee River and Fort Donelson on the Cumberland River. Both of these forts were in northern Tennessee, near the Kentucky line, and had been sited before Kentucky's neutrality was violated.

The inadequacy of Johnston's line, as

Below: *The USS* Hartford, *Flag Officer David Farragut's flagship of the West Gulf Blockading Squadron, steams beyond Fort St. Philip during the naval battle of New Orleans in 1862.*

well as the incompetence of some of the officers under him, was made all too clear only 19 days into the new year. Confederate General Felix Zollicoffer, a newspaperman with little military experience, led a force of about 4,000 men out of the mountain protection of Cumberland Gap to a precarious position, with their backs to the Cumberland River, at a place called Mill Springs, or Logan Crossroads. There he was soundly whipped by a force under General George H. Thomas in a battle that cost Zollicoffer his life. For the Union, the nation's

confidence in the Western troops was strengthened. Pro-Confederate sympathies in Kentucky, a state severely divided in loyalties, was weakened.

Then, in rapid succession, U.S. Grant's forces, which included the river navy of Flag Officer Andrew H. Foote, captured Forts Henry and Donelson (on February 6 and 16, respectively). The Confederates evacuated Bowling Green and their Columbus fortifications, and then Nashville, the Tennessee capital city, was occupied by Federal forces on February 25. By June the Federals even held

Cumberland Gap. Further west, across the Mississippi in northwestern Arkansas, Confederate forces under General Earl Van Dorn were defeated in the battle of Pea Ridge, March 7-8, dashing their hopes of reestablishing a Confederate foothold in Missouri. Like Kentucky, Missouri was an important border state divided in loyalties.

On April 6, Albert Sidney Johnston tried a similar attempt to regain territory by launching a surprise attack from northern Mississippi against Grant's troops along the Tennessee River in southwestern Tennessee. Fighting was desperate around

Shiloh Church and the Yankees were pushed back steadily on the 6th, but, reinforced during the night, Grant managed to win the day on the 7th. The Battle of Shiloh was a close call for the emerging Union hero of the West, and with combined casualties of nearly 24,000, including General Johnston, the battle proved to both sides that this was going to be a long and bloody war.

Thus, 1862 opened with Union successes in the Western Theater, some of which were strategically decisive, and witnessed the emergence of Ulysses S. Grant, a man so full of self-doubt at the beginning of the war that he was certain no one would give him a command of any significance. One of the principal strategies of the Union was a blockade of Southern ports and the splitting of the Confederacy by seizing control of the Mississippi River. Grant's success in Kentucky and Tennessee contributed in no small degree to opening the Mississippi by loosening the Confederacy's grip on these vital areas. On March 14, Union General John Pope captured New Madrid, Missouri, and laid siege to nearby Island Number 10 in the Mississippi, which fell on April 7. By June the Federal fleet captured Memphis.

Operating against the other end of the river was a huge fleet under Flag Officer David G. Farragut, which began bombarding Forts Jackson and St. Philip

Below: *Thomas J. Jackson's forces struck the Orange and Alexandria Railroad on the evening of August 26, 1862, and captured the Union supply depot at Manassas Junction. This surprise move forced John Pope's Army of Western Virginia into an abrupt retreat.*

below New Orleans on April 18. A week later Farragut landed at New Orleans. And so began a long occupation of the Confederacy's largest city. Now only Vicksburg was an obstacle to the Union control of the "Father of Waters."

On the East Coast, the modern age of naval warfare was ushered in with the first clash of ironclad vessels as the USS *Monitor* and CSS *Virginia* (built from the hull of USS *Merrimack*) battled to a stalemate at Hampton Roads, near Norfolk, Virginia. Elsewhere along the Atlantic coast, Federal troops under General Ambrose E. Burnside made amphibious landings on the North Carolina shoreline and pushed inland and along the coast, seizing the port city of New Bern (March 14) and capturing Fort Macon (April 25).

In contrast to the brilliant successes of Union forces in the West, General McClellan's Army of the Potomac turned in a dismal record for 1862. Constantly prodded by Lincoln to do something at least threatening in the direction of the Confederates, still encamped at Centreville, not far from the capital, Little Mac seemed content to drill and organize, to the point that on March 11, he was demoted from General-in-Chief of all Federal armies (Scott's old job) to commander of just the Department and Army of the Potomac, still an enormous responsibility. When McClellan did get moving, he moved ponderously, giving "chase" to the retreating Confederate army of Joe Johnston as it fell back from Centreville to a new and presumably better position on the Rappahannock River. "On to Richmond!" became the battle cry of the Army of the Potomac.

When the Confederates in May 1861 relocated their seat of government to the Virginia capital of Richmond, it was predestined that the intervening ground would become blood-soaked before the war ended. But in his first major offensive, McClellan's approach was not overland, but seaward. In devising the Peninsula Campaign, he turned his back on Johnston's army in northern Virginia. Instead of a direct confrontation, McClellan loaded his massive army on transports for a trip to Union-held Fortress Monroe, on the tip of the peninsula between the York and James rivers. It was a tremendous undertaking, but the transfer of 100,000 men and ordnance was immaculately executed by McClellan, the master planner, and by April 5, he was laying siege to Yorktown. Nearly a month later he was still sitting before Yorktown, pleading for reinforcements, though he never held worse than a two-to-one edge over the Confederates during the whole campaign.

In order to hold the attention of Union forces in northern Virginia after Johnston's relocation, and to prevent reinforcements from being sent to McClellan, Confederates under Stonewall Jackson in the Shenandoah Valley created one of the finest strategic diversions in military

Below: *In February 1863, 19-year-old Colonel Charles Rivers Ellet, commander of the Union Ram Fleet, volunteered to attack the big Confederate steamer* City of Vicksburg. *Ellet put a pair of small Parrott guns on to the USS* Queen of the West *and banked her with cotton bales to make her shot-proof. Ellet successfully sped through heavy enemy fire, and mortally damaged the enemy steamer.*

history. Jackson's legendary "foot cavalry," managed in a series of lightning marches and surprise attacks to create the illusion of much greater numbers, and in so doing, in one month's time, tramped some 350 miles, fought five battles (McDowell on May 8, Front Royal on May 23, Winchester on the 25th, Cross Keys on June 8, and Port Republic on the 9th), in which three different Union armies were defeated, inflicted twice their own number of casualties, even though outnumbered two-to-one, or worse, and managed to hold the attention of an estimated 60,000 potential reinforcements for McClellan.

Once McClellan finally got his army moving on the Peninsula, he made good gains, entering an evacuated Yorktown on May 3. Pushing the Rebels out of Williamsburg (May 5th), by the end of the month Richmond was in sight. There Johnston finally turned to lash back at the pressing Federals, who were at the moment vulnerable, straddling the Chickahominy River east of Richmond. In the ensuing Battle of Seven Pines (or Fair Oaks), fought May 31–June 1, Johnston was severely wounded. He was replaced by President Davis' military advisor, General Robert E. Lee. The change in command would prove momentous.

It turned out that Lee had been the mastermind behind the Shenandoah Valley diversion, so ably executed by Stonewall Jackson. Their relationship would grow, for even the secretive Stonewall trusted Lee, and perhaps no one else. The Battle of Seven Pines ended in stalemate, and McClellan's army remained lurking on the outskirts of the Confederate capital. Lee went on the offensive. In a series of battles

known as the Seven Days, June 25-July 1, Robert E. Lee began to emerge as the premier commander of the South.

Skirmishing on June 25 proved indecisive. Meanwhile, Stonewall Jackson's men arrived from the Shenandoah Valley to reinforce Lee. The next day the Confederates struck hard at Mechanicsville. On the 27th, the Battle of Gaines' Mill was another offensive by the Army of Northern Virginia, which saw Federals again in retreat. At Savage Station (June 29th), McClellan's rear guard was struck, forcing him to leave

behind nearly 3,000 sick and wounded men. The Battle of Frayser's Farm (or White Oak Swamp) on June 30 was a confused fight in which Lee attempted a double-strike from the north and west through a desolate swamp. Lee's campaign to save the capital ended on July 1, at Malvern Hill. The ill-advised attacks in this battle were extremely costly for Lee and drew severe criticism.

The next phase of fighting in the Eastern Theater was the Second Manassas (or Bull Run) Campaign. The three forces of Union troops so roughly handled by Stonewall

Jackson in the Shenandoah were subsequently consolidated and styled the Army of Virginia. It was placed under General John Pope.

With McClellan's army still on the Peninsula below Richmond, Pope's mission was to march into Virginia and create a new front for the Confederates to contend with. Jackson had since joined

Below: *William T. Sherman's famous (or infamous) "bummers" scoured the countryside for food, booty, and contraband on the march through Georgia.*

Lee for the Seven Days. Nevertheless, with Jackson out of the way, Pope had ample space in which to operate. He started marching on July 14. In response, Lee demonstrated his contempt for McClellan, who was sitting largely inactive at his new base on the James River, by dispatching Jackson northward, soon followed by General A.P. Hill's troops, and eventually Lee's whole army.

The same northward shift soon occurred in McClellan's army, with significant consequences to Little Mac and the whole command structure. As units arrived back in Washington they were funnelled out to Pope and thus taken from McClellan's control. The resulting battles of Cedar Mountain (August 9), Groveton (August 28), Second Manassas (August 29-30), and Chantilly (September 1) constituted the one and only campaign of the short-lived Army of Virginia. Pope was soundly whipped by Lee's army, and the Yankees rushed to the Washington defenses.

Lincoln then made an important command decision. Lee had to be stopped; Confederates were again in position to threaten the capital. Despite not leading them to any great victories, McClellan was adored by most of his troops. Because of the current emergency he seemed the best choice. The Army of Virginia was dissolved, and McClellan resumed command of an even heftier Army of the Potomac. But what about Pope? Conveniently, during August the Sioux Indians had gotten restless in Minnesota. Off went Pope to Minnesota.

Late summer of 1862 saw three northward thrusts by the Confederates, none of which were successful. In early September, Lee raided north into

Maryland and came close to disaster. His plans had fallen into enemy hands, but the "enemy" was McClellan, who reacted predictably slowly, but he still managed to place Lee in a perilous situation with a huge Union army bearing down on the dangerously divided Confederate forces. Sharp fighting at South Mountain (September 14) held off the approaching Army of the Potomac long enough for Jackson to capture Harpers Ferry on the 15th. This allowed Lee to concentrate his army for a stand along Antietam Creek, at Sharpsburg, Maryland.

The battle there on September 17 was the bloodiest single day in American history, with 24,000 casualties in blue and gray. McClellan failed to smash Lee's much smaller army, but did force the Confederate leader to retreat back into Virginia, thus spoiling what ultimately proved to be the Confederacy's best prospects for British recognition. Lincoln used this victory to issue his Emancipation Proclamation against slavery.

Across the mountains, Confederate Generals Braxton Bragg and Edmund Kirby Smith struck north through Tennessee and Kentucky, nearly to the banks of the Ohio River, before squabbles between the two generals brought the invasion to a standstill. The Battle of Perryville (October 8) ended the otherwise successful invasion. It was a stalemate. In Mississippi a thrust intended to carry Confederate forces under Earl Van Dorn

Below: *The Army of the Potomac clashes with the Army of Northern Virginia at the Battle of the Wilderness in May 1864. After two days of desperate fighting the Confederates were finally forced to flee the battlefield.*

into western Tennessee was turned back by General William S. Rosecrans at Corinth (October 3-4.

The onset of winter didn't discourage military operations in 1862. At Prairie Grove, Arkansas (December 7) in the ongoing struggle for control of Missouri, Union forces under Generals James G. Blunt and Francis J. Herron defeated Confederates under General Thomas C. Hindman. Earl Van Dorn, whose defeat at Corinth had gotten him demoted to a cavalry commander, launched a successful raid on Grant's supply base at Holly

Springs, Mississippi (December 20). Grant, who was engaged in operations against Vicksburg, lost 1,500 men as prisoners at Holly Springs, and $1.5 million in supplies.

In the Virginia theater, Lincoln finally had all he could stand of McClellan's "slows" after Antietam, and on November 7 replaced him with Ambrose Burnside, who openly expressed doubts about his ability to command such a huge army. He proved himself right at the Battle of Fredericksburg (December 13) where the slaughter of his men in futile attacks was

so great that it prompted Lee to contemplate how one might grow too fond of war. In Tennessee, the year ended with fighting along the banks of Stones River near Murfreesboro. Union commander William Rosecrans emerged the victor. Bragg, his opponent, left the field on January 3.

For the Union, the year began and ended with victories in Tennessee. East of the mountains, though, Lee reigned supreme.

The new year opened with Lincoln's Emancipation Proclamation taking effect. For the moment it was largely a useless

document as far as the institution of slavery was concerned, but it was packed with political clout on the international front. It caused some upheaval in the armies of the North as soldiers re-evaluated their reasons for fighting—preserving the Union was one thing, an abolitionist crusade was another. As the document read, slaves in territories still at war with the United States were now called "free," but the Proclamation did not disturb slavery in areas behind Union lines. The moral and psychological impact of the Emancipation Proclamation was

hailed internationally as a bold and brilliant stroke for Lincoln.

The Union generals and their armies, not politicians, would be the great emancipators, conquering territory and thus freeing the slaves therein. This created huge caravans of blacks trailing behind the Western armies. Lincoln's proclamation also allowed former slaves to be admitted to the armed forces. Eventually an estimated 200,000 blacks entered Federal service, and Lincoln later claimed their participation contributed significantly to preserving the Union.

Some commanders, such as General William T. Sherman, refused to accept black units, except as garrison troops in rear areas, and he criticized government

Below left: *Brigadier General Alexander Hays was killed in the first day's fighting of the Battle of the Wilderness on May 5, 1864.*

Below: *Fortifications at Petersburg. Grant hoped to take Petersburg, below Richmond, and then approach the Confederate capital from the south. The bungling by General Benjamin Butler resulted in a 10-month siege.*

officials who attempted to recruit black regiments in his department. Black soldiers were never really accepted as equals by most of their white comrades in arms; their units were officered by whites, and until 1865 they were paid less than whites. Risks were greater in black units, too. The Confederate government decreed that white officers commanding black units were guilty of inciting slave uprisings and thus subject to execution if captured.

Meanwhile, at Fredericksburg General Burnside was still bringing shame to his Army of the Potomac with a miserable campaign that literally bogged down in the muck of a Virginia winter, entering the history books as "Burnside's Mud March." The general had overstayed his welcome and was replaced by General Joseph Hooker. The egotistical "Fighting Joe" had made his reputation at Antietam.

With the coming of spring Hooker stole a march on Lee and got behind him. Then, however, Hooker lost his nerve and allowed the Lee-Jackson team to out-general him at Chancellorsville, May 1-4, sending the Potomac boys heading for safety behind the Rappahannock River. It was yet another disaster for Union forces in the East. Lee boldly split his army three separate times in the face of a superior foe, and in the end a flanking force under Stonewall Jackson provided the decisive blow. Chancellorsville has been called Lee's greatest victory, though a very costly one. Mighty Stonewall was accidentally wounded by his own men and died of complications on May 10.

Lee reorganized his army from two corps to three for an invasion of the North, dividing Jackson's old corps between Generals Richard S. Ewell

(Second Corps) and A.P. Hill (Third), while James Longstreet retained command of the First Corps. In command of Lee's cavalry was General James Ewell Brown "Jeb" Stuart.

There were several reasons for Lee's invasion of the North. First and foremost, Virginia was trampled and desolate after two years of war. The Old Dominion needed a rest. By moving into Pennsylvania, Lee would relieve pressure on Richmond and his army could live off the enemy's land. Furthermore, a victory on Yankee soil might garner more support

for Northern Peace Democrats, known as "Copperheads." Most of these individuals sought a politically negotiated end to the war through certain concessions to the South, while at the extreme was the notion to allow the South to go its own way. That same victory might entice European recognition and support.

The beginning of their northward thrust was delayed and nearly exposed at its outset when Stuart was caught napping at Brandy Station, Virginia. Stuart had been lax with the dispositions of his units, allowing General Alfred Pleasonton's

Union horsemen to catch him fully unawares on June 9, the day the northward march was to commence. Only after hard fighting and superb leadership did Stuart manage a tactical victory in what was the largest cavalry fight on the North American continent.

The Army of Northern Virginia swept northward after Brandy Station. On June

Below: Confederate defensive works in front of Atlanta, Georgia. General John Bell Hood abandoned Atlanta on September 1, 1864. Sherman occupied the city the next day.

14–15 they whipped a Federal force under General Robert Milroy at Winchester in the Shenandoah. Confederates were across the Potomac and on Pennsylvania soil by June 24. There was one problem. The army was spread far and wide for strategic as well as foraging purposes. Stuart, the "eyes" of Lee's army, was off on another of his daring rides leaving Lee's infantry blind in enemy territory. Meanwhile, Hooker had been relieved of command of the Army of the Potomac and replaced by General George G. Meade (June 28). The Army of the Potomac gave pursuit and

Lee's invasion culminated in a chance meeting at the crossroads town of Gettysburg in south-central Pennsylvania.

In three days of desperate fighting, July 1-3, 1863, Meade's army turned back the best the South had to offer in the greatest battle of the war. Over 50,000 casualties resulted, and a turning point in the war was at hand: in addition to the Army of the Potomac's success at Gettysburg, another great Union victory was achieved in the West. While Lee began his retreat from Gettysburg (July 4), Ulysees Grant accepted the surrender of Vicksburg,

Mississippi, after a lengthy siege. Since early May, Grant had Vicksburg in his sights, with fighting at Port Gibson (May 1), Raymond (May 12), Jackson, the capital of Mississippi (May 14), Champion's Hill (May 16), and at the Big Black River (May 17). These engagements merely got Grant into position before Vicksburg, and the siege began on May 18. Siege operations were also underway at Port Hudson, Louisiana, lower down on the Mississippi, where the last Rebel garrison on the river held out until July 8. The Union now held the great river from

its headwaters in Minnesota to its mouth at the Gulf of Mexico.

Elsewhere in the South, Union attacks on Fort Wagner near Charleston, South Carolina brought into battle one of the first black units raised in the North, the 54th Massachusetts. The July 18th assault was very costly to the regiment and failed to take the fort. A month later, on August 17, in a reversal of roles from the opening guns of the war, Union batteries erupted on Confederate-occupied Fort Sumter, Fort Wagner and Battery Gregg. The bombardment continued in earnest

through the 23rd. After 5,000 rounds the Confederates miraculously still held out. Sporadic fire continued until the 27th, with still no white flag at Fort Sumter; however, the Confederates evacuated Fort Wagner on Morris Island on September 6. Two days later, a heroic stand was made by a handful of determined Texans, manning a mud fort. They turned back an amphibious invasion force at Sabine Pass.

In the North, draft riots in New York City claimed lives and property. The summer of 1863 also saw a new star added to the flag of the United States as

delegates in western Virginia elected to form their own state, West Virginia, loyal to the Union. Confederate General John Hunt Morgan raided through Ohio in July and did more damage than good for the Southern cause. The majority of his command was eventually captured, including Morgan himself, and his raid

Below: Confederate works at Potter House, Atlanta, in 1864. After three and a half months of maneuvering and hard fighting, the Union forces forced the Confederates to abandon Atlanta, their munitions center.

through "Copperhead country" created such a scare that many Peace Democrats converted to staunch avengers. Three months later they helped elect a strong war governor in Ohio.

In Kansas, Confederate guerrilla William C. Quantrill exercised no manly restraint in an August raid on the anti-slavery town of Lawrence. Quantrill's force was more of a gang than an organized military unit. Veterans of this border violence would write a new chapter in American history—with names like Jesse and Frank James.

Things remained surprisingly quiet in Tennessee after the Battle of Stones River (or Murfreesboro), which had concluded January 2, and left the Union in possession of the battlefield. As Grant plotted the fall of Vicksburg and the Army of the Potomac fought one major battle and was on the verge of another in the East, General Rosecrans sat with his army at Murfreesboro, fortifying, and raising fears in Washington that Lincoln might have another McClellan on his hands. Bragg's Army of Tennessee was concentrated in and around Tullahoma, Tennessee, less than 40 miles

away, and it was feared in Washington that Bragg might send reinforcements to Vicksburg unless he were otherwise occupied. Rosecrans prepared to move against Bragg.

The Tullahoma Campaign, (June 23-July 3) was extremely well executed by the Union commander, incurring few casualties as he outmaneuvered Bragg at every step, forcing the Confederates over the Tennessee River into Chattanooga, near the Georgia border. Rosecrans stopped pursuit and waited a month and a half before attempting to wrestle Bragg

out of his new position. Again after some prodding by Washington, Rosecrans planned a new offensive that would take his army across the Tennessee River south and west of Chattanooga and trap Bragg between his army and a force under General Burnside moving south from Kentucky into East Tennessee. Bragg evacuated Chattanooga on September 6, and on that day Burnside occupied Knoxville. Maneuvering and blundering culminated in the Battle of Chickamauga, September 19-20 in North Georgia. Reinforced by most of James Longstreet's

corps of Lee's army, Bragg drove the Union army from the field just when Southern spirits needed a lift. Rosecrans limped into Chattanooga, in the shadow of Lookout Mountain. The town proved to be a strong defensive position, but he was now trapped by the mountains, the Tennessee River, and Bragg's army.

The Confederates occupied Lookout Mountain and Missionary Ridge and appeared immovable. Bragg laid siege and Rosecrans was stymied. A change in command was necessary. General Grant arrived (October 23) as the new

department commander, and General George H. Thomas succeeded Rosecrans as army commander. By the end of the month a "cracker line" was open, bringing ample supplies into the city. Reinforced with troops from other theaters, Grant soon launched a series of attacks to break out of Chattanooga.

On November 24, troops under General Hooker scaled Lookout Mountain and fought what has been called the Battle

Below: *The Federal supply depot at Johnsonville, Texas, in December 1864.*

Above the Clouds, because of the dense fog clinging to the mountainsides. Next morning the Stars and Stripes fluttered conspicuously from high atop Lookout Mountain. Later that day Union forces struck the Confederates on Missionary Ridge. Momentum on the Federals' part, and apprehension among the Confederates turned the attack into a foot race as charging Yankees swept startled Rebels completely from the ridge. Bragg's retreat did not stop until Dalton, Georgia, and all of Chattanooga belonged to Grant. It would serve as a base for further operations into Georgia and the all-important Confederate supply center at Atlanta.

The American Civil War was two and a half years old. There were green troops entering the ranks daily but they lined up next to battle-hardened veterans of countless engagements. The whole complexion of warfare as the world knew it was changing. By 1864 men's hearts and minds had grown cold, their actions machine-like on the march and in battle, and the glory of war no longer held as much fascination as in those early days back in 1861. In short, they were better killers now.

One instance of putting harsh necessity ahead of humanitarian instincts was the Union's decision to halt prisoner exchanges in order to exploit the South's manpower shortage. New prisons were built and old ones expanded in an attempt to accommodate the anticipated influx of prisoners, North and South, as the campaign season drew near.

Feeding and supplying an army were constant logistics headaches: cut an army's supply line and it would have to retreat.

That notion was tested in February and March as General William T. Sherman embarked on a campaign from Vicksburg across the State of Mississippi to Meridian on the Alabama border, generally destroying railroads and other resources in central Mississippi that the Confederacy might need. In the unusual, one-month, statewide march to Meridian and back, Sherman fought several skirmishes, took 400 prisoners, destroyed miles and miles of track, burned countless bales of cotton, commandeered 3,000 horses and mules, and all the while mostly lived off the enemy civilian population. It was a lesson that Sherman learned well and would try again on a larger scale.

Something else Sherman learned was that the South had a remarkable cavalry commander named Nathan Bedford Forrest, who fought from instinct rather than formal training. In conjunction with Sherman's trek across Mississippi he was to have been assisted by a cavalry force of 7,000 under General William Sooy Smith raiding south from Memphis. Smith never arrived. Hampered by the pesky Forrest, Smith tangled with him at West Point, Mississippi, on February 20, and he was soundly whipped by the Confederate commander on the 22nd at Okolona, one of Forrest's brightest moments. Forrest is

Bottom: *Flag of the 1st and 3rd Regiments, Florida Volunteer Infantry, issued in 1864.*

Top: *Flag of the 57th Regiment, Georgia Volunteer Infantry.*

Below: *State Regimental Color of the 138th Pennsylvania Volunteer Infantry who were stationed before Petersburg in 1864.*

considered by many to be the best horse soldier in American history.

Meanwhile, U.S. Grant was promoted to the revived grade of lieutenant general and placed in command of all Federal armies. He decided to locate his headquarters in the field, in the East with Meade's Army of the Potomac. Now the premier commander in the West would meet the premier commander in the East. Robert E. Lee of course had seen enemy generals come and go. The last one who had come from the West was John Pope. The last anyone had heard of him, he was way up in Minnesota fighting the Sioux.

The Army of the Potomac, under Grant's direction but still technically commanded by General Meade, left its winter camp around Culpeper, Virginia, and crossed the Rapidan River on May 4, entering a marshy tangle of trees and underbrush known as the "Wilderness." Lee struck ferociously and this set the tone for the rest of the campaign as tough veterans fought desperately at close quarters. The usual response to such a brutal and confused match as this was a hasty retrograde by the Army of the

Potomac to refit and reorganize. But not with Grant supervising things. He plunged ahead, and the rank and file cheered him.

Grant's Overland Campaign stalled for two weeks in May at Spotsylvania Court House as Lee's army constructed elaborate fieldworks and prepared to fight and die. Many did, and casualties mounted on both sides at a staggering rate as Grant vowed to fight it out on this line if it took all summer. Finally Lee pulled out and gave ground slowly as the Army of Northern Virginia fell back. The two armies battled constantly from

Spotsylvania to the North Anna River, then Cold Harbor, then, by mid-June, to the James River and Petersburg, below Richmond, where the Confederates dug in for a do-or-die stand to protect their capital. Grant resorted to siege operations and he'd spend the next nine months confronting Lee on this line.

Considerable drama was provided along the siege lines on July 30, when the Federals exploded a mine under the Confederate works where the lines were very close together. The blast tossed humans, parts of fieldworks and huge chunks of earth into the air. The resulting attack, in which a number of black units participated, was horribly unsuccessful and Lee's troops quickly sealed the breach in their line. The affair entered the history books as the Battle of the Crater.

Grant's cavalry was under another commander brought from the West, General Philip Sheridan. Dispatched toward Richmond while Grant was stalled at Spotsylvania, Sheridan fought Stuart's cavalry at Yellow Tavern, north of the Confederate capital (May 11). Stuart was mortally wounded at Yellow Tavern and died the next day. A month later Sheridan was defeated by Stuart's successor, General Wade Hampton, at Trevilian Station as the Union force raided railroads in Lee's rear.

In the West, where General Sherman assumed overall command with Grant's departure for the East, the invasion of Georgia was about to begin from the Federal base at Chattanooga. The key to the campaign was control of the railroads. Several of them criss-crossed at Atlanta,

Below: *A dead Rebel at Petersburg in 1865. This is how the war ended for so many young men.*

bringing in and shipping out supplies to points all over the South. One railroad, the Western & Atlantic, led south from Chattanooga to Atlanta. Along this route Sherman would advance. He had three armies under him: George Thomas' Army of the Cumberland, James B. McPherson's Army of the Tennessee, and John M. Schofield's tiny Army of the Ohio. All told, the three armies were still smaller than the Army of the Potomac, but larger than the Confederates' Army of Tennessee, still at Dalton. But Braxton Bragg had long since departed, resigning after the Missionary

Ridge debacle to become President Davis' military advisor in Richmond. Bragg's replacement was Joe Johnston.

In a series of engagements through North Georgia, from Rocky Face Ridge to Resaca, then in and around Dallas, to the Kennesaw Mountain line, Sherman skillfully outmaneuvered Johnston by constantly thrusting at the Western & Atlantic Railroad, Johnston's supply link to Atlanta. President Davis and an anxious South watched through May and June as Johnston fell back from one defensive position to another, much the way he had

done on the Peninsula facing McClellan back in 1862.

The president and the general had never seen eye to eye, but now they must reach an understanding. When or where would Johnston strike back at Sherman? Did Johnston have a plan to defeat Sherman? When Johnston evaded the question once too often, Davis relieved him, in mid-July, and appointed General John Bell Hood to command the army. Hood was a known fighter, schooled as a tough division commander under Lee in Virginia. Hood sought to emulate the battle-winning

exploits of his mentor and the great Stonewall Jackson. But his best laid plans for July attacks at Peachtree Creek, and along the Georgia Railroad east of the city (called the Battle of Atlanta), and at Ezra Church, outside the western defenses of Atlanta, all proved disastrous, and Sherman tightened his grip on the vital supply, rail and manufacturing center. A month more of skirmishing and maneuvering, and a two-day battle at Jonesboro (August 31-September 1) on the Macon & Western Railroad south of Atlanta, and the city formally surrendered to Sherman's men on September 2, but the Federals had failed to destroy the Confederate army. Hood's battered command marched south to regroup.

While the first day's fighting raged at Jonesboro, in Chicago the Democrats nominated General George B. McClellan for president on the so-called "peace at any price" platform. Much of what transpired in Georgia over the next 48 hours led to McClellan's defeat in the November election, as a war-weary North could finally see victory in sight. Lincoln was re-elected for another term. Other contributing factors to Lincoln's victory at the polls were Farragut's victory at Mobile Bay in August, and Phil Sheridan's successful campaign of destruction in the Shenandoah Valley. Back in Georgia during October, Hood had become restless and decided an offensive into Tennessee and perhaps Kentucky might erase Federal gains in the theater. He marched north

Below: *The chaplain's quarters at Drewry's Bluff (Fort Darling) in April 1865. A battle here in May 1864 blocked a Union attempt to capture Richmond, the Confederate capital.*

from Palmetto, swung wide around Union-held Atlanta, crossed the Chattahoochee River, and fought Sherman's troops at Big Shanty, Acworth, Allatoona and Dalton, all north of Atlanta on the Western & Atlantic Railroad. Thus the armies had changed places from the Atlanta Campaign's start.

Sherman pursued Hood through North Georgia and into Alabama, then decided that whatever threat Hood posed could best be handled by troops gathering in Tennessee. He sent his trusted lieutenant George Thomas to Nashville to take command, and dispatched two corps under General John Schofield to assist in Tennessee. Sherman then abandoned his long and vulnerable supply line for a new base on the Atlantic coast. In mid-November he put the torch to Atlanta's warehouses, factories, and all other structures that might be used for war-making. Fires raged out of control and burned many public and private buildings.

The "March to the Sea" across Georgia by 60,000 veterans, living off the land and the civilian population, and burning anything that could aid the Confederacy's war effort, ended with the capture of Savannah (December 21), which Sherman thought was a fitting Christmas gift for President Lincoln. Meanwhile, Hood's Tennessee Campaign met disaster at Franklin on November 30, after a missed opportunity at Spring Hill, below Franklin, allowed Schofield's two corps to get between Hood's army and Nashville. Any hope of Confederate success in Tennessee was dashed at the Battle of Nashville, December 15-16, where Thomas routed Hood's forces. But a remnant of Hood's army slipped away

with a little fight left in it.

As the last winter of the war approached, the Confederacy had little hope of making up for the losses of 1864. Lee had his back to Richmond, Atlanta was lost as a vital manufacturing and supply base. And west of the Mississippi, a last-ditch effort to take Missouri by Confederate General Sterling Price had failed. But, when all seemed lost to Southerners that year of 1864, there were incidents that had stirred the heart, such as the tiny Confederate submarine *Hunley* sinking the Federal sloop *Housatonic* near Charleston, South Carolina, in February; Virginia Military Institute cadets charging in a fight at New Market; yet another stunning victory for Forrest at Brice's Crossroads in June; a July raid by General Jubal Early that took his Confederates to the edge of Washington's defenses; and Confederate cavalry commander John McCausland taking the war back into Pennsylvania and burning Chambersburg.

But most of the news was bad for the South. In addition to setbacks already described, the famous Confederate raider *Alabama* was sunk by the *Kearsarge* off the coast of France; the raider *Florida* was captured off Brazil; and the ram *Albemarle* was sunk at its moorings in North Carolina. Confederate operatives in Canada launched several raids along the border and North Coast, with little success. A September raid on the Johnson's Island prisoner of war camp in Lake Erie ended in failure. The next month an attempt was made by Rebel agents to burn New York City, and this time a raider

Below: *The ruins of Richmond, the Confederate capital, in April 1865.*

went to the gallows. Coincidentally, in New York performing in a production of Shakespeare's *Julius Caesar* as the Confederates set fire to the building next door, was John Wilkes Booth, a young actor who passionately hated Lincoln. The two were on a collision course. As the new year dawned, the siege of Petersburg was over six months old. Rather than the quick marches and fluid maneuvers of the early war, the Civil War in the East had literally dug itself straight down into the earth. Down the coast at Wilmington, North Carolina, the last major port still operable

for the Confederacy, Federal land and naval forces pounded away at Fort Fisher. On January 19 Sherman's troops began leaving Savannah on what proved to be a most destructive march up through South Carolina. By the end of the month, Lee was named General-in-Chief of all Confederate armies, hardly a desirable position considering the condition of things all over the Confederacy. "Marse Robert" remained with his beloved Army of Northern Virginia and did what he could to advise far-flung commands, hard-pressed at every point.

On February 3, a conference was held aboard the *River Queen* near Fortress Monroe, with Lincoln and Secretary of State William H. Seward attending on behalf of the United States, and Vice President Alexander H. Stephens the chief emissary for the South. What were the Confederacy's prospects and options for a negotiated peace? Lincoln held firm for the unconditional preservation of the Union, but implied liberal treatment of Southerners, a message repeated in his inaugural speech a month later.

February brought the fall of

Wilmington, the evacuation of Charleston, and the capture of Columbia, South Carolina by Sherman's "bummers," the name his Westerners had acquired from foraging liberally off the land. The better part of Columbia was burned in a huge fire started by smoldering cotton bales left by retreating Confederates, then spread by high winds and arsonist Yankees of Sherman's command. In any event, tall, stark columns reaching to the sky from the ashes of Columbia's once elegant mansions and public buildings stood as monuments to the new era of warfare.

Sherman's troops entered North Carolina just after March 1. Confronting him there were troops assembled under his old foe Joe Johnston. There would be some fighting at Kinston, Fayetteville, Averasboro and Bentonville, but the war in this part of the country was all but over.

On March 13, President Davis signed into law a bill authorizing the recruitment of black troops to fight in Confederate service in exchange for their freedom. A year ago, when black units might have helped the Rebels, General Patrick R. Cleburne proposed the recruitment of

blacks and was severely denounced. He might have been drummed out of the army had he not been one of the best commanders the South had. Cleburne possibly was denied corps command because of his controversial idea, but now it was law, and Cleburne had died a division commander at Franklin the

Below left: *Piles of ammunition in the ruins of a Richmond iron works in 1865.*

Below right: *President Jefferson Davis of the Confederate States of America.*

previous November. The beginning of the end for the Confederacy began with rustling in the Army of the Potomac's camps in the last days of March. Lee's lines were stretched to breaking point at Petersburg, and break they did at the critical road junction of Five Forks when attacked on April 1. This action on Lee's extreme right flank exposed the South Side Railroad (a principal artery of supply and retreat) to Grant's grasp. Bad news reached President Davis on April 2: Richmond and Petersburg must be given up, and Lee was trying to extricate his army safely and get it moving westward. Many miles away, in Selma, Alabama, Nathan Bedford Forrest's command was beaten this same day. The last days of the Confederacy had arrived.

Everything of military value in Richmond was put to the torch by retreating Rebels. Grant's hordes marched through Petersburg and Richmond in pursuit of Lee's army on April 3. Lee's army struggled westward in need of supplies. He expected to find them at Amelia Court House, but they were not there. His army was deserting him, while the remnant still intact sought crossings of the Appomattox River. Then even worse news arrived, if that were possible—a substantial part of the army was cut off and captured at the Battle of Sayler's Creek (April 6). Three days later it was all over. Lee surrendered to Grant at Appomattox Court House, Virginia, on April 9, 1865. This effectively ended the Civil War, for the remaining armies of the South soon followed suit, most notably Johnston's Army of Tennessee, which surrendered to Sherman on April 26, near Durham Station, North Carolina. The last

land battle of the war occurred thousands of miles away near Brownsville, Texas, on May 12 and resulted in an inconsequential yet fairly won Confederate victory.

Two tragedies remained, even though the wholesale slaughter of Americans by Americans on the battlefield ended at the peace table at Appomattox. On the evening of April 14, the actor John Wilkes Booth, embittered by the Union victory and emboldened by the fact that his family, mostly actors, had come to immortalize assassins, shot President Lincoln at Ford's Theatre.

The president died the next morning. A cohort of Booth nearly killed Secretary of State Seward at the same time Booth struck, but the planned assassination of Vice President Andrew Johnson had little chance of success, due to an unwilling assassin. Three other co-conspirators were hanged. Booth was trapped on April 26, and shot by a cavalry sergeant. He died a short time later.

A cruel fate had one black card yet to play. A steamer loaded with returning prisoners of war from the Confederate prison camps at Andersonville and Cahaba was churning its way up the Mississippi River. Later that night the *Sultana's* boilers exploded, killing upwards of 1,800 people, the worst maritime disaster in American history. Thus, the Grim Reaper gathered a final harvest of death even as peace and calm settled over a nation reunited.

Below left: *An infantry monument at Chickamauga National Military Park.*

Below: *War graves at Lookout Mountain National Military Park.*

WAR COMMANDERS

WHEN SIMPLE MEN ARE CALLED FORWARD BY GREAT EVENTS, sometimes remarkable things happen. Many of these young men—and many who were not so young—put aside their careers, their education, and all their other hopes and dreams of the future, to set forth on the great adventure of their generation.

Yet mere participation hardly guaranteed that a man would rise to command. That required something else entirely. A few of them, North and South, had to learn not just how to be leaders, but how to be generals or admirals, when the full weight of command both practical and moral would settle upon a single man's shoulders. There was a great deal more to leadership in the Civil War than scene after scene of stirring command and bravery, as many American men were to discover.

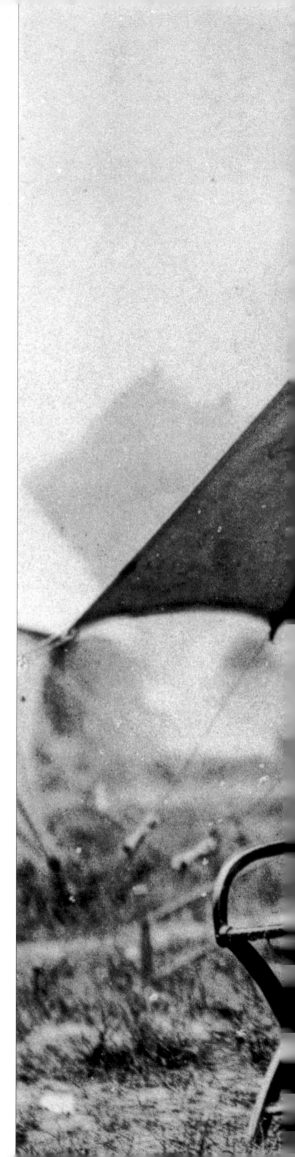

Above: Major General's dress epaulettes belonging to Major General George G. Meade.

Right: George G. Meade, photographed here as a brigadier before being made commander of the Army of the Potomac.

P. G. T. Beauregard

No Confederate general began the war with brighter promise, yet few at the end had been dogged by more controversy or unrealized potential.

Pierre Gustave Toutant Beauregard was born on a Creole, one of the Louisianans of French descent, below New Orleans, on May 28, 1818. The "Napoleon in Gray" grew up studying the great French leader and was attracted to the military. He entered West Point and graduated in 1838 with a fine record. He served with distinction during the war with Mexico, then spent the 1850s in routine engineer duty. Beauregard was assigned superintendent at West Point in January 1861, three days before his native Louisiana seceded.

Beauregard resigned his commission almost immediately and became a brigadier in the South. He was assigned to Charleston to deal with Fort Sumter. On April 12, 1861, his batteries began the war when they opened fire on the fort.

He followed this with a shared victory with Joseph E. Johnston in the first Battle

of Manassas on July 21. This won him promotion to the highest rank of general.

Beauregard, however, was haughty and proud. He clashed with President Davis, and initial disagreements turned into outright enmity on both parts. At his own request he was reassigned from the Virginia theater, and became Albert Johnston's second in command. When Johnston was killed at Shiloh in April 1862, Beauregard assumed command, but lacked the resources to follow up his initial advantage, and retreated. Reassigned to Charleston again, he repelled land and naval attacks in the spring of 1863. In 1864, as commander in North Carolina and southern Virginia, he probably saved Petersburg and Richmond from capture by Grant. Beauregard's feud with President Davis ensured he never held a major field command again.

After the war he turned to railroading and supervised the Louisiana lottery. His real passion was his continuing feud with Davis, which he fought out in the pages of his partisan and contentious memoirs. His death in 1893, however, did not end the controversy over his capabilities.

Below left: Pierre Beauregard was nicknamed "The Napoleon in Gray" and he liked it when people called him that. His military career, however, was blighted by criticisms and acrimony with President Davis.

Below: Confederate Artillery batteries in Charleston open fire on Fort Sumter in April 1861. Pierre Beauregard, as a brigadier general assigned to Charleston, was responsible for ordering this bombardment. This action, and the subsequent surrender of the fort made Pierre Beauregard the Confederacy's first military hero of the American Civil War.

George and Thomas Crittenden

❖

IT WAS OFTEN CALLED THE "BROTHER'S war" and with good reason. Yet there were some families that took sibling rivalry just a bit far, virtually pitting brother against brother. If one such family could symbolize the conflicting loyalties that tugged at all of them, it had to be the Crittendens of Kentucky.

John J. Crittenden spent half a century in state and national politics. When secession came after the election of Lincoln, Crittenden introduced resolutions in the Senate designed to give North and South a compromise that would avert disunion and war. The Crittenden Compromise failed, and Crittenden thereafter went home to try to keep Kentucky from seceding.

But now the national tragedy repeated itself in his own family. His oldest son, George Bibb Crittenden, born on March 20, 1812, graduated from West Point in 1832. He served in the Black Hawk War, then with the army of the Republic of Texas, and fought in the war with Mexico. By 1861 he was a lieutenant colonel in the

US Army but resigned his commission and went to join the Confederacy. President Davis made him a brigadier general.

His younger brother Thomas Leonidas Crittenden, born on May 15, 1819, made the law his career, though he served during the war with Mexico. His loyalty was to the Union and he became a brigadier general in September 1861.

Only misfortune prevented the two brothers facing each other in action. George, soon promoted to major general, lost the only battle in which he ever commanded, at Mill Springs, Kentucky, in January 1862. Accused of drunkeness at the battle, he was court martialed, but soon commanded the reserve corps of the army marching to battle at Shiloh. Just days before the fight he was found drunk and relieved of command, and resigned his commission in October 1862. His brother Thomas was at Shiloh, and soon rose to the rank of major general. He was given command of the XXI Corps, but the collapse of his command at Chickamauga in September 1863 ruined him. Thomas, like his brother, also resigned his commission in December 1864.

Happily both brothers were reunited after the war, George serving as state librarian before his death in 1880, and Thomas as state treasurer before he returned to the army, dying in 1893.

Below left: War graves at the Shiloh. Both brothers were supposed to have been present at the Battle of Shiloh in April 1862. George Crittenden was removed after being found drunk shortly before the battle.
Below: Union commander Thomas Crittenden led his troops impressively at Shiloh in 1862. Over 23,000 men died during the battle.

George Armstrong Custer

❖

A FELLOW OFFICER ONCE DESCRIBED HIM as a "circus rider" gone absolutely mad. With his black velvet sailor shirt, long reddish ringlets, and a red bandana, it was obvious to one and all that George Armstrong Custer liked attention.

This bold and daring officer was born near Scio, Ohio, on December 5, 1839, and dreamed from youth of being a soldier. He grew up with his sister's family and entered West Point in 1857.

Legend has it that Custer finally got an appointment thanks to the influential father of a local girl because he did not appreciate George Custer's attentions to his daughter.

George Custer achieved one of the worst records—short of dismissal—in its history, finishing last in his class in 1861. Nevertheless, with the war just starting, Custer was immediately commissioned and first saw action at Manassas in July. Custer somehow got a staff appointment with General George B. McClellan, commanding the Army of the Potomac, and later with General Alfred Pleasonton,

commander of the army's cavalry.

After displaying remarkable courage, especially at Aldie in Virginia on June 17, 1863, he was elevated several ranks to brigadier general. Two days later he was leading a brigade at Gettysburg.

Custer participated in all of the cavalry fighting of the army subsequent to Gettysburg until he was transferred to the Shenandoah in the fall of 1864. There Custer led a division in battle at Winchester and Cedar Creek, then returned to the Army of the Potomac for the final campaign to Apomattox.

Custer's division was instrumental in blocking the path of Lee's retreat, and compelling the surrender.

Although George Custer finished the war a major general, he reverted to lieutenant colonel of the new 7th United States Cavalry, and with it his destiny would be linked until he and 200 of his men were killed on the Little Big Horn on July 25, 1876. Though this spectacular death always overshadowed his Civil War service, he had been, for all his faults and vainglory, one of the finest "boy generals" of the war.

Below left: *George Armstrong Custer is best remembered for his heroic stand at the Little Big Horn in 1876. "Autie", as he was always called from youth, however, was also an outstanding Civil War cavalry officer.*

Below right: *George Custer (far right) in conversation with Generals Sheridan, Merritt, Devin, and Forsyth, in 1865. Custer gained a reputation for being a bold and daring cavalry officer. He quickly acquired a distinguished service record and on June 29, 1863, with little warning, was suddenly appointed to brigadier general and given command of a brigade.*

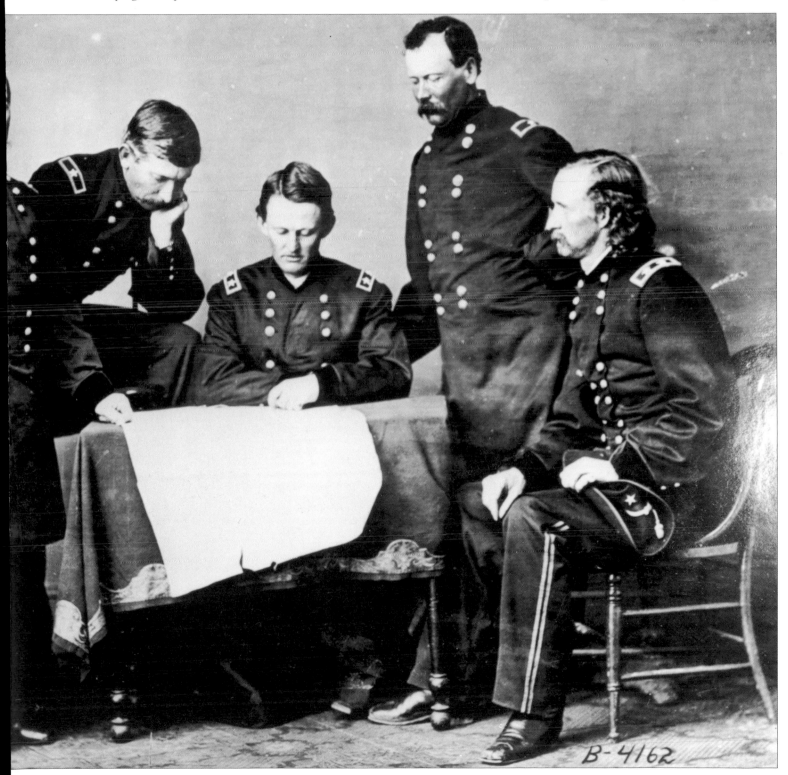

B-4162

Percival and Thomas Drayton

❖❖

The war split families and brothers in every conceivable way, but none more bizarrely than two men from South Carolina who were destined to face each other in battle. The Draytons were an old family from Panaletto State. Thomas Drayton was born on August 24, 1808, and his brother Percival was born on August 25, 1812. Thomas entered West Point in 1824, served for eight years in the army, then became a planter and politician in South Carolina.

His brother joined the navy, became a midshipman in 1827, and was a commander when the Civil War began.

Thomas Drayton remained with the Confederacy and became a brigadier general. This appointment arose from his connections to President Davis, a friend from his time at West Point. He never escaped the odium of getting his commission thanks to favoritism, and his poor performance did not help. He led a brigade at Second Manassas and Antietam so badly that Lee took the brigade away from him.

Percival, by contrast, did well for himself. Having spent most of his adult life at sea and in Philadelphia, he sided with the Union. In October 1861 Percival commanded the USS *Pocahontas*, then in the summer of 1862 rose to captain commanding a warship in the South Atlantic Blockading Squadron, when he aided in the 1863 naval attack on Charleston. He eventually rose to fleet captain under David G. Farragut, commanding the USS *Hartford* in the Battle of Mobile Bay.

The defining moment for them came on November 7, 1861. Percival Drayton's USS *Pocahontas* was in the vanguard of an attack on Confederate Fort Walker at Port Royal in South Carolina. The fort was commanded by Thomas Drayton. Knowing this, his brother took the USS *Pocahontas* closer to the fort than any other ship, for fear that his superiors would think he quailed from attacking his own brother. The Federals won, but the Drayton brothers were never reunited. Percival Drayton died in 1865, with the Civil War barely over, while Thomas lived until 1891.

Below left: *Union naval commander Admiral David Farragut's columns of monitors passing an enemy fort during the Battle of Mobile Bay on August 6, 1864. Percival Drayton served gallantly in command of the USS Hartford, Farragut's flagship, during the engagement. He was subsequently appointed Chief of the Bureau of Navigation in April 1865 and died in that post shortly afterwards.*

Below right: *Thomas Drayton became a brigadier general after the outbreak of the Civil War. He proved, however, to be a poor commander in the field.*

David G. Farragut

❖

On a dramatic day in August 1864, one of the Union's mightiest machines of war, the ironclad monitor USS *Tecumseh*, suddenly lurched in the water of Mobile Bay, Alabama, and sank within seconds, taking all but one man aboard to the bottom. She had struck an underwater mine, then called a torpedo. Looking on from his perch in the shrouds of the flagship USS *Hartford*, a native Southerner who had become the Union's greatest naval commander refused to allow the danger of other mines to avert him from his attack on the Confederate fleet awaiting him. "Damn the torpedoes!" said James Glasgow Farragut.

He was born July 5, 1801, not far from Knoxville, Tennessee. It was a long way to the sea in any direction, but his ferry-operator father soon moved to New Orleans for a navy position. The Farraguts became involved with the family of David Porter, one of the nation's first naval heroes. The Porters helped win Farragut an appointment as a midshipman in 1810. In 1814 he changed his name from James

to David in appreciation.

Farragut commanded his first prize ship in the War of 1812 at the age of 12 years. After the war Farragut served in the Mediterranean, then the West Indies, slowly rising in rank until he settled in Norfolk, Virginia, in 1823, where he married and remained until the Civil War broke out.

In 1861 Captain Farragut left Virginia when it seceded and took over the West Gulf Blockading Squadron in January 1862. He built up the fleet that captured New Orleans (April 1862), and helped in the attack on Vicksburg, meanwhile closing all Confederate ports on the Gulf except Mobile. While his foster brother David Dixon Porter helped Grant take Vicksburg (July 1863), Farragut bombarded Port Hudson and helped secure its surrender shortly after.

David Farragut's last great objective was Mobile, heavily defended by forts and warships. On August 5, 1864, he steamed past the forts, ignored the torpedoes, and captured or dispersed the enemy fleet. He became the nation's first vice admiral and then two year later Congress created the rank of full admiral for him. The war ruined his health, however, and he died in 1870, still on active duty.

Below left: *Admiral David Farragut is regarded as the Union's finest naval commander. His inspiration was David Porter, one of the nation's first naval heroes.*

Below right: *The gunboat USS* Galena *was one of the vessels used in David Farragut's 1864 attack on the Confederate vessels and fortifications in Mobile Bay. This was the last great naval battle of the Civil War.*

Ulysses S. Grant

◆◆◆

HE WAS A MAN WHO FAILED AT ALMOST everything, but when he found the one thing he could do well, he did it perhaps better than anyone else of his time. Hiram Ulysses Grant was born at Point Pleasant, Ohio, on April 27, 1822.

His father secured him an appointment to West Point, but an error led to his name being mistaken as Ulysses Simpson Grant, a change that he found simpler to adopt than to correct. Grant was placed into the infantry although he was a good rider.

He first served under Zachary Taylor with the 4th United States' Infantry in the war with Mexico. He then served under Winfield Scott, and saw action that won him promotion.

The peacetime that followed found Grant at a Pacific coast outpost, far from his wife, where he became depressed and began drinking. He resigned in 1854 and tried a succession of trades. Then the war came and he was commissioned colonel of the 21st Illinois Regiment. By August he was a brigadier and commanded at Cairo, Illinois, and then occupied Paducah,

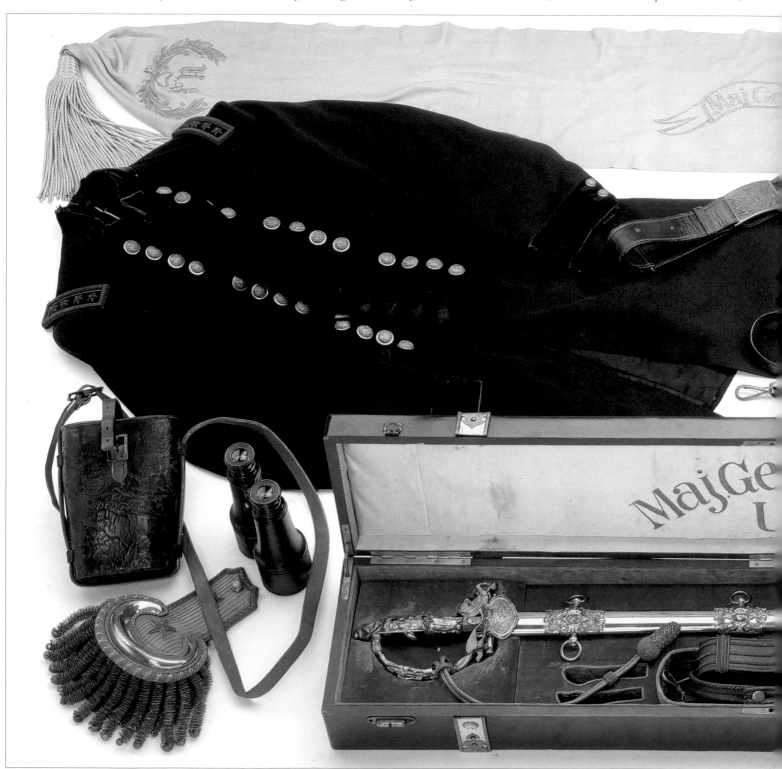

Kentucky, in September. In November he skirmished at Belmont, Missouri.

In February 1862 he captured Forts Henry and Donelson, opening up most of Tennessee to the Union and forcing the Rebels to evacuate western Kentucky. He was victorious at Shiloh in April and then focused his attention on taking Vicksburg and controlling the Mississippi. On July 4, 1863, he captured Vicksburg. By now he was a major general. Grant then lifted the siege of Chattanooga, and defeated Braxton Bragg at Missionary Ridge.

Lincoln responded by making him a lieutenant general, the first since Winfield Scott, in March 1864. As commander of all Union armies he thereafter planned offensives across the continent. He was largely responsible for directing the Army of the Potomac at the Wilderness, Spotsylvania, Cold Harbor, and the crossing of the James River. He narrowly missed taking Petersburg. After a long siege, he was forced to retreat adn surrendered to Grant at Appomattox.

Grant was a four star general at the end of the war. He later served two terms as the nation's president and died in 1885.

Below: *The uniforms and personal regalia of the celebrated Union commander General Ulysses S. Grant. This includes his general's silk embroidered sash, and a silver and gilt sword made by Schuyler, Harley & Graham, New York, in an ivory-banded case. The ivory-handled pen commemorates Grant's promotion to lieutenant general in November 1863. His wool frock-coat (left) has the insignia of full general, a rank awarded to him in 1866. The wool frock-coat (right) was made by John Wanamaker Co., Philadelphia. Button groupings show that it is that of a full general. The frock-coat dates from around 1866.*

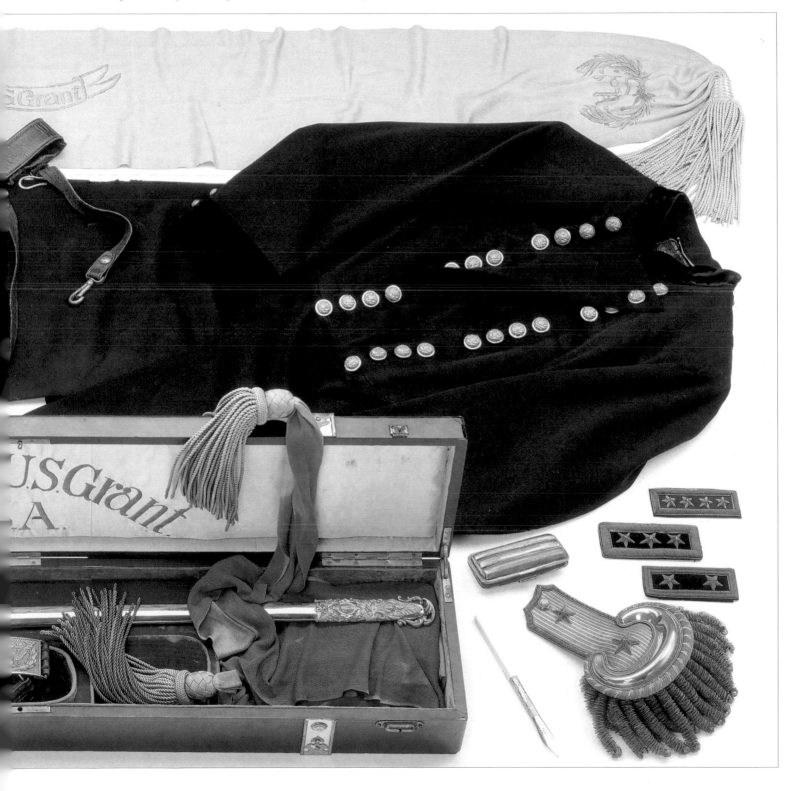

Thomas J. Jackson

❖

Only Robert E. Lee himself has attracted more reverence than his most famous lieutenant, the man called "Stonewall". So great is his hold on the american imagination, that he is the only Confederate general who, some believe, had his life been spared, might have changed the outcome of the war.

Thomas J. Jackson came from the humblest beginnings. Born January 21, 1824, in Clarksburg, Virginia, Jackson was left an orphan by his father's early death, and was raised by a cold and unloving uncle.

Jackson secured an appointment to West Point in 1824. He struggled as a student but graduated a respectable 17th in his class in 1846.

Almost immediately Jackson went to Mexico where he performed well in action. The years after the war proved disappointing, however, and in 1851 Jackson resigned to take a position as a professor at the Virginia Military Institute at Lexington. This would be his home for the rest of his life.

He was an uninspiring teacher. When Virginia seceded in April 1861 he followed his state into the Confederacy.

What followed is the stuff of legend. After a brief period drilling recruits in Richmond, he was commissioned a brigadier and assigned command of the 1st Virginia Brigade.

He led the brigade at the First Battle of Manassas, or Bull Run, and there they earned an immortal sobriquet when another Confederate general likened their stand in battle to that of a stone wall.

Promotion came quickly and, as Major General Jackson, Stonewall led his command back to the Shenandoah where he defeated three separate Union forces greater than his own in the spring of 1862. He fought with Lee in the Seven Days Battles, and then in August won a considerable victory at Cedar Mountain on his own.

At Second Manassas he set up Lee's victory, then fought at Antietam and Fredericksburg, by now a lieutenant general commanding the II Corps of Lee's Army. His greatest day, and his last, came on May 2, 1863, at Chancellorsville, where he led the corps in a wide flanking march around the Union right. During the battle he was hit by accidental shots from his own side and died eight days later.

Below: The personal memorabilia of the Confederate commander General Thomas Jonathan Jackson. This includes the black, waterproof coat and leather gauntlet worn by Jackson at the moment of his wounding at the Battle of Chancellorsville in May 1863. There is also a fine cased, British-made Adams revolver with accoutrements, and a hand-made, embroidered scarf presented by an admirer.

Robert E. Lee

I F EVER A MAN WAS BORN TO BE A HERO, it was Robert E. Lee. Born January 19, 1807, in Westmoreland County, Virginia, he was the son of a hero. "Light Horse Harry" Lee of the Revolution, and a descendant of one of the "First Families" of the Old Dominion. Being a Virginian would dominate his life.

Robert E. Lee entered the United States Military Academy in 1825, and graduated second in his class in 1829, to spend the next 36 years in uniform. Lee saw wide and varied service, but it was in combat that he excelled.

In the war with Mexico he served on the staff of General Winfield Scott, performing dangerous scouting missions that were integral to American successes. Peacetime found Lee in quieter roles, including superintendent at West Point, though in October 1859 he commanded the contingent that fought and captured John Brown's raiders at Harper's Ferry.

In 1861 Lee had the opportunity for high command with the Union, but with Virginia's secession he followed her

fortunes. Briefly he commanded the state militia until President Davis commissioned him a brigadier, and later a full-rank general. But Lee's Civil War did not start well. He failed in a command in western Virginia, then commanded the defenses of South Carolina, and by early 1862 was stuck as military advisor to the president in Richmond.

When Joseph E. Johnston fell wounded at Seven Pines in May, Lee got his chance. Davis gave him the command of what would become the Army of Northern Virginia, and the general and the army were never apart for the rest of the war.

In a dazzling campaign Robert E. Lee drove the Federals away from Richmond, then struck north, defeating them on the old Manassas battlefield before launching his first invasion of the North, ending at Antietam. Despite that setback, Lee inflicted a severe defeats at Fredericksburg (December 1862) and at Chancellorsville (May 1863). A further invasion was stopped at Gettysburg.

At the Wilderness and Spotsylvania, the North and South Anna, and Cold Harbor, Lee repeatedly stymied Grant, who nevertheless kept coming. By June 1864 Lee had his back to Richmond and was besieged. For ten months he held Grant at bay. Lee and his army then made a dash to the west, but Grant caught Lee at Appomattox on April 9, 1865.

Below: *The personal possessions of General Robert E. Lee. These include a camp bed and blanket used by Lee during the siege of Petersburg in 1864, and a table used at the winter headquarters near Orange Courthouse, 1863–64. The pen was used to sign the surrender at Appomattox in 1865.*

George B. McClellan

❖

HE WAS CALLED "THE YOUNG Napoleon" but George Brinton McClellan never lived up to his nickname. He was born to affluence in Philadelphia on December 3, 1826, and went to West Point in 1842. Four years later McClellan finished second in his class and subsequently served as an engineer during the war with Mexico.

McClellan, sometimes called "Little Mac", then taught at West Point, went to observe the Crimean War in Europe, and worked on surveys for the future transcontinental railroad. He also designed a cavalry saddle that bore his name and remained in use well into the twentieth century.

After leaving the army in 1857 he worked for the Illinois Central Railroad but was made a major general of state militia in Ohio in 1861. President Lincoln then made him a major general in the regular army. After a successful minor campaign in Virginia, he was called to Washington to assume command of the beaten army from First Manassas.

"Little Mac" had an unusual gift for infusing elan into the men. He trained and equipped them into the Army of the Potomac. But when it came to leading them in the field, he proved hesitant and was forever convinced that the enemy outnumbered him. He was appointed general-in-chief in November 1861.

When he moved on Richmond in the spring of 1862 he was badly defeated in the Seven Days battles. He blamed Washington for the failure, attempted to dictate civil policy to Lincoln, and failed to support General John Pope in northern Virginia, leading to another defeat at Second Manassas.

McClellan somewhat redeemed himself when he stopped Lee's invasion of Maryland at Antietam, but virtually allowed him to get away after being trapped. Thereafter he delayed and complained again, and was finally relieved of his command in November.

In 1864 McClellan was nominated by the Democratic Party to oppose President Lincoln's reelection but was soundly defeated. McClellan resigned his commission and served as governor of New Jersey. George Brinton McClellan died in 1885.

Below left: *George B. McClellan and his staff. He was a fine organizer and greatly inspired his men, but was disappointing in battle.*

Below: *McClellan was one of a group of selected officers sent to Europe as an observer during the Crimean War. There he had the opportunity to examine the equipment of European troops, and upon his return to the United States he developed a saddle for the army. His design was a great success.*

George G. Meade

THE LONGEST SERVING COMMANDER OF the Army of the Potomac was sometimes referred to as a "goggle-eyed snapping turtle". It is argued that he does not rank with the great captains of the Civil War in part because of his eclipse in the last year of the conflict by the presence of Grant with his army, and a journalistic conspiracy of silence.

George Gordon Meade was born in Cadiz, Spain, on December 31, 1815. His father was an American merchant. Meade entered West Point in 1831 and graduated four years later. He had no wish, however, to remain in the army and resigned in 1836 to train in civil engineering.

Meade rejoined as a second lieutenant in the Corps of Topographical Engineers in 1842. During the war with Mexico he was made a first lieutenant and was later promoted to captain.

Meade was made a brigadier general of volunteers in Pennsylvania. He then joined George B. McClellan on the Peninsula in June 1862. During the Seven Days' battles he fought at Mechanicsville, Gaine's Mill,

and Glendale where he was severly wounded in two places almost simultaneously. Despite these injuries he led his brigade at Second Manassas.

At South Mountain and Sharpsburg Meade commanded a division. He then commanded the 3rd Division at Fredericksburg. After this he took command of the V Corps for the battle at Chancellorsville.

In June 1863 Meade took charge of the Army of the Potomac. This force prevailed at the Battle of Gettysburg under his leadership and the decimated forces of the Confederacy were compelled to retire toward the Potomac on July 5.

They crossed the river on July 13. Many criticized Meade for allowing them to "escape" and he offered to resign. The administration did not accept this offer and instead made the talented officer a brigadier general.

In 1864 Meade fought through the Wilderness, Spotsylvania, Cold Harbor, and the siege of Petersburg. He was rewarded with the rank of major general.

At the close of the war Meade was assigned, successively, to the command of departments and divisions in the East and South. George G. Meade died in 1872.

Below: *The uniform and effects of Major General George G. Meade. These include a Model 1839 Topographical Engineer officer's saber and scabbard made by N. P. Ames, Springfield, Massachusetts. The officer's slouch hat was worn by Meade during the Battle of Gettysburg in July 1863. The coin silver forks, made by Filley and Mead, are from a mess set used by Meade during the Mexican and Civil Wars. His major general's forage cap was worn during the 1864 campaigns.*

John Hunt Morgan

❖

THIS CONFEDERATE COMMANDER WAS born IN Huntsville, Alabama, on June 1, 1825. He saw service in the Mexican War, and after discharge from the Army he entered the family business in Lexington, Kentucky, becoming active in the Lexington Rifles, a local militia unit. At the outbreak of the Civil War Morgan took his small unit to Bowling Green and offered his services to General Buckner. Dashing and colorful, he was soon promoted to colonel of the 2nd Kentucky Cavalry and proceeded to establish himself as one of the most feared Confederate cavalry leaders. Morgan's raids into Kentucky, Tennessee, Ohio, and Indiana caused great concern to the Federals.

In the summer of 1863 Morgan led his cavalry across the River Ohio and into Indiana and Ohio. Quickly, the Federals were on his train, and on July 26 they brought Morgan and a few hundred of his men to a halt, forcing them to surrender.

On August 1 he was sent to the Ohio State Penitentiary at Columbus, where he was searched and had pocket knives and

other useful articles confiscated. But in late November Morgan escaped with a few other prisoners.

In a well-thought-out plan, devised by Captain Thomas H. Hines, an escape group excavated a tunnel that began underneath the officer's cell. The enterprising team cut their way through a layer of cement, then beneath that six layers of bricks, before reaching the basement chamber.

They then tunnelled through the foundations into an open yard beyond. All the time Hines sat in his room keeping guard and signalled to the diggers below by rapping on the floor.

Morgan switched places with his also-incarcerated brother, Col. R. C. Morgan, who was on the ground floor of the prison, scaled a high wall, walked to a station and boarded a train that rode through the night to Cincinnati. Morgan then took a ferry across the Ohio River to his native Kentucky, and from there worked his way south to Tennessee and friendly lines.

In September 1864 he was surprised by Federal cavalry while en route to attack the enemy at Knoxville. The brigadier general was killed during the engagement.

Below: *The personal memorabilia of the Confederate commander Brigadier General John Hunt Morgan. This includes a general's frock coat, an officer's silk sash, a Model 1851 Federal officer's sword belt, and a pair of buckskin gauntlets. There is also a pair of fine, ivory-stocked, engraved Colt Model 1860 Army revolvers, and a cased Tranter revolver with accoutrements for loading and cleaning. The Housewife (sewing kit) was made by John Hunt Morgan's mother in 1861.*

William T. Sherman

❖

FRIENDS CALLED SHERMAN "CUMP". His father admired the great Shawnee leader Tecumseh, and so honored him by naming his son for him.

William Tecumseh Sherman was born February 8, 1820, in Lancaster, Ohio. He was orphaned at an early age and raised by friends, including Senator Thomas Ewing, who got him an appointment to West Point in 1836.

In 1840 he finished sixth in his class but missed seeing action in the war with Mexico as he was posted to California where little happened. Slow promotion impelled him to resign in 1853. He then went into banking in San Francisco, then the law, and finally took the post of superintendancy of the Louisiana State Seminary and Military Academy.

Sherman was in Louisiana when the state seceded and had a genuine fondness for the Southern states. But Sherman stayed loyal to the Union and became colonel of the 13th United States' Infantry, and by the summer commanded a brigade at the First Manassas.

Unlike many people, he predicted a long and bloody war. Sherman was promoted brigadier in August and later went to defend Kentucky.

After suffering a minor nervous breakdown he went on to command a division under Ulysses S. Grant at Shiloh. Thereafter Sherman's fortunes were linked with Grant's, each a perfect complement to the other.

Following his promotion to major general in May he played a key role in capturing Vicksburg. Sherman then went with Grant to relieve the siege of Chattanooga in November 1863, conducted his own campaign to Meridian, Mississippi, that winter, and in the spring of 1864 he assumed command of several armies in the western theater and planned and conducted the famous Atlanta Campaign. Thereafter he marched his armies across Georgia and South Carolina to Savannah, cutting the Confederacy in two, and finished the war in North Carolina where he accepted the surrender of the Army of Tennessee.

After the war Sherman succeeded Grant as general-in-chief and four star general.

He retired in 1884 and died in 1891 as one of the most famous American generals.

Below left: *Cannon in the Manassas National Battlefield Park. William T. Sherman commanded a brigade at Bull Run, near Manassas, in July 1861. The Rebels, however, won this first significant engagement of the war.*

Below: *Union general William T. Sherman outside Atlanta. Sherman was responsible for planning the 1864 Atlanta campaign. After a bitter struggle he forced the Confederates out of their munitions center at Atlanta.*

J. E. B. Stuart

❖

THERE WERE STORIES THAT HE GREW A beard to conceal a weak chin, rumors countered by his teenage nickname "Beauty". This was replaced in later life by the single syllable Jeb.

He was a Virginian. James Ewell Brown Stuart was born February 6, 1833, and secured an appointment to the United States Military Academy. In 1854 Jeb Stuart graduated and gained a commission in the cavalry.

From then until the outbreak of the war he served mainly on frontier duties in Kansas. He was in the east in October 1859, serving temporarily as aide to Colonel Robert E. Lee of the 2nd United States Cavalry, when they were ordered to put down the John Brown Raid.

Stuart chose to go with Virginia when she seceded, and took command of the 1st Virginia Cavalry, which he led at the First Battle of Bull Run. He was promoted to brigadier general two months later.

The following spring he was sent by Robert E. Lee, now commanding the Army of North Virginia, to reconnoiter

the Yankee army on the Peninsula. Jeb Stuart rode entirely around the enemy positions and gained valuable intelligence. Lee rewarded Stuart with command of all the army's cavalry. Stuart would hold this post until his death.

He proved to be an almost ideal cavalryman, and a team player who worked well within the chain of command despite occasional outbursts of adventuring. As a major general he harassed enemy armies, gathered vital intelligence for Lee, and created a legend of dash and daring. He helped win the

Second Manassas campaign, performed ably in the invasion of Maryland, and at Chancellorsville in May 1863 actually took command of the Second Corps after the wounding of Stonewall Jackson.

Jeb Stuart met his first real check at Brandy Station in June 1863. He was surprised and almost defeated by Federal cavalry forces. In the Gettysburg Campaign Jeb Stuart did not live up to Lee's expectations entirely, but the fault was as much Lee's as Stuart's. Certainly Lee never lost any confidence in this commander who was mortally wounded

at Yellow Tavern on May 11, 1864. Jeb Stuart died the next day.

Below: *The personal possessions and memorabilia of General James Ewell Brown. Stuart. These include Stuart's field glasses and case. After being wounded at Yellow Tavern in May 1864 the general gave these to his aide-de-camp Lieutenant Theodore S. Garnett. The general's silk sash was also worn by Stuart at Yellow Tavern. His plumed, felt officer's hat was made in Paris, and his Model 1860 cavalry saber is also French. The flag is the First National Pattern and was flown at Stuart's headquarters.*

THE OFFICERS

❖

LEADERSHIP IS A QUALITY STILL INDEFINABLE AFTER THOUSANDS of years of study. No one can predict with certainty who will or will not make an able commander in war or a capable statesman in peace. Events themselves so often bring out the qualities lying dormant within the individual that any attempt to forsee the emergence of a great leader in advance, or to explain it afterward, is almost futile.

Certainly it was so in the American Civil War. Out of a nation torn in two, and out of a pre-war military that was practically non-existent, tens of thousands of leaders, from the mightiest generals to the most obscure lieutenants, virtually appeared out of the crowd.

Above: Model 1850 staff and field officer's sword, with scabbard.

Right: Robert Tyler and staff, Culpeper, Virginia, in 1863. Tyler entered the Confederate service as quartermaster of the 15th Tennessee in the Fall of 1861. On April 16, 1865, with a handful of extra-duty men, militia, and soldiers en route to rejoin their commands, he defended a small earthwork on the west side of town against a full brigade of Federal Cavalry, part of the corps of Major General James H. Wilson. In the course of the storming of the work, called Fort Tyler now, he was killed by a sharpshooter.

Leading The Charge

B Y THE END OF 1862, THE TEST OF BATTLE had been applied all across America, and the men who led and those who followed could look down into their souls and see what courage was. "Oh everyone is brave enough," wrote one Federal speaking of the officers in his army; "it is the head that is needed." How right he was. In all the preparation, sometimes amounting to months of training and campaigning before a unit saw its first action, it was the intelligence of their leaders that accomplished or failed to accomplish their preparation for battle. And when finally an officer led his men into the fight, for all that personal courage was a necessity, still more requisite was a cool head and the ability to think under the severest kind of pressure man can experience. Many a brave officer got himself and his men killed through bold foolishness. The commander who knew when to temper his courage with discretion, who knew how to control his men by means other than mere personal example, who knew how to control

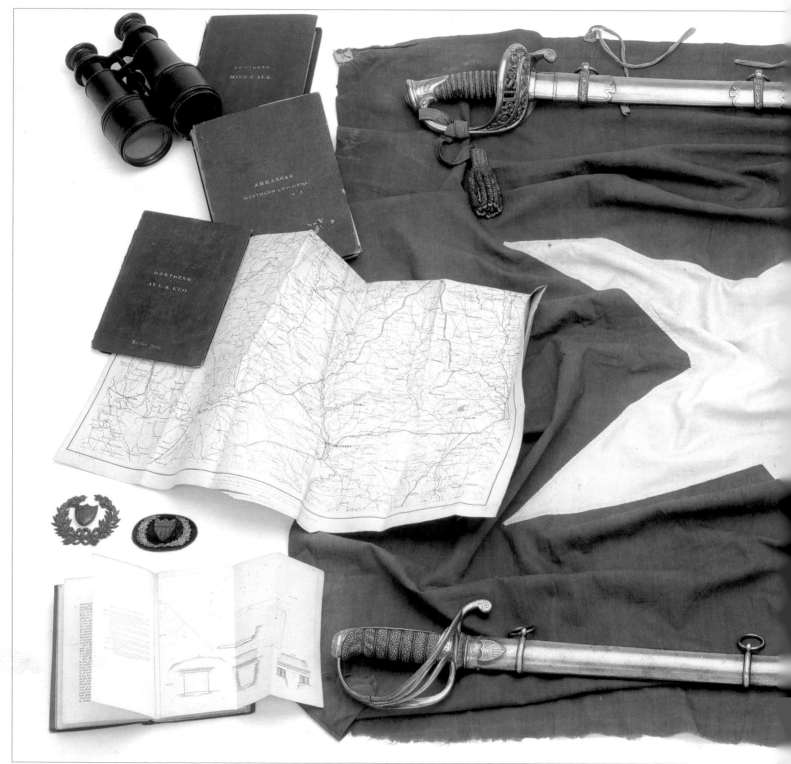

himself, was the one who achieved the greatest goals with the means that were available to him.

Much had to do with simply knowing how to control the men, whether on the march or before going into battle. Mere use of the authority of rank was rarely effective, for the simple fact was that most of the volunteers never equated rank with the right to command, and they always felt at liberty to question the directives of an officer if they did not agree. Thus the martinet had a difficult and often insurmountable task before him. Simply stated, the men would never yield. If they could not stymie him one way, they would find another. In the worst extremity, if their claims be believed, they threatened to, and perhaps did, exact their revenge in battle.

"Many a wearer of shoulder-straps was to be shot by his own men in the first engagement," wrote a Massachusetts boy speaking of the expressed intentions of comrades in the ranks. However, once under fire, most men found themselves occupied pretty much full-time by the enemy, so the threats may have been hollow. Still, many enlisted men believed such things had happened, and the stories were told and retold, and no doubt magnified, in hushed tones around the campfires. "Such officers," said one man

Below: Union Signal Corps and Engineer officers' uniforms and equipment. The Signal Corps originated in the early days of the Civil War as a special unit. Their mission was that of setting up and maintaining communications. While their uniforms and equipment of the corps were basically the same as other Federal units.

referring to a martinet he had seen, "received a stray ball occasionally on the field of battle." Indeed some claimed to know officers who were afraid to go into battle at all, and not for fear of the enemy. If it actually happened, no one can say with certainty.

Undoubtedly some officers were killed by their own men. But for the most part such extreme means were not necessary. They could get an offending commander's attention much more effectively by less violent means. Many were the companies that staged mock funerals in camp with

the officers they disliked hanging in effigy before being placed in a coffin covered with dire records of his offenses. Seeing how his men felt about him, many a tyrranical officer either changed his ways or else resigned before the mock coffin had to be exchanged for a real one.

At the same time, an officer dared not to be too easy or lenient with his men, else he could not command their respect, and only hope that they would obey important commands without question. Consequently, the leader had to walk a fine line between being sufficiently

detached and authoritarian to remind the men that he was different, while at the same time not assuming to be so self-important that the men still did not think of him as one of them. He had to understand and to some degree empathize with their problems—even if he could do little to remedy complaints, he had to appear to sympathize with them. He had to be very reluctant to criticize their faults openly, and show a lot of discretion in doling out reprimands or punishment when required. He had to be able to read his men to anticipate how they would

accept his actions, and most of all, he had to fall back upon cold and final military law only as a last resort. That was a lot to expect even from Regulars who were accustomed to command. When it had to come from civilians-turned-officers, more often than not it sprang from basic instinct for leadership rather than any training they received.

The trick was to instill a little bit of fear along with respect, and it came more often in isolated gestures than from the daily regimen or drill. On the march men were generally under orders not to fire their weapons, or even to have them loaded. When one man shot down a buzzard, his lieutenant immediately and profanely reprimanded him in front of his company. Later during a halt, the officer returned and apologized to the offender for losing his control. Thus he had achieved two ends. His initial outburst showed that there was fire in the man, and that similar infractions in the future might elicit the same response. His apology showed him to be a man of good heart and fair play, and won him the admiration of his men.

The purpose of mastering this kind of psychology was all, in the end, directed to making the enlisted man a part of a team, his company, regiment, and ultimately his army, and all to prepare him to be his most effective when he went into battle. This was one of the things that many enlisted men never understood; that all of

Below left: *Brigadier General John White Geary and his staff at Harper's Ferry, Virginia. His son, Edward Geary, was killed in action in 1863.*

Below: *Union officer's cloak coat.*

the boring routine was designed, not just to keep him occupied, but to condition him to immediate response to an order when his own and the lives of his companions might depend upon it.

However much success at it the officers might think they were having when the armies were in winter quarters or field camp, they could quickly discover that the men would behave differently when on the march or heading toward the enemy. Whether 100 men or 100,000, they were easier to control in the confines of an encampment where sentries and provosts could keep an eye on them. But string them out over expanses of dusty country roads, marching past wells when they were thirsty or well-stocked farms and barns when hungry, and the men proved almost impossible to control. Every farmer's fence rails looked like excellent firewood and henhouses and cornfields appeared to be there for the taking. Many Confederates, specifically ordered not to take farmers' hogs, simply decided to call the hogs bears instead, and then gleefully boasted of the abundance of wild "bears" they shot and ate on the march.

Straggling—lagging behind the rest of the company and not maintaining the rate of march—was epidemic in both armies. Officers of every rank had constantly to ride along their lines urging the men to keep up. The two most frequently heard words out of the mouth of Confederate General Thomas "Stonewall" Jackson were "close up, close up" as he pushed his infantry forward. Sometimes a frustrated commander even drew his saber and smacked the laggard on the head or shoulders to force them forward, though not without risk. One officer made ready

to strike a slow soldier with the flat of his blade, and was told "Put up your sword or I'll shoot you."

As busy as he was when his command lay in camp, an officer's duties seemed to multiply tenfold when the army was on the march. Often no more than two or three days' notice were given from army high command. The officers had to see that the prescribed number of rations were issued for the march, cooked if necessary before leaving, the ordered rounds of ammunition passed out, any defective or missing weapons replaced, and the men

Union Infantry Officers' Uniforms and Equipment.

1: Officer's slouch hat of 1st Lieutenant John Beall, 94th Ohio Infantry
2 and 3: Officer's slouch hat insignia
4: First Lieutenant's insignia
5 and 6: Officer's cotton shirt and housewife
7, 8, and 9: Forage caps
10: Smoking pipe
11: Colonel's insignia
12: Forage cap
13: Officer's slouch hat
14: Model 1850 foot officer's sword

15 and 16 : Beall's frock coat and vest
17: Monocular glass
18: Officer's short jacket
19: Officer's frock coat
20: Sword belt
21: Leather haversack
22: Beall's trousers
23: Brass spurs
24: Private purchase shoes
25 and 30: Officer's sash
26: Model 1850 sword
27: Officer's trousers
28: Buff gauntlets of Major General Amos Eaton
29: Brass stencil

carefully inspected one last time to weed out those who cold not stand the march. The officer supervised the breaking down of the encampment, the storing of impediments not being taken on the march, saw that the company wagons—if there were any—were in shape to haul tents and heavy baggage, and looked to the condition of the horses and mules. A week's worth of inspections, it seemed had been accomplished in a single day. Moreover, there were constant demands from higher authorities for daily—even hourly—status reports, mostly to soothe the nerves of anxious regimental and brigade commanders who fidgeted before the final jump-off of the campaign. The last evening before the march began, the company and regimental officers had to circulate through all their encampments, calming the anxieties of the enlisted men, perhaps exchanging stories or jests with them, maintaining quiet so that sleep—for those who could—might come early.

The day of the march, the whole column might be up a few hours after midnight not because commanders really expected to march at that hour, but because the larger an army, the longer it took to get it moving. If the column were only a few regiments, it might get going with relative dispatch. If it were an army of 50,000 or more then it would move in several columns from four or five different general encampments using parallel roads when possible rather than stringing itself out endlessly on a single road. The march was often a series of fits and starts, with the officers all the while riding or walking along the line trying to keep the men from bunching up or leaving the column.

Matters became more tense as the

column approached the intended scene of action, especially if the battle was already under way and the men had heard the boom of cannon for a few hours as they neared the action. With every step towards the battlefield, the challenge to maintain discipline and order became greater.

Those final hours before the fight, when the officers and men alike knew that they were about to launch themselves into the inferno, could be either the most difficult of all or—oddly—the easiest, for many men achieved a kind of peace before battle. It was now that the individual strengths and personalities of the company and regimental officers revealed themselves most fully. The martinets stayed in their tents or busied themselves with issuing orders and even punishments, right up to the last minute. The officer who understood leadership more perceptively walked among his men, encouraging them, comforting those with the inevitable premonitions of death, and attempting to assure all that each would do his duty and emerge unscathed. The officer knew, of course, that for many his words were hollow or meaningless, but still it often helped the men to hear his reassurances.

In the last minutes before the fight, the officers felt exactly the same as their enlisted men. Tension. Dry mouth and

Below: *Major General Andrew Humphreys (center, with buttons arranged in rows of three on his frock coat) and his staff in June 1865. This commander was a career officer in the military and served in both line and staff positions throughout the Civil War. By the end of the Civil War he had seen action on most of the major battlefields in the East.*

throat. Sweaty palms. The actual place of an officer in battle in the Civil War varied, chiefly according to rank by regulations, but more by temperament of the individual officer. It was foolhardy for generals to risk going into battle, although Johnston did at Shiloh. Corps and brigade commanders belonged at the rear. Only the regimental colonels really had any business going into the fight, and even they were better used by staying close to the battleline but out of the line of fire. Company captains and lieutenants, however, truly belonged with their men.

Many officers learned that so far as their careers were concerned often there was little to gain by conspicuous bravery, for battlefield promotions were effectively non-existent. But of bravery, in the end, there was more than enough to go around, and chivalry, too, though many of the nonsensical old notions about glorious war dissolved in the blood-sodden fields of Virginia and Tennessee. It was just as brutal for an officer as for an enlisted man. The sight and stench of a battlefield after the fight did not distinguish between the eyes and nose of a private or general. The

disillusionment, depression, shame, guilt, and exhaustion that battle's aftermath imposed on almost anyone also struck the officers. The officers were not immune to the effects of what they saw; unlike their men, however, they were expected not to show it.

Like their men, however, they never lost their humanity. Out in Virginia's Shenandoah Valley in 1862, a Pennsylvania private had just drawn a bead on the dashing Confederate cavalryman, General Turner Ashby, Stonewall Jackson's right-hand man.

Before the Yankee soldier could pull the trigger on a certain shot, the colonel of his regiment knocked aside the private's rifle, thus saving the unsuspecting general. "Ashby is too brave to die in that way," said the colonel.

Ashby would die in battle that same year anyhow, but an act of nobility by a foe preserved him for the South a little longer, and at the same time revealed a great deal about the kind of men who led soldiers North and South into the war. Those Civil War soldiers were well served by those they served.

Confederate Headgear and Epaulettes.

1: 1858 Hardee hat of Colonel Francis Bartow, 7th and 8th Georgia Regiments
2: 1858 Hardee hat with N.C. palmetto insignia
3: Rubberized rain hat
4: Full dress bear-skin chapeau
5: Civilian slouch hat worn by a lieutenant
6–9: Forage caps
10: Cotton havelock of W. Kirkpatrick
11: Non-regulation cap of Captain David Smoot, Alexander Artillery, Virginia
12: Forage cap of Brigadier General George Wythe Randolph

13: Colonel's epaulettes of Major General Alexander Galt Talliaferro
14: Captain's epaulettes of Major General H. Clayton
15: Captain's epaulettes of Captain James Lee, Company B, 1st Virginia Infantry

While regulations were quite specific, the Confederate officer wore whatever hat was available at the time. Replacements were difficult to obtain, so many pieces of equipment were used until they were little more than rags. Surviving material was used up after the war due to the desperate economic conditions.

The Union Officer

❖

AFTER THE OUTBREAK OF THE CIVIL WAR the loyal Old Army officers who did not resign stayed at their posts awaiting news. These officers were posted all across the continent. Those scattered across the West hoped for orders to report to the East. It would have been unnatural for these men, most of whom had only known peacetime service with its boredom and glacial rate of advancement, not to be anxious to participate in the excitement in Virginia and elsewhere.

It was in the East that careers could be made, promotion won, and real experience gained. "After the news of Fort Sumter," said Captain John Gibbon, 4th Artillery, at Camp Floyd in the Utah Territory, "days and weeks now dragged their slow length along and all eyes were turned eagerly eastward for more news, while orders for our recall to the States were anxiously awaited."

The only "rapid" communication came by way of the famed Pony Express, which sent its riders from the westernmost telegraph line at Fort Kearny, on the Platte

River in the Nebraska Territory, on to the Pacific Coast. Every arrival of the Pony Express brought more news, none of it good for the Union, and produced more and more excitement and frustration among the men. They were torn between anger at what was happening to their country, and fear that the war would end too soon for them to participate.

When finally Gibbon's orders arrived, he was directed to march to Fort Leavenworth in Kansas. Stores and supplies that could be carried with his marching column were sold locally, and all

Below: *Brigadier General FitzJohn Porter (standing in the center) and his staff. Most of the officers pictured are wearing Union officers' frock coats. This dress generally followed the Uniform Regulations of 1851 and 1861. They were made of dark blue wool and were lined with dark polished cotton or silk fabric. Rank and branch of service were designated by shoulder straps or epaulettes bearing rank insignia on specific color backgrounds, single- or double-breasted construction, and button placement. The coat was double-breasted for general and field officers and single-breasted for company grade officers. The frock coat, which* was very serviceable and probably the most frequently encountered style of officers' dress, had a skirt extending from two-thirds to three-fourths of the distance from the top of the hip to the bend of the knee. Generals had velvet collars and cuffs. There were two interior pockets in the lining of the rear of the skirt and a left-hand breast pocket. Staff officers' buttons for major generals and above had two rows of nine buttons arranged in groups of three. Brigadier generals had two rows of eight buttons arranged in groups of two. Field officers had two rows of seven buttons each. Company grade officers had one row of nine buttons.*

excess arms and ammunition were destroyed. On July 27 they started on their two-month dusty march, and four days later were startled to see a Pony Express rider hastily hand a slip of paper to an officer as he raced past. All gathered to hear the man read an account of the battle of July 21st along Bull Run, the war's first major engagement. He read of the initial success of Irvin McDowell's Union army as it pushed back the Rebels, commanded by Beauregard and Joseph E. Johnston.

Once Captain John Gibbon's column reached Fort Leavenworth, more personally tragic news began to reach the Old Army men. Few were touched by it as John Gibbon, when he opened two month's worth of mail. He learned that his three brothers were all entering Confederate service, following their allegiance to North Carolina, which had seceded. Gibbon never saw or spoke to them again until after the war.

When Captain Gibbon finally reached Washington, he met the same sight that confronted many of his brother officers. The army and the country were in disarray. "Everywhere were troops, camps, baggage-wagons, the sound of martial music, and saddest of all, the constant boom of distant guns which told the story of our distracted country."

For a number of officers, even those already in the Regular Army, personal politicking had to be resorted to in order to get a field assignment. Never in any other conflict in American history was personal influence—local, financial, family, and other connections—to play so large a role in determining who was to receive a commission.

Never before or afterward did the

ingenuity or persistence of the prospective officer himself have so much to do with his success in getting a place—often more to do with it, in fact, than any training or experience he might have had.

Yet with barely 1,100 actual serving officers in uniform when the Civil War broke out, and with 300 of those resigning to go South, demand for leaders clearly outstripped supply. Even counting United States Military Academy graduates who had left the service and might be brought back, such as Grant and Sherman, that only offered another potential 200 or so

Union Officers' Camp Equipment.

1, 2, 8, 15, and 21: Silverware
3: Brass travelling candlestick
4, 17, 18: Ledger
5: Tin document tube
6, 22, and 37: Newspapers
7: Military forms
9: Ceramic cup
10: Sand shaker
11: Quill pen and ink
12: *Carte-de-visite*
13: Military documents
14: Ledger

16 and 24: Desks
19: Map
20 and 28: Decanters and travelling liquor case
23: Army blanket
25, 26, 27, and 34: Officer's uniform, swords, and boots
29, 30, and 31: Hand mirror and straight razor
32 and 35: Field chest and folding camp chair
33: Military manuals
36: Binoculars and case
38: Patent cast-iron camp stove
39: Tin coffee cup
40: Tin coffee boiler

for the Union, and even fewer for the Confederate State's Army.

President Abraham Lincoln's initial call for 75,000 volunteers after the fall of Fort Sumter in 1861 would alone require at least 2,500 officers, easily double the number of trained men currently in uniform or in retirement. Obviously he and Confederate President Jefferson Davis would both have to lean heavily on state militia officers, private military school faculty and graduates, and even politicians who, if nothing more, knew how to run election campaigns well.

In the end, both the Confederate and Union governments utilized a host of means in choosing officers. The rule of the day was that there were no strict rules of procedure. What was policy was simply whatever means succeeded in getting a man a commission in the army.

It would have helped immeasurably in the Union Army if the remaining Old Army officers had been parceled out evenly over the new volunteer units. Certainly it would have made hundreds of lieutenants and captains delighted to become colonels of their own regiments.

Had such been done, then these professionals could have overseen training their own officers, as those Regulars who took volunteer commands often did. But Washington decided to keep the Regular Army units intact, with as many of their officers as possible, expecting them to be the stiff backbone needed to keep volunteer outfits in line in battle, a largely needless function as it turned out. Here, at least, the Confederacy fared better, for having no pre-established regular army of its own, all former Regular officers who joined the cause could be put in charge of

volunteer units.

Some states, like Michigan, did establish camps of instruction, and sent their officers to them first before the enlisted men followed. More often than not, however, fresh Union officers and men were both simply dumped into the maelstrom of camp life and training, and left to learn and fend for themselves. The results were usually comical and not infrequently tragic.

However much North and South may have failed to recognize and act upon the need for systematic training of their

Below left: A front and rear view of a 6th Pennsylvania officer's jacket. Union officers' shell jackets appeared in both double- and single-breasted styles. Most were waist length but some have been noted slightly longer. Besides these three general styles in use with the bulk of the army there were also unit specific styles.

Below: Brigadier General Orlando Willcox (seated in the center) and his staff enjoying a cock fight at their headquarters in front of Petersburg in August 1864. Willcox graduated from West Point in 1847, fought in the war with Mexico and the Seminole War, and resigned from

the army in 1857 to practise law in Detroit. In May 1861, he was appointed colonel of the 1st Michigan Regiment, which participated in some of the earliest campaigns of the Civil War, including the capture of Alexandria and the Battle of Bull Run, where he was taken prisoner. Willcox was exchanged in the summer of 1862 and promoted to the rank of brigadier general of volunteers. He returned to battle as part of Burnside's army, fighting at Antietam, Fredericksburg, and in the final campaigns at Wilderness, Spotsylvania, Cold Harbor, and Petersburg. After the war, Willcox remained with the army for the next 21 years.*

volunteer officers, both sides never let up in their steady production of professionally trained men to send forth for leadership in their armies. The United States Military Academy at West Point continued its operations without interruption, and so did the United States Naval Academy, though its proximity to danger in secession-sympathizing Maryland necessitated its temporary removal to Newport, Rhode Island.

West Point, of course, led all the rest for the sheer number of graduates that it turned out and for the number that

contributed to the opposing armies, especially the Union.

The course at the United States Military Academy during the Civil War did not differ substantially from the kinds of classes that cadets had studied for decades. Sciences—both natural and physical—mathematics, history, and the like made up the liberal arts aspect of the regimen. In military sciences, every cadet was exposed to engineering, infantry, cavalry, and artillery studies and tactics, and for most some studies in French, in order to master the latest European military manuals.

West Point lasses continued through the fall and spring term, with a summer encampment a traditional event before the war, and one especially essential once hostilities commenced.

Both the departure of many undergraduate cadets to the Confederate cause and the growing needs of the burgeoning army in the field, impelled the War Department to accelerate the rate of graduation of cadets. There was resistance at first, for Secretary of War Simon Cameron thought he saw in the large number of West Pointers who either

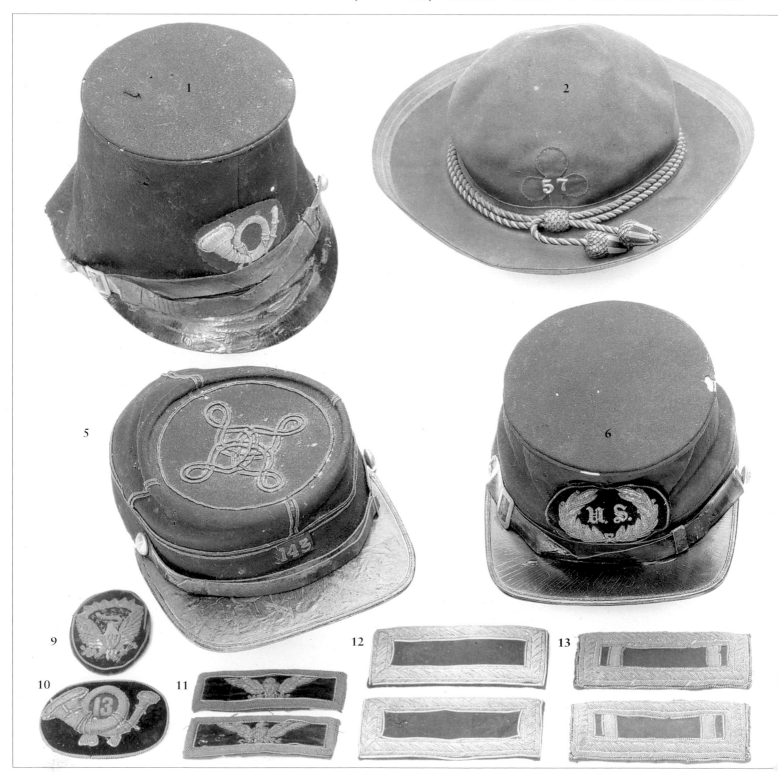

resigned from the Academy or from service in the army, "an extraordinary treachery displayed," and asked if it "may not be traced to a radical defect in the system of radical education itself." The criticism did not last for long, especially when supporters of the United States Military Academy reminded critics that at least 66 Southern-born graduates had not resigned but remained firm to the Union.

Indeed, soon the War Department was singing the tune that accelerated graduation was a necessity, for there were not enough officers for all the places to be

Union Officers' Headgear and Insignia.

1: Standard infantry officer's McDowell pattern forage cap with infantry insignia
2: Slouch hat with badge of the 2nd Corps, 1st Division
3: Patent havelock cap or "whipple hat" with battery insignia.
4: Forage cap with 10th Corps insignia
5: Chasseur's pattern cap with regimental insignia
6: Staff officer's forage cap
7: Chasseur's pattern cap with regimental insignia

8: Forage cap with regimental patent air vent in the crown
9 and 10: Hardee hat national and regimental insignia
11: Colonel's shoulder straps
12: Second Lieutenant's shoulder straps
13: First Lieutenant's shoulder strap insignia
14: Captain's shoulder straps
15: Lieutenant Colonel's shoulder strap insignia
16: Colonel's shoulder straps
17 and 18: Hardee hat national and regimental insignia

filled—exactly the opposite of the pre-war Old Army experience. Whereas there were only 142 West Point students at the start of the war, Cameron urged that the number be raised to 400, and that funds be spent to increase that to 500.

The United States Military Academy actually graduated just 159 officers during the war, though the total student body at any time was well over 200; never close to Cameron's hoped-for 500. Far from reducing its appropriations, as might have been inferred from remarks made in 1861, Congress augmented funds earmarked for

the institution, to the point that during the last year of the Civil War expenditures exceeded $200,000.

Maintenance and upkeep were expanded due to the demands of real practical instruction being given at West Point. The Academy library holdings were increased, the officers' quarters dressed up, and even gas pipes and fireplaces repaired. For targets for artillery practice, academy instructors spent $100 and another $1,000 for new mounts for cavalry and artillery practice.

By the end of the conflict, Secretary of

War Edwin Stanton was also trying assiduously to get Congress to change the 1843 authorization that limited the number of appointments to West Point. "Military science and art cannot be disseminated throughout the country," he complained when the number of graduating cadets was so limited. And, he urged, the standard of admission should be raised, after seeing "the difficulties that have been experienced for years past in training the minds and bodies of the young gentlemen sent to the Academy" who were not equal to its demands.

Thus it was that the United States Military Academy emerged from the Civil War with enhanced prestige, and a considerable momentum for growth in the last half of the century. Though the total number of its graduates that made up the Union Army's officer corps might have bccn small as a percentage, their influence went far beyond their numbers.

Every one of the major army commanders would be a graduate of the United States Military Academy at West Point. Most of the corps and department leaders would be as well.

Ulysses S. Grant, William T. Sherman, Philip Sheridan, Lorenzo Thomas, and more, the men who won the war, all learned much of their craft at the Academy, and so did that small legion of lesser officers who served them so well. And Robert Lee, Albert Johnston, Joseph Johnston, Pierre Beauregard, Braxton Bragg, and the rest of the Confederate high command owed their schooling to West Point. Indeed the story of the West Pointers in the Civil War could be taken for the story of the war itself, for they were never out of the big action.

Below: *Major General George Meade (seated, center) and his staff. For most of the war there were only two grades of general in the Union Army, brigadier and major general. In 1864 the rank of lieutenant general was reactivated and given to Grant. However, confusion entered the scene thanks to what were called "brevets". They were essentially honorary promotions given in recognition of outstanding acts, but which were not recognized for the purposes of rank or command. Some 1,367 men were made brevet brigadier and major generals, when their real ranks never exceeded those of colonel, lieutenant colonel, major, and even captain.*

The Confederate Officer

❖

When the South Carolina batteries fired on Fort Sumter, all West Point cadets came to a final examination not previously part of the school's studies. Secretary of War Simon Cameron immediately ordered that all cadets, officers, and faculty at the Military Academy should swear an oath of allegiance. It was essential to weed out at once the disloyal and the wavering. The new plebe class, the first year cadets, were the first required to so swear, and it was an affecting scene. Under the assumption that there would be some who would refuse the oath, causing some drama, most of the Academy's upper classmen were present as well to witness what happened. The plebes gathered in the chapel before the assembled military and academic staff, all in full uniform. Their names were read aloud, and each of the plebes stepped forward to swear his oath. The first time a Southern boy refused, fellow Southerners stamped their feet in applause, while the rest of the assembly of spectators began a loud hissing. Ten young men could not

take the oath, and were soon dismissed. The Civil War had split "the corps."

Of course, the decision of whether to stay or go had been faced by men at the Academy as far back as January 1861, a few days after South Carolina seceded in December. One young man actually asked Beauregard during his brief tenure if he should resign. Still hoping to stay himself, the superintendent counselled the boy, "Watch me, and when I jump, you jump. What's the use of jumping too soon?"

Some had already "jumped". On November 19, 1860, Henry S. Farley of South Carolina became the first cadet to resign. Another South Carolinian followed him four days later, then a Mississippian, and an Alabama boy. As the resignations continued into 1861, the lame-duck president James Buchanan ordered that all cadets suspend studies on February 22, to go to the chapel and hear read to them Washington's farewell address, and to think upon his admonitions of "the immense value of your national union". Later that evening, cadets of opposing views began to shout cheers for the rights of the Union or the South.

In the end, out of 278 cadets at the Academy at the beginning of November, 65 left either by resignation or from being discharged for refusing to take the oath.

Perhaps, because so many leading Rebels were graduates, and certainly because of the long-standing military tradition in the South, the new Confederacy was not yet even established

Below left: Officers of the South Carolina's Washington Light Infantry.

Below: Confederate Colonel of Engineers.

before leading secessionists began to call for a Southern military academy. On January 26, 1861, the Misssissippi secession convention passed a resolution calling on its representatives in any new confederation "to use their influence to have a military academy similar to that of the United States at West Point."

Once the Confederacy was formed, its Congress waited only until May 16, 1861 to approve an act providing that cadets could be appointed by the president on an interim basis, "until a military school shall be established for the elementary instruction of officers for the Army." Not long thereafter, on October 7, 1861, in a treaty concluded with the Cherokee Indians, one of the inducements used to woo the tribe into an alliance with the Confederacy was the promise that one Cherokee youth would be selected every year "to be educated at any military school that may be established by the Confederate States."

For all the good intentions, certainly heartily approved by old West Pointer and now President Jefferson Davis, the South simply never had the time or the wherewithal to set up its own military academy. The act allowing Davis to appoint cadets was as far as Congress got, and he did, indeed, appoint quite a few.

They were attached as supernumaries to existing volunteer or Regular companies, where the cadets, presumably, learned as much of the art of war as would allow them to be commissioned into active service. Several of these men became second lieutenants in the Regular Army and probably more took commissions in the Provisional Army of the Confederate States.

Fortunately for Davis and his cause, he had other sources of excellent trained young officers. The South literally teemed with private and state military schools. Furthermore, a number of colleges and universities offered intensive courses of military instruction, meaning that there were actually thousands of non-West Point-trained men in the Confederate reservoir of potential officers. Indeed, looking just at the field of officers—regimental men of colonel's, lieutenant colonel's, or major's rank—in Lee's Army of Northern Virginia, it appears that out

Confederate Infantry Officers' Uniforms and Equipment.

1: Uniform frock coat of Colonel L. Keitt
2: Forage cap of Colonel W. Clark, N.C. troops
3: Uniform frock coat of Colonel Ellison Capers
4: Caper's overcoat
5: Gray felt officer's hat
6: Uniform frock coat of Captain C. Fleming
7: Leech and Rigdon foot officer's sword
8: Sash of Captain W. Oliver, 9th Va. Cav.
9: Haversack
10: Sword belt
11: Boyle, Gamble and Co. sword

12: Two-piece Confederate States plate
13: Officer's sword
14: Fleming's silk sash
15: Keitt's trousers
16: Slouch hat
17: Sash of Colonel James Martin
18: Tin drum canteen of Captain W. Bachman
19: Wooden canteen
20: Officer's haversack
21: Haversack of O. Jennings Wise, Richmond Light Infantry Blues
22–26: Effects of Wise's haversack
27 and 28: Uniform jacket and vest of Adjutant J. Bidgood

of a total of 1,695, some 208 were graduates of such schools. Adding to that the 73 West Point field officers gave Lee a very respectable nucleus of trained leaders.

In the first instance, however, both governments turned first to the professionals, to current and former officers of the Old Army. From the outset the high-level vacancies created in the new regiments and brigades were chiefly filled by these professionals. Thus it was no surprise that many of the more esteemed Old Army officers found themselves wooed by both sides in what at times almost amounted to a bidding war in which the prize was not money, but rank. Simon Buckner of Kentucky was offered brigadier generalcies by both Lincoln and Davis in the summer of 1861. He sided with the latter. Another Kentuckian, Ben Hardin Helm, was offered first a major's commission in the Union Army, then took the colonelcy of a new Confederate infantry regiment. Robert Lee, of course, had reportedly been offered command of the Union Army by Winfield Scott but took the command of Confederate Virginia's state troops instead. Even as he was resigning his commission to go to the South, Albert Sidney Johnston was wooed by Washington to remain in the Federal service, to no avail.

For men of the South, when news of their native states' secession came through, or for those who had decided to take Confederate service in any case, the sometime pain of the decision was at least compensated for by the immediate control they could take of their own destiny. A simple letter of resignation, once posted, freed them of any sense of further obligation or necessity to wait around.

These officers were free to make their way to the Confederacy, saying farewell to their remaining brothers of the Old Army who had to wait where they were for orders to come.

Thus it was that Albert Sidney Johnston made his journey all the way from Los Angeles to Richmond, Virginia, after May 1861. While he may have equivocated about simply staying out of the war altogether, once his adopted state of Texas seceded he knew he had to go. On June 16 he joined other officers in a daunting trek across the southwest by horseback that

Below left: *A Confederate and a Union officer, clutching their swords, urge their men to close with their enemy during the siege of Vicksburg. It was the men who knew how to lead who got their regiments through the test of battle and brought them home again.*

Below: *Auburn Guards Officer, Alabama Militia, 1861. Easily the most colorful of all the units coming into the Confederate Army were the local militia and privately raised outfits that took arms for the South in 1861. With no prescribed uniformity, they arrived in uniforms of almost every color of the rainbow—green, red, buff,*

brown, and most frequently of all, blue. Among the most colorful were the Auburn Guards of the Alabama Volunteer Militia. Their blue trousers and short jackets were glorious, covered with bright brass buttons, set off by a white crossbelt, epaulettes, white gloves and facings, red sash, and a gleaming black leather Pattern 1851 Albert shako topped by a red and white feather pom-pom. The rigors of campaigning played havoc with such uniforms, and these beautiful outfits did not last long in the field. As they wore out they were steadily replaced by Confederate regulation gray or butternut.

took them to Fort Yuma, then along the Gila River, south on the Rio Santa Cruz to Tucson, then due east to Picacho on the Rio Grande. This trek on foot and horseback was made in the worst of the summer through scorching deserts. It took more than a month for the trip, and once in Texas it took Johnston another month to reach New Orleans, and another week, perhaps, to get to Richmond.

Albert Sidney Johnston went straight to the executive mansion, only to learn that President Jefferson Davis, his old friend, was upstairs ill. But Davis was awake, and he heard the traveler's boots in the hall below. "That is Sidney Johnston's step," the President exclaimed, "Bring him up." In less than a week, Johnston was a full general and the second ranking officer in the entire Confederate army.

Literally dozens of other officers preceded or followed Johnston in the exodus of the Old Army men to the Confederacy. While few others traveled so far or through such danger and hardship, still each had his own story.

Leaving the Old Army, however, was not always an easy choice. "No act of life cost me more bitter pangs than mailing my resignation as a captain in the United States Army," lamented Henry Heth of Virginia, "separating myself from those I loved, bidding adieu to my splendid company, my pride, and the finest regiment in the arm." It was a commonly held and expressed emotion.

Not infrequently, other friends in the Old Army had attempted to persuade Southern men not to go South. When Lieutenant Edward Porter Alexander reported for duty in San Francisco to his close friend Lieutenant James B.

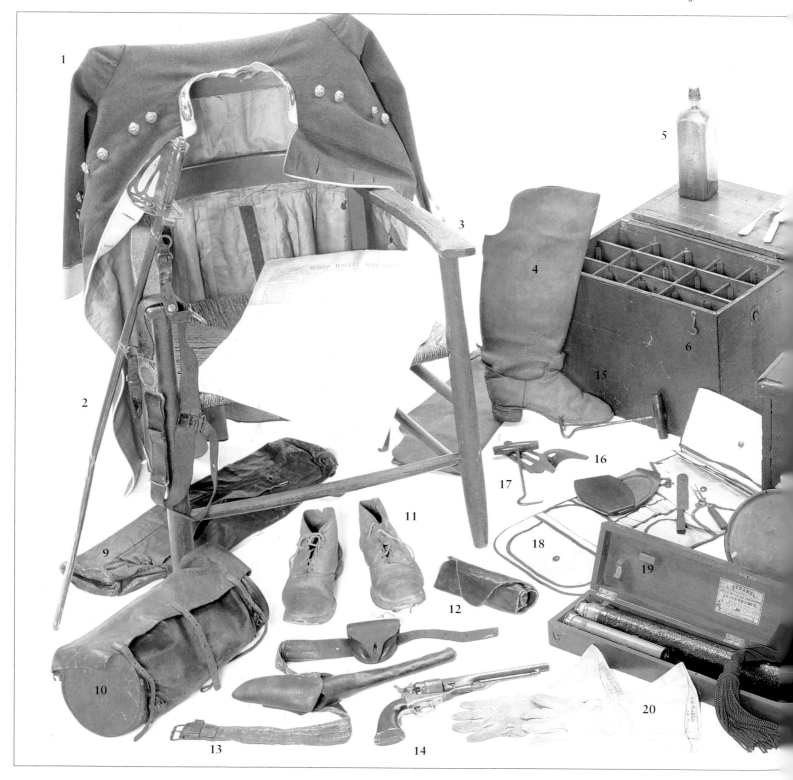

Confederate Officers' Camp Equipment.

1: Frock coat of Brigadier General James Connor
2: Connor's English Model 1822 infantry sword
3: Camp chair used by General Robert E. Lee, 1863
4: Boots of J. McKenna
5: Bourbon whiskey bottle
6: Walnut wine chest
7: Ammunition box
8: Wooden trunk of General Joseph Johnston
9 and 10: Saddle roll and valise
11: Leather brogans
12: Leather dressing case

13: Belt and plate of Captain William Wright
14: Colt 1860 Army revolver of Dr. H. McGuire
15, 16, and 17: Boot pullers
18: Dressing case of Major General Robert Ransom Jr.
19: Field glasses of General Pierre Beauregard
20: Cavalry gauntlets
21: Officer's sash
22: Hat of Captain John Hudgins, 30th Virginia Infantry
23 Confederate tobacco
24: Carved dogwood pipe
25: Shaving glass of Brigadier General Henry Wise

26: Velvet housewife of Colonel Nathan Davis
27: Wooden inkwell of Governor John Gary Evans, S.C.
28: Evans' pen
29: Pearl-handled dagger
30: Bone-handled knife
31: Field desk of General "Jeb" Stuart
32: Walnut desk of Lieutenant General Richard Ewell
33: Wooden cane

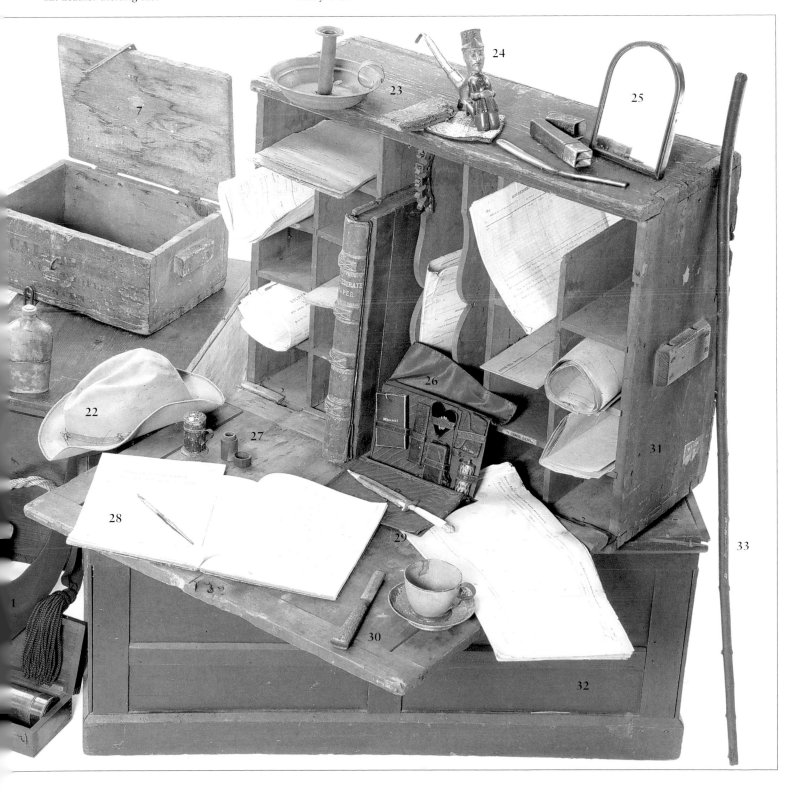

McPherson, there was no question that the Georgian Alexander intended to leave the army. He talked with McPherson telling him of his intention and asking him to accept his resignation.

"Aleck if you must go," said his friend, "I will do all I can to facilitate your going. But don't go." He promised that Alexander would be able to remain on the Pacific coast, far from the war, honorably continuing his service without having to fight against his own people.

"Now this is not going to be any 90 days, or six months, affair," McPherson continued. If Alexander went South, with his training he would certainly wind up in the front lines. "God only knows what may happen to you individually," he said, "but for your cause there can be but one possible result. It must be lost." McPherson tried to explain how Alexander's promotion would be rapid as other officers were drawn away to the war. He even suggested that the Georgian could make good investments in the expanding land business in San Francisco.

"In short, remaining here you have every opportunity for professional reputation, for promotion, and for wealth," McPherson concluded: "Going home you have every personal risk to run and in a cause foredoomed to failure."

Alexander was deeply impressed by McPherson's words, "A crisis in my life was at hand," he recalled later. He was utterly helpless to avert it, however. "Mac," he cried, "my people are going to war, and war for their liberty. If I don't come and bear my part they will believe me a coward—and I will feel that I am occupying the position of one. I must go and stand my chances.

"So I wrote my resignation of my beautiful position in the Engineer Corps," Alexander remembered. McPherson gave him a leave of absence to return to the East to await its acceptance, and then as his last gesture of friendship, helped arrange Alexander's passage home at a reduced steamship rate. The two never met again. Alexander would serve with the Confederates in Virginia, from first Manassas all the way to Appomattox; McPherson, during the Atlanta campaign in the summer of 1864, would be the only Union commander to be killed in the field.

Below left: *Captain, Rutledge's 1st Tennessee Light Artillery. Sometimes volunteer Confederate outfits combined their own regulations with those of their enemies in their uniforms. The officers of Rutledge's 1st Tennessee Light Artillery wore both collar insignia and shoulder straps or epaulettes, like this captain, each carrying badges of rank. The style of his cuff facings is also different from prescribed design. In time, and thanks to the idiosyncratic nature of Confederate uniforms in general, men and fellow officers came to recognize and accept almost all such differences. Indeed, it made for a colorful variety in the command structure of the Rebel Army. Especially unusual in an artillery officer is the broad brimmed hat worn in the place of the customary kepi. Units from west of the Alleghenies generally showed more variation in headgear and uniform styles. By the war's end the only thing all had in common was tatters.*

Below right: *Colonel John Singleton Mosby of the 43rd Virginia Partisan Rangers. Few raiders of the war could even attempt to approach the record of the "Gray Ghost." Mosby's raids, including the capture of two generals, became legendary. He seemed invincible and unstoppable, and indeed he was.*

THE SOLDIERS

❖

In order to understand the Civil War it is necessary to look at the men in the ranks who first to last bore the brunt of the fighting. It is they, not their officers, nor the statesmen behind the lines, who stood the fire, who kept up their determination in the face of hardship and defeat, who had the will to make any sacrifice along the road to victory. Individually their names are all but forgotten except by their descendants. A very few are remembered for some special act of heroism, or because they left a particularly revealing memoir. Most are recalled only collectively, for no one will ever forget the celebrated exploits of the Army of the Potomac, the Army of Northern Virginia, or the Army of Tennessee. But one must not forget that the common soldier in blue and gray *were* those armies.

Above: A Cook and Brother musketoon, with ramrod.

Right: Company G of the 114th Pennsylvania Infantry infront of Petersburg, August 1864.

A Call to Arms

❖

SOME 3 MILLION MEN MARCHED TO WAR during 1861–65. Barely one of them knew what to expect. They were a new people in a new era, facing a very new sort of conflict. These men of North and South, innocently answering the call of flag and country, had never mustered in legions in crowded encampments, or been away from home for months and years at a time, living out under the open heavens, marching in unison step, and slavishly following the orders of more privileged officers they often regarded as fools. Army food was as yet an unrevealed mystery to them, as were the horrors of military medicine awaiting the sick and wounded, or the prison hells ready to swallow up the captured. The routine of army life for the common soldier would be an awakening for them all, relieved only by those inerasable traits ingrained in the nature of all America's lowly; their folk-humor, rowdiness, the love of sport and frolic, and fear of their God.

And out of their four years of war, these Johnny Rebs and Billy Yanks would forge

a legacy uniquely their own. But they rarely became soldiers. They remained always simple civilians, temporarily "reassigned". Reb and Yank alike carped incessantly at the army and everything in it, and became masters at looking out for themselves while in uniform.

Most of all, they knew who they were. These simple soldiers were not the planters and politicians who made the war. Yet while they grumbled about it being "a rich man's war and a poor man's fight", they did not shrink from that fight. Though at the same time, they had a sense that what

they did and suffered might never be recognized. Barely had the war come to an end before one proud Confederate lamented that amid all the outpouring of boastful memoirs and florid accounts of battle and leaders, few "would hardly stop to tell how the hungry private fried his bacon, baked his biscuit, smoked his pipe". They accepted it as part of the lot of the common soldier, a price they paid toward a greater end. Yank and Reb alike could agree with Sergeant Ed English of New Jersey when he wrote in 1862 that, "A man who would not fight for his

country is a scoundrel! I cannot get tired of soldiering while the war lasts." he confessed. He had to be there, for all his unsung trials.

As the war dragged onward year after year, a time would come when gold was about all that would buy a man into the army. The first volunteer enlistments were

Below: *Union troops in camp. Of the many things that soldiers both blue and gray would remember in later years, their fondest memories would be of those hours spent taking their ease with comrades in camp.*

for terms usually of 90 days—a year at most—when everyone expected the war to end before the summer of 1861 was out. When it did not, many regiments simply ceased to exist, while many more re-enlisted, first for a year, and later on for three years or the term of the war, both North and South. But in the first great rush of enthusiasm and patriotism that followed the secession, the fever to volunteer for the fight fed virtually upon itself. Thousands of young men on both sides sensed intuitively that this was a great event. Spurring them on from every

press and pulpit were the fiery exhortations of the zealots who helped bring the conflict in the first place. Aroused by their incentive, the young manhood of the nation could hardly fail to respond. To encourage and profit by the spirited wave sweeping over the continent, every public square and courthouse lawn sprouted mass meetings with stirring martial music, posturing politicians, swaggering recruiting officers, and an excess of swooning damsels. Aging veterans tottered to stand to remind one and all of their proud traditions.

Then it was time to enlist. The whole event was played to the tune of the most shamelessly unselfconscious display of patriotism yet seen. Even some of those in the press who did their best to encourage the feeling had to admit that at times it seemed a bit overdone.

They stepped forward for all manner of reasons. For some, in their enthusiasm, enlisting just seemed the right thing to do. Standing back would let down friends and community, even family, risk missing all the fun and glory and, worse, hazard the chance of being branded a coward. The

pressure on a young man's pride and sense of honor was profound. Enlisting friends urged their comrades to follow them. Fathers on both sides gazed toward the rifle on the wall and lamented that they were too old to go. Worst of all were the sweethearts.

More than this appeal to pride and shame, thousands of young men enlisted simply to see a change. The army was something different from struggling behind a plow or scrivening at a desk. War was adventure, the great adventure of their generation. There would be glory,

excitement, new places to see. Many of these boys had never been outside their own home counties. The wild life of the army promised enticements that few of them had ever known. And even to men who had seen battle before, the allurement of adventure was the same.

Even economics played a part in luring men into the ranks. To be sure, the pay of a Union private was not particularly generous, just $13 a month, while for a Confederate man it would be $2 less. Yet North and South alike were suffering from widespread unemployment and

Below left: *Federals in front of their tents and improvised shelters. The soldier took such shelter as he could, or as much as the quartermaster allowed him. Tents varied in size and shape, though they all succeeded in being drafty.*

Below: *Privates, North Carolina Infantry. Rebel troops from North Carolina were among the best clothed of all Confederates, and enjoyed perhaps the greatest degree of uniformity of dress among their regiments. North Carolina could produce its own textiles and had ports for blockade-items, so it could arm and equip its men effectively.*

recession, and army pay was enough to live on—and it was supposedly steady. Better yet, many states were paying enlistment bounties or bonuses to those who joined—and later those who re-enlisted—often amounting to several hundred dollars. Pay, however, would not always be as regular as the men supposed. In the South some men would go a year at a time without being paid, only to find their currency so inflated that it bought next to nothing anyway.

Certainly there were loftier motives on both sides for enlisting. For some

Northerners the war became in time a crusade to end slavery. Some would even look upon the early years of Yankee failure on the battlefield as punishment for acquiescing on the issue for so long. Yet their sentiments were much in the minority. Among the 2 million men who would wear the blue of the Union Army, less than one in 10 felt any real interest in emancipation. And for every Federal man who voiced his sympathy for the plight of slaves, there were a legion of others who disagreed and saw it as a war to preserve the Union.

Far more pervasive was the sense of duty to their country. In the Southern territories that meant the defense of its lands and institutions after secession.

Bred for generations to view Northerners as hypocritical fanatics bent on destroying the Constitution, most Southerners were thoroughly convinced of the righteousness of their cause. Further, theirs was a militant society, and they looked upon themselves as by nature better soldiers and fighters than Yankee shop keepers. Defense of the South, to them, was a holy a task as the American

Revolution, and the enlistees vowed to bear hardships as great as Washington's before they would fail.

While military inclinations did not dwell in the North in the same degree as they did below the Potomac, still they abided much in the western frontier, where Lincoln's call for volunteers met with a more enthusiastic reception. Yet, as in the new Confederacy, militarism stood well behind a sense of duty and purpose in impelling those young men to rush forward and sign the muster rolls.

For all the differences that brought about the war, and those that impelled the men on either side to enlist, the Northerners and Southerners who rushed to take up arms were more alike than not. They came overwhelmingly from the farms of rural America; and not just in ones or twos. Whole companies and regiments were raised in the same locality, bringing with them their own local values and customs.

Fully one half of the men who donned the blue had been farmers, and almost two-thirds of the new Confederates were trading the plow for the gun. Carpenters, clerks, laborers, and students made up much of the remainder, but in fact over 300 different occupations were represented in the Union Army, and over

Below left: *A Union 1863 New York National Guard jacket.*

Far left: *A Union 1861 New York State jacket, with rear view.*

Below: *Union troops in camp. Soldiers spent most of their service finding ingenious ways to make camp life more tolerable.*

100 in the Confederate.

Just as the majority on both sides were white, native-born, Protestant, and unmarried, so were they all primarily young men. While the youth of the soldiers enlivened camp life and infused a enthusiasm in battle that enhanced morale, the armies took some stability from the maturity of soldiers at the other end of the allotted three score and 10.

Whatever their age, many men were healthy individuals, inured by the hard life of the fields or the factories. The ruggedness of military life posed few

challenges to their hardened constitutions. The men tended to be lean when they enlisted, and to stay that way. No one grew fat on army rations and marching.

Whatever made them different or the same, most of the men North and South who answered the call were native-born Americans. Yet stepping forward with them, to lend their own special talents and accent to Civil War soldiering, were tens of thousands of foreigners. Company H of the 8th Michigan numbered among its men, 47 New Yorkers, 37 Michiganders, 26 other "native" Americans, 7

Canadians, 5 English, 4 Germans, 2 Irishmen, 1 Scotsman, 1 Dutchman, and one mysterious fellow who simply listed his nationality as "the ocean".

Often overlooked in both armies were the small numbers of native minorities who wore blue and gray. Perhaps as many as 12,000 American Indians served the Confederacy, most of them members of the Five Civilized Tribes living out in the Indian Territory. In all, the Rebels would raise some 11 regiments and seven battalions of Indian cavalry, not to mention a few hundred men scattered

among other Confederate regiments. Around 6,000 Indians wore the blue.

Blacks, too, would step forward to the recruiter, though not without the trials and setback that accompanied their progress in the United States. Yet they would fight and prove themselves.

Many openly argued against enrolling blacks, both among civilians and white soldiers. Besides fears that arming Negroes would degrade the army, and even risk rebellion among them, most asserted that it would be a threat to white rule.

By late 1861 abolitionists and politicians began to argue that the Union Army could use black numbers to bring a speedy conclusion to the war, and at the same time the army would teach them discipline and prepare them for their place in postwar society—whatever that place was to be. Black soldiers were finally enlisted into the Union Army in January 1863.

Below left: Enlisted man with officer, 83rd Pennsylvania Volunteer Infantry. The men who raised and equipped some Union regiments strained their imaginations to create new looks, and borrowed shamelessly from the styles of other regiments. Probably no Federal regiment presented a more mixed bag of elements in its private soldiers' uniform than the 83rd Pennsylvania. The enlisted man at left wears epaulettes normally only worn by general officers, a somewhat shortened version of a blouse similar to those worn by some zouave outfits, and exceptionally baggy zouave pantaloons gathered in at the ankles by gaiters. The lieutenant, by contrast, is entirely standard regulation, with nothing distinctive.

Below: A group of troops, probably from Massachusetts, taken early in the war.

The Union Soldier

❖

WHEN THE AMERICAN CIVIL WAR began the Union Army had the North's superior industrial resources to call upon for their supplies. As a result, the dress and equipment of the Federal soldier tended to be more standardized than that of his counterpart in the Confederate States Army, while the basic materials were of a higher quality. The Federal forces also started the conflict with the advantage of the Old Army as a basis for their traditions, and for the design of their uniforms and equipment.

There were, of course, exceptions to such uniformity in the Federal ranks, particularly in the early days of the Civil War when men joined the army from the state militia system. These militia formations, drawn from specific counties, towns, or even neighborhoods of cities, practically encouraged individuality of uniforms and equipment.

The results were often multi-colored, brocaded, plume-bedecked costumes that were taken extremely seriously by the wearers, but which may have appeared

comical to onlookers.

The common Union soldier and his officers were quick to recognize that bright, colorful attire attracted enemy attention. This was frequently followed by hostile fire. The realities of war, therefore, soon relegated such dress to the footlocker, ceremonial events, the band, or home guard.

While such extravagances rapidly diminished in popularity, nevertheless the branch of service of an individual soldier was shown by colored piping and badges of rank, and this continued throughout the

Below: *The 48th New York Infantry at Fort Pulaski. This regiment was made up of men from New York City and New Jersey. Formed shortly after the fall of Fort Sumter, in the Summer of 1861, the 48th was assigned to the Department of the South. It served for three years on the coasts of South Carolina, Georgia, and Florida. The 48th occupied Fort Pulaski from April 1862 until June 1863. In July of 1863 the 48th and other units assaulted Battery Wagner on Morris Island at Charleston Harbor. The attack failed, and the 48th suffered 284 casualties out of about 500 present for duty. In February 1864 the unit fought at the Battle of* Olustee. *It was then transferred to Virginia and to the Army of the James. The 48th fought at Bermuda Hundred and Drewry's Bluff. They then moved to the Army of the Potomac and fought at Cold Harbor, Deep Bottom, Strawberry Plains, Hatcher's Run and the siege of Petersburg. The 48th was then assigned to the Fort Fisher Expedition in January 1865. They then joined Sherman's Army of the Ohio as it marched up from North Carolina. By the end of the Civil War, the 48th New York had lost many of its original members and sustained 859 battle casualties. Having done their duty, in the spring of 1865 the survivors went home.*

American Civil War, although there were variations. The basic colors were red for artillery, blue for infantry, and yellow for cavalry units.

Federal enlisted men's coats and jackets can be found in the same basic styles as officers': the frock coat, sack coat, and shell jacket. The garments were usually of lesser quality, manufactured at arsenals and by numerous contractors.

Many early coats were said to be made of "shoddy," a kind of remanufactured material. Some of these coats were so poorly made that they literally fell apart or dissolved in the rain. This was the result of manufacturers' profiteering, which was soon corrected by a system of Quartermaster Inspectors. As the war continued it became evident that efforts were being made to establish a standard of dress for the whole army.

The 1858 Regulations authorized and required a single-breasted dark blue frock coat with nine brass buttons for all enlisted soldiers. The 1861 Regulations stated that the skirt extended one-half the distance from the top of the hip to the bend of the knee and the stand-up collar was hooked at the neck. Brass scale epaulettes were worn on the shoulders for dress functions. There were pockets in the rear skirt of the coat and one in the breast. Lining was usually polished cotton. Many coats were government issued but there were some that were privately purchased by those who could afford them, and these were found to be of officer quality in some cases. The collar and cuffs with two brass buttons were piped with cord or welt in branch of service color.

These frock coats were relegated to garrison duty by many units. Some

regiments, however, such as those in the Iron Brigade, proudly wore their long coats in the field.

The dark blue sack coat was the trademark of Billy Yank. It was adopted for fatigue duties in 1859 and became the uniform of choice of the Union Army by late 1861. Tens of thousands were manufactured during the war at Schuylkill Arsenal in Philadelphia, Cincinnati Arsenal, and a host of private and commercial contractors. The coat was made of loose fitting dark blue flannel extending half way down the thigh. It was

Below left: *Private, 56th Colored Infantry. It was inevitable that the Union government would find a way to take the ex-slaves, whose cause had been so great a part in starting the war, and turn them into a weapon for winning it. Thousands wanted to take up arms to fight for their brothers still in bonds in the Confederacy, and eventually several tens of thousands were enlisted in more than 100 all-black regiments; though at the beginning they were regarded more as laborers than combat soldiers. The uniforms and equipment for these units was virtually the same as that for this private of the 56th United States Colored Infantry, and in fact, no different*

from the average white soldier. Dark blue wool jacket, light blue wool trousers, blue cloth kepi, Springfield rifle and accompanying bayonet were all standard issue. Most glaringly different was the fact that for most of the war, until at least 1864, black soldiers were paid less than their white counterparts.

Below: *The flag of the 125th Ohio Infantry pictured with officers of the unit. Unit flags were the soul of the regiment, guarded by men chosen for stature and previous valor at great personal risk, the rallying point in time of crisis and the focal point of fire from opposing forces.*

single-breasted with four brass buttons and an interior breast pocket, and came in lined and unlined styles. The sack coat was easy to manufacture, inexpensive and practical, an ideal military garment. Because of these factors, most were worn-out in service, and it is a rare coat today.

Artillery and cavalry shell jackets were of the same pattern. The 1861 Regulations stated that they would be made of dark blue cloth with one row of twelve small brass buttons and a stiff stand-up collar hooked at the neck. Brass scale epaulettes were worn on the shoulders for dress

functions but were not worn in the field. The jacket extended to the waist and the collar, cuffs and all edges were piped with three-eighths-inch wide tape in the color of branch of service. The jacket was supposed to be lined with white flannel but a variety of colored fabrics have been observed too. Many volunteer artillery and cavalry units came into service with their own state issue of these regulation patterns, and these exhibit many subtle variations. There existed some very few dragoon and mounted rifle shell jackets in the early months of the war. These were

according to pattern with lace in color of branch of service. Musicians of these branches wore the same shell jacket with the addition of an elaborate pattern of tape in the form of a plastron on the breast.

New York State 1861 issue shell jackets were another variation of this pattern. These jackets had cloth epaulettes and a belt loop on the left side. The epaulettes, belt loop and sometimes the collar were piped in branch of service color.

Somewhat less conspicuous were the chasseur coats, copies from those of the

French Light Infantry. These were worn by some Pennsylvania, New York, and Massachusetts units and were made of dark blue cloth, slightly flared and longer than a shell jacket but not as long or shapeless as the sack coat. Lining was dark polished cotton and similar fabric. Most had epaulettes, belt loops, and colored piping, and some were actually imported from France.

On all of these uniforms chevrons in branch of service color above the elbow indicated noncommissioned officer rank.

Trousers for enlisted men, like those of

Union Infantry Equipment.

1: Hardee hat

2: Infantryman's overcoat

3: Neck stock

4: Forage cap

5: Soft knapsack

6: 2nd Corps Headquarters flag

7: Model 1840 Non-commissioned Officer's sword and shoulder belt

8: Enlisted man's shoulder scales

9: .69 caliber cartridge box

10: Haversack

11: Model 1858 covered tin drum canteen

12: Brogans

13: Sack coat

14: Infantryman's uniform trousers

15: Model 1842 rifled and sighted musket

16: Infantry accoutrements: belt, cap box, bayonet and scabbard, and cartridge box

17: Soft knapsack

18: Soft knapsack

For the men who served in the Union Army, equipment was usually plentiful and of standard quality. Only the more remote units of the Union Army had real trouble replacing essential pieces of uniforms or equipment.

officers, were found in mounted and dismounted patterns. All trousers were made to be loose fitting with the cuff spread well over the boot. The seat and inside of the trouser leg were reinforced for mounted personnel.

The 1861 Regulations ordered all trousers to be dark blue cloth with the exception of Light Artillery units, whose trousers were to be sky blue kersey. General Order No. 108, Headquarters of the Army, dated December 16, 1861, said every enlisted man except those of the Ordnance Branch would wear sky blue

kersey trousers. Union ordnance personnel retained the dark blue trousers.

Trousers for foot soldiers were usually not lined and had metal, bone or porcelain buttons for fly closure and suspenders. Pockets were either side seam or mule ear and there were never any rear pockets or belt loops.

Noncommissioned officers had worsted leg stripes in branch of service color. Sergeant's stripes were one-and-one-half inches wide and those for a corporal were a half-inch wide.

Shirts for the soldier were always a

pullover pattern, often of coarse wool material or sometimes flannel, and cut very full. Colors varied from shades of white and gray to dark blue and many civilian shirts of plaid and striped patterns were worn when issue items were not available. These shirts were considered undergarments and rarely worn without the coat. Most had two to four bone buttons at the neck and one bone button on each cuff. There were no pockets in military contract shirts but many civilian shirts had one or two.

Like the sack coat, shirts were worn-out

in service and are seldom seen today. Three shirts a year were supposedly issued to each enlisted man. Prolonged periods in the field made this very difficult to accomplish. These garments were secured from a multitude of contractors and surviving specimens are very diverse. Several states also issued shirts to their regiments and they, too, show considerable individuality.

The 1851 and 1861 Regulations specified all enlisted men were to have a leather neck stock "of the pattern then in use." It was thought that such an item

Below: *12th New York State Volunteers. They were ordered by the Governor of the State in August 1861 to be mustered in the United States service for the unexpired period of its term of State service. They went to Washington, D.C., in May 1861 and subsequently took part in the following engagements: Blackburn's Ford, Va., July 18, 1861; Bull Run, Va., July 21, 1861; Upton's Hill, Va., August 27, 1861; Near Big Bethel, Va., March 27, 1862; the siege of Yorktown, Va., April 5–May 4, 1862; Yorktown, April 11 and April 13, 1862; Hanover Court House, Va., May 27, 1862; Seven Day's Battle, Va., June 25–July 2, 1862; Gaines Mill, June 27,* 1862; *Malvern Cliff, June 30, 1862; Malvern Hill, July 1, 1862; General Pope's Campaign, Va., August 27–September 2, 1862; Bull Run, Va., August 30, 1862; Antietam, Md., September 17, 1862; Near Shepherdstown, Va., September 20, 1862; Fredericksburg, Va., December 11–15, 1862; Richards Ford, Va., December 30–31, 1862; Rappahannock River, Va., April 30, 1863; Chancellorsville, Va., May 1-3, 1863; Gettysburg, Pa. July 1-3, 1863; Mine Run Campaign, Va., November 26–December 2, 1863; Wilderness, Va. May 5–7, 1864; Spotsylvania Court House, Va. May 8–21, 1864; North Anna, Va. May 22-26, 1864; Totopotomoy, Va. May 27–31, 1864.*

would keep the soldier's head up and give him a more martial bearing. It was little more than a band of leather with a small buckle worn under the collar, very uncomfortable in practice. Most were left in garrison or thrown away in the field at the first opportunity.

The 1858 Pattern enlisted men's hat, known as the Hardee hat, was made of black felt and had a double row of stitching instead of binding around the edge. The brim was looped up on the right for mounted men and on the left for foot soldiers, and a black feather was worn on the side opposite the loop. The hat had a worsted branch of service color hat cord with tassels and branch of service insignia on the front. All insignia, unit numeral, branch of service plate and eagle plate, were made of die stamped brass. Many Hardee hats were field-modified by soldiers to be almost unrecognizable.

The enlisted Pattern 1861 forage cap was the hat worn by most Federal soldiers throughout the war. Civilian contractors sold over 4 million of them to the Quartermaster Department and another 41,000 were manufactured at Army Depots. Enlisted men also wore chasseur pattern forage caps with a lower crown. Branch of service insignia, company letter, and regimental numerical designation and corps badge were on the top of these hats rather than the front. With the exception of the corps badge, all insignia was die stamped brass.

Early in the American Civil War forage and chasseur pattern caps were often covered by havelocks made of cotton or linen. These covers supposedly provided protection from sun and dust on the march but actually added to the

discomfort of the wearer. Most of these covers were discarded or the material put to some other use. Waterproof or foul weather covers made of oilcloth or vulcanized rubber were used and welcomed by sentries and videttes during periods of bad weather.

Civilian slouch hats were very popular particularly with Western Theater troops. These hats were usually dark, nondescript and shaped to the whim of the soldier. Some had appropriate regulation military insignia affixed. Other special units wore specific headgear.

Below left: *The color guard of the 118th New York Volunteer Infantry. The unit was organized at Plattsburg, New York, and mustered in August 1862. The 118th were present at various actions, including Cold Harbor, Petersburg, Fair Oaks, Drewrys Bluff, Fort Harrison, Swift Creek, Richmond, and were present at the Appomattox Court House for the surrender of Lee's army. The 118th was mustered out on June 12, 1865.*

Below: *Sergeant, 79th New York Infantry "Highlanders", 1860–61. Few Yankee regiments of the war were quite as distinctive—or as*

ridiculed—*as the famed 79th New York Infantry, the "Highlanders". Modeling itself after the 79th Cameron Highlanders of the British Army, its initial core of four companies was formed in 1859 entirely of Scots immigrants. With the outbreak of the Civil War its strength was increased with enlistments of English and Irish, as well as other foreign-born men, but its dress would remain distinctly Scottish. In the field the men of the 79th New York Infantry quickly changed to light blue trousers, which they are reported to have worn at First Manassas, or Cameron tartan trews; dark blue blouses, and a regulation kepi.*

The Confederate Soldier

◆

WHEN ARMED CONFLICT BEGAN, LACK of uniformity in dress of troops was a major problem. Many Rebel units did not have gray, so they fought in what they often termed "butternut" uniforms. Close to the end of the war, North Carolina textile mills turned out a big batch of Confederate uniforms before taking care that they had suitable dyes on hand. When no gray could be found, these were dyed blue—and shipped off for use by Confederate units. This inevitably led to numerous instances in which comrades fired upon comrades.

What the Rebel soldier wore showed the deplorable state of Confederate supply. Scores of regiments equipped themselves locally before going off to war, but as clothing and equipment wore out it was often up to the private soldier to replace it himself. Even what the Richmond government did manage to distribute was often of wildly varying quality.

Although the shell jacket was the standard upper garment, soldiers were also issued frock coats and sack coats. All

were made of wool, wool and cotton twill, wool jean cloth or kersey. Some shell jackets were trimmed with branch of service colored tape on collars and cuffs and some units chose a color because it was fashionable. Single-breasted frock coats were worn through the war but were more common in the early years. North Carolina issued distinctive sack coats to state troops and managed to clothe its regiments adequately throughout the war.

Huge quantities of cloth were imported from England, and Peter Tait of Limerick, Ireland, sent bales of ready-made cadet gray kersey uniforms with buttons of his own manufacture through the blockade on his own ships. Regulations authorized the wear of the forage cap but southern soldiers also wore a variety of slouch hats and palmetto straw hats. Forage caps were made of cotton or wool jean cloth, with brims of leather or oilcloth and chinstraps of similar material. Some caps were made in branch of service color or had a band of that color, but most were gray or butternut.

Slouch hats came with brims turned up or down, one side pinned up or both sides pinned up, and were adorned with brass, silver, pewter or embroidered insignia at the discretion of the wearer. It seemed no

Below: *Rebel troops at a camp at the Warrington Navy Yard, Pensacola, Florida, in 1861. Much Confederate camp equipment was civilian material pressed into service, such as household or camp utensils. During the summer of 1861 a considerable variety of shelters appeared in the armies, both North and South. The tent was extremely important to the soldier as he could expect to spend three seasons of the year under canvas.*

two were alike. Color was usually black or some shade of brown, and the favored insignia was a star or state badge. A substantial number of English slouch hats were imported.

Large numbers of Federal Jefferson bootees or brogans and Wellington boots were worn by Confederate foot soldiers and mounted troops, and had to work very hard. Capture of quartermaster supplies and the stripping of dead (and sometimes living) Federal troops at every opportunity made these fine brogans and boots available.

Confederate-manufactured brogans copied the same Jefferson pattern and were supplied by many contractors in varying quality to the Quartermaster Department. In addition, significant numbers of officers' boots were civilian private purchases.

Britain supplied thousands of pairs of shoes to the Confederate fighting man. One pattern was square-toed with hobnail pegs in the soles. Another pattern had buckle closure rather than lace and eyelets. British footwear was admired for its sturdy quality.

Sword belts and waist belts were the two primary types of Confederate belts. The sword belt suspended an edged weapon and was worn by officers of all branches of service, and by mounted troops. The waist belt was an integral part of a set of accoutrements and suspended the cap box, cartridge box and bayonet with scabbard.

Sword belts were made of leather or canvas, painted or unpainted, and had two sword hangers affixed. The belt was usually between 1.5–2inches wide with brass mountings and was secured by a

belt plate.

Leather belts were constructed of a single thickness or sometimes folded over a cloth core and sewn on the reverse. Most were black or dark brown although white and black enameled examples have also been noted.

Waist belts were also made of leather or painted or unpainted canvas and were usually the same width as the sword belt, and similarly were secured by a belt plate. Methods of construction were similar to that used for sword belts, but colors were again normally restricted to the usual black or dark brown.

Both types of belts were fabricated at government arsenals and by many private contractors, and a substantial number were imported along with much other material and weapons from England through the Federal blockade.

Confederate soldiers wore several hundred different styles of belt plates, including brass frame, rectangular, oval, and two-piece interlocking patterns. Substantial numbers were imported from Britain, while thousands of captured Federal plates were also utilized.

Below left: *Southern and Confederate buckles and plates. From the outset, Rebel forces were issued with an array of distinctive central government accoutrement plates, usually oval or rectangular in shape and made of brass.*

Below: *Confederates, like Yankees, often enlisted in groups, even families, like these Rebel soldiers proudly displaying their muskets. These Rebel troops are wearing crudely manufactured "butternut" frock coats. When the war began the lack of uniformity in dress of troops was a major problem. Many Rebels did not have gray and wore "butternut" uniforms.*

The General Service plates were produced in numerous foundries all over the Confederate states. These plates were either generic brass frame buckles in several sizes or sheet brass plates, both generally rectangular in shape, used on both sword and waist belts.

Frame buckles were made with forked, double or single tongues. Sheet brass plates had hooks in various configurations soldered to the reverse for belt attachment. These buckles were by far the more common types in Confederate service.

Plate and buckles bearing the letters "CS" or "CSA," state seal or state letter designation were also made in quantity but nowhere near that of General Service plates. Styles were rectangular, oval and two-piece interlocking. Brass, pewter, sheet iron and even precious metal examples have been noted. The rectangular CSA plate fabricated at the Atlanta Arsenal and the two-piece interlocking CS plate made in Richmond were the most common, if any Confederate plate may be called common.

Thousands of snake buckles were imported from Britain. There were also British-made plates that had the state seals as well as the arms of the Confederate States Navy.

Uniform buttons worn by Confederate military personnel numbered in the millions and were very diverse. prewar southern militia and Federal issue buttons were very prominent. Civilian buttons of all types were used and enormous numbers of buttons imported from England and a lesser number from France saw use. Local Confederate and southern state production added to this number.

There were three-piece, two-piece buttons, and those that were solid cast with drilled shanks, all produced by manufacturers throughout the Confederate states. Material used was primarily die struck sheet brass and some had tin backs, while there were some cast pewter and turned wood buttons. A very few special orders were made of precious metals. The face of the button presented the letter of branch of service, a staff eagle or state seal or some variant of the seal.

English-manufactured buttons included all branches of army service as well as the

Confederate Infantry Equipment.

1: 1st Sergeant's frock coat
2: Forage cap
3: Linen havelock
4: Trousers for 1st Sergeant's frock coat
5: Uniform vest for 1st Sergeant's frock coat and trousers
6: Shirt
7: Cartridge box
8: Cap box
9: Fayetteville rifle
10: Brogans
11: Wooden canteen with the name of the

owner inscribed on it
12: Haversack
13: Model 1860 Colt Army revolver and holster
14: Side knives

After some initial confusion, the Confederate forces adopted gray as the color for uniforms. Pattern of clothing varied throughout the Civil War. Various shades of gray spanned the spectrum into blacks and browns. Confederate uniforms exist in most Southern state collections and the superb display housed at The Museum of the Confederacy in Richmond boasts over 100 items from the period.

Confederate States Navy.

These buttons were imported by the gross on blockade-runners and substantial numbers were still available on original cards in the 1960s. Some dies still exist and many buttons have been re-struck and others have been manufactured in England and elsewhere abroad in recent years. Fine collections of Southern buttons may be viewed at the Museum of the Confederacy, Richmond, Virginia.

The Confederate soldier's uniform gave very little protection against the elements during the harsh winter temperatures. Nor did the Rebel uniforms provide any comfort in hot and dry, dusty camps during the summer.

In the summer of 1864, one Confederate soldier likened a walk through camp to a stroll through an ash heap. "One's mouth will be so full of dust that you do not want your teeth to touch one another." A canoneer wryly remarked that whenever a grasshopped jumped up, it raised such a dust that Union lookouts reported that the Confederate forces were on the move again.

The dust blew through holes in their worn clothing and caked to the sweat on their bodies. "I have no seat in my pants," lamented a Virginian Rebel soldier, "the legs are worn out, have had but one pair of socks which are worn out completely, my shirt is literally rotted off me". A new issue shirt proved to be so louse-ridden that he could not bear to wear it.

Clothing deteriorated badly, and there were frequently no reissues. As a result, by the end of the Civil War many Confederate uniforms had ceased to mean anything. The men simply dressed themselves with whatever they could find to hand.

Far left: *Private and Sergeant, 1st Texas Infantry. Men from the Confederacy's western regiments often wore very individualist dress, and even uniforms of whole regiments could vary considerably from regulations. The battle shirt, for instance, could sport oversize breast pockets, usually outlined against their plain or checked home-spun background. The 1st Texas was one of the better clothed western outfits, and at the beginning of the war sported gray frock coats and trousers, trimmed with blue, and gray kepis with stars and regimental numerals on the crown. Armed with Enfield rifles, they saw heavy service in the Army of Northern Virginia* with the Texas Brigade, from Seven Pines in 1862 to the end at Appomattox. Consequently, clothing deteriorated with scant reissues and men simply wore anything they could find to hand.

Center: *Men of the 9th Mississippi near Pensacola in 1861.*

Below right: *Private, 11th Mississippi Infantry, Confederate State Army. The 11th Mississippi Infantry presented one of the handsomer variations on the standard gray uniform of the Confederacy. The regiment was made up chiefly of prewar volunteer militia companies, many of* which wore entirely different garb. Most eventually wore slight variations of the sate militia dress, the mid-thigh length gray blouse with red collar and red frogging on the breast, red cuffs and trouser stripes. Their headgear was predominantly the Hardee-style hat worn by this enlisted man, pinned up on the right or left side, according to the individual taste of the wearer. Some wore a distinctive state seal beltplate, but this private had only an ordinary buckle. The Mississippians used their rifles well. At Antietam they held the line near the Dunker Church until all their field officers went down, and still repulsed assault after assault.

Below: *Private, Co. E, 23rd Virginia Infantry, Confederate States' Army. Four years of heavy service characterized the 23rd Virginia, and by the end it showed on those fortunate few who could still answer the roll. They were typical of units that had been raised in 1861. Formed chiefly from companies locally raised in Virginia and called such names as the "Brooklyn Grays" and "Louisa Grays", the 23rd Virginia Infantry wore gray frock coats and trousers, with blue or black trim and distinctive yellow loops on their collars. Their leather belts and accoutrements were originally white, but hard service quickly soiled them.*

Right: *Confederate battleflags. The battleflags of the Rebel states are easily one of the most recognizable symbols worldwide. Many people believe it to be the only Confederate flag, and unfortunately this symbol of a no longer extant military organization has been associated with various extremist political groups. Specimens exist in many Southern state collections.*

Below right: *Confederate photographer Jay D. Edwards captured this scene of raw recruits being drilled in Fort McRee, Pensacola, Florida, early in 1861. These men present a uniformity rarely seen in the Rebel armies.*

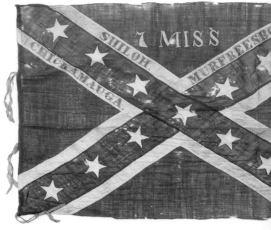

The Zouaves and Sharpshooters

◆◆◆

ZOUAVE (ZOO-AHH-VAH) WAS THE name given to native North African troops employed by the French Army as mercenaries. Their dash, spirit, and heroic style of warfare caught the fancy of many military observers.

The distinctive zouaves outfit was derived from the tribal dress of the Zou Oua, a fiercely independent Kabyli tribe living in the rocky terrain of Algeria and Morocco. In 1830 the French hired the Zou Ouas as mercenaries and they were formed into two auxiliary battalions. The the indigenous fighters, however, kept their tribal dress, which consisted of baggy trousers, a tight vest, and a turban or fez.

The French authorities slowly weeded out the indigenous troops, and renamed the unit the French Zouaves, but retained the unusual dress with one modification: they changed it to the French national colors. What had once been dress of light beige, tan and white became the bright red and dark blue of the French Army. This was the beginning of a long, and very colorful tradition.

In 1852, President Louis Napoleon instructed that the zouaves be reformed into three regiments of the regular French Army. Only Frenchmen would serve in these formations.

During the Crimean War, Captain George B. McClellan (later to become a senior commander during the American Civil War), saw the French Zouaves in action. He was much impressed with these distinctive warriors and regarded them as "The finest light infantry that Europe can produce....the beau-ideal of a soldier." He fell in love with the fighting style and the

Below left: A wounded Union zouave is offered a canteen of water by another soldier.

1: Distinctive jacket of the 9th New York, "Hawkins' Zouaves". The unit was formed by Rush C. Hawkins. His men wore a sky-blue overcoat over a darker blue jacket and chasseur patterned dark blue trousers.

2: An officer's cap of the 114th Pennsylvania Volunteer Infantry, "Collis' Zouaves de Afrique". The unit was raised by Charles Collis in August 1861. Collis dressed his men in the traditional garb favored by the fierce French

Zouaves, and hoped his unit would emulate them as much as possible.

3: Officers cap of the 5th New York Volunteers, "Duryée Zouaves". This cap was worn by Lt. Col. Gouverneur G. K. Warren. The unit was formed by Abram Duryée and was outfitted in a colorful variation of the zouave uniform.

4: A Union zouave fez. The French Algerian Zouave troops often wore a turban or fez. This particular style of headgear was frequently copied by the zouave militias that were formed in America.

1

2

3

4

uniform, and brought both back home to the United States. What followed can only be called a craze to rival any modern fashion trend.

The widespread popularity of the zouaves is largely due to Elmer Ephraim Ellsworth. He was a prominent member of the state militia who met a veteran of the French Zouaves, Charles DeVilliers, in 1857. This meeting led to Ellsworth exploring the zouaves and he established the "United States Zouave Cadets" in Chicago. The members were to be "morally upright", and to abstain from

alcohol or tobacco. By 1860 Elmer Ellsworth's men were considered to be the finest Midwest militia outfit.

This zouave formation rose to national prominence after Ellsworth challenged the militias of a dozen states to compete in a drill competition. Ellsworth took 50 of his finest zouaves on a tour of 20 cities where thousands of people watched their immaculate displays of drill.

The *New York Times* noted "Their bronzed features, sharp outlines, light, wiry forms, muscular developments and spirited, active movements, give them an

appearance of dashing ferocity."

"Ellsworth's Zouaves" began a craze that rapidly spread across the United States. American zouave companies were established across the country wearing adaptations of Ellsworth's version of the original French uniform.

As the country moved towards war, Ellsworth went to New York where he raised an entire zouaves regiment, the 11th New York Infantry. These men were recruited from Manhattan's Volunteer Fireman whose stature and stamina made them ideal recruits for his elite formation.

They received an enthusiastic send-off as they marched down Broadway on April 29, 1861. When they arrived in the capital, President Lincoln, a friend of Ellsworth, personally welcomed them.

The zouave uniform became immensely popular, and influenced everything from state militia uniforms to children's wear.

Those state militia units, at the outset of the war, became the basis for many of the zouave formations who fought during the conflict. The zouave-style uniforms were difficult to obtain in the United States, so manufacturers of specialty clothing were

Below: Zouaves of the 114th Pennsylvania Infantry, Petersburg, Virginia, August 1864. The unit was originally mustered into service on August 17, 1861, only three days after Charles Henry Tukcer Collis received authorization from Assistant Secretary of War Thomas Alexander Scott to raise a company of zouaves "...for three years or during the war" as Collis' Independent Company "Zouaves De Afrique". The majority of the 114th Pennsylvania Volunteers were neither farmers nor foreigners. Colonel Charles Collis was a Philadelphia lawyer and most of his enlisted soldiers were skilled laborers. Because of their skilled background, the Pennsylvania

Volunteers were more highly educated and more financially stable than the typical Yankee soldiers. Colonel Charles Collis' soldiers had an extremely distinctive uniform. They were dressed in baggy brick red trousers, short dark blue jackets with red tape trim forming two tombeaus on the chest. The men had dark blue vests or the Zouave shirt, which is most evident in photographs of the regiment. The men of 114th Pennsylvania Infantry also wore the brick red fez with a large golden yellow tassle and white turban. A french blue sash around the waist, white leggings and leather jambieres to protect the legs completed the outfit.

employed to make the uniforms. There were many distinct styles and colors, depending on the designs submitted by the main benefactor of a given regiment.

Zouave shell jackets were all based on the jacket worn by the elite French North African units. Almost all had the decorative device known as tombeaux on each breast and the collarless, short, close fitting jacket did not button but had an integral vest worn beneath the coat. The tombeaux were normally bright red on the dark blue jacket. These jackets, along with other striking pieces of zouave uniform,

made the soldier so attired a handsome target. Some zouave trousers were, in fact, pantaloons, again in the style borrowed from the North African dress of their zouave units. The leg came only below the knee and was bloused in the gaiters or jambiéres worn with this uniform. Many of the pants were cut very full. Others were tailored more like conventional trousers but each regiment had its own distinctive style. Some of the pantaloons were bright red, others shades of blue. Combined with other pieces of the uniform, these made the zouaves very

conspicuous on the battlefield.

Money for the uniforms of a new zouave regiment was donated by numerous people. John M. Gosline, a prominent citizen of Philadelphia who raised the 95th Pennsylvania or "Gosline's Zouaves", secured sufficient funds to purchase a full set of clothing for 1,000 men and had enough extra to insure that the uniforms could be replenished as they were worn out during the course of the war.

When the uniforms of the 114th Pennsylvania Infantry began to wear out, Colonel Charles Collis used his influence

with political friends in the state legislature to secure state money to supply new uniforms to the unit's men who needed them.

Other zouave regiments were not so lucky. By the time of the battle of Gettysburg, many of these regiments had lost or worn out their uniforms, and adopted the standard Union uniform. A handful of them kept only a portion of the zouave uniform, such as the jacket. There were even some Union regiments such as the 146th New York Infantry and 155th Pennsylvania Infantry, that did not start

Union Zouave Uniforms and Equipment.

1: Zouave fez
2: Uniform pantaloons
3: Short jacket with insignia and badge
4: Jambiére, or outer legging of leather
5: Uniform gaiter
6: US brass belt plate
7: Uniform jacket of 72nd Pa. Vols
8: Corps badge
9: Model 1845 French Infantry Bugle
10: Wooden small arms ammunition box for 1000 rounds
11: Embroidered uniform jacket

12: Pantaloons
13: Fez
14: Fez complete with regimental badge which belonged to Private Lathen Avery Fish, Company C, 9th New York Volunteer Infantry
15: Screwtop tin drum canteen

Numbers 1 to 5 were worn by Corporal Walter H. Mallorie, Company B, 76th Pennsylvania Volunteers, "Keystone Zouaves". Numbers 11 to 13 were worn by Private Thaddeus Paxon, Company F of the 11th Pennsylvania Volunteers, "Collis' Zouaves" who died of disease on January 11, 1863.

out as zouave regiments, but later adopted zouave uniforms.

The sharpshooters were the elite shots of the Civil War. These soldiers had the skills to hit high-priority targets like officers or color guards at long range.

The Confederate army formed their best riflemen into a formation known as the "Whitworth Sharpshooters". This unit was formed in 1862 to undertake flank security and skirmishing roles.

These sharpshooters excelled at long-range precision fire. Many of these Confederate sharpshooters used the

Sharps rifle imported from Britain. This was a .45 caliber, high-velocity longarm and was originally designed as a top of the range hunting rifle.

The Sharps rifle was imported in small quantities and cost at least $500 in gold. This included some 1,000 rounds as well.

The rifle used a bullet shaped to suit the hexagonal rifling of the bore. Each rifle had a ladder-style-sight and many had a fine Davidson 4X scope on left side of the stock. Although the Sharps rifle was very accurate at long range, it fouled easily and was slow to reload.

The "Whitworth Sharpshooters" displayed incredible skill and accuracy despite the low velocity of the bullets, the loose powder, low-power optics, and the general hindrance of battlefield conditions. They achieved this remarkable level of ability because they were firstly recruited from the rural communities where a man depended on his shooting skills for protection and food. Once they joined the sharpshooters these men would continuously practice range estimation as well as other skills required to be an expert rifleman. The sharpshooters constantly

worked to perfect their skills.

In the Federal army the sharpshooters were formed into two regiments under Hiram Berdan. Hiram Berdan was a national champion marksman and when war broke out he formed a Union regiment of skilled riflemen to undertake scouting and flank protection duties. The selection process consisted of two sequences of fire, both at a target. The soldier was required to fire 10 shots at the target from a rest, at a range of 200 yards, then a further 10 rounds at an identical target from the standing, off-hand

Below left: *Private, 9th New York Infantry Regiment, "Hawkins' Zouaves". In 1861 Rush C. Hawkins, a veteran of the Mexican War went to work finding men for a new regiment. Starting with members of the old prewar Company of New York Zouaves, he enlisted enough men to muster his 9th New York Infantry on May 4, 1861. Thanks to their uniform, they were quickly dubbed "Hawkins' Zouaves". The regiment fought at Big Bethel in June 1861, then went on to campaign in North Carolina before returning to take part in the Battles of Antietam and Fredericksburg. They were mustered out in May 1863. The uniforms*

that gave them their name were typical of zouave outfits: skullcap, short jacket and baggy pants tucked into white leggings. Armed with 1861 Springfields and bayonets, they lent color to their army. Though how colorful it was in 1863 is open to debate. Hard wear and a uniform that looked as it it were made for Rebel target practice may have toned it down.

Below: *A group from the 11th New York Volunteer Infantry, "Ellsworth's Fire Zouaves". The Regiment lost 3 officers and 48 enlisted men killed and mortally wounded and 3 officers and 12 enlisted men by disease during the war.*

position, at 100 yards. All the 10 rounds within each string needed to be within the circle. This required impressive accuracy.

Many of the successful applicants to the regiments were peacetime shooters who brought along their own match rifles. These precision longarms, however, were unsuitable to military use.

Berdan's men were notoriously unruly and free-spirited. The sharpshooters often had contempt for the regular soldiers and were extremely confident in their abilities. This independent nature was seen when the 1st and 2nd Sharpshooters were issued

with the standard Springfield rifle-musket. They refused to carry this longarm and were instead issued with a repeating rifle. The sharpshooters were issued with the Colt revolving rifle. This design had been extremely successful in pistol form but proved problematic when adapted into a rifle. The sharpshooters almost started a mutiny and were issued with the .52 caliber Sharps breechloader instead.

This longarm had been around since 1848, it loaded from the breech which enabled Hiram Berdan's soldiers to reload from a concealed position. The Sharps

breechloader also had a high rate of fire. Some 10 shots per minute could be fired compared to just two or three rounds from a Springfield in the same period.

Berdan's men had dual "set" triggers on the rifles. These were normally used on target longarms and were adjustable to enable the hammer to be released with very light pressure.

The Federal sharpshooters were formed into four-man fire teams rather than the company-sized formations of other units. Sharpshooters did act in the sniper role but normally undertook skirmishing and

gave flank security. Two-man teams would alternate their fire. While the first man to fire was reloading the second would fire. This tactic ensured that sustained fire was maintained against enemy targets.

The sharpshooters on both sides of the Civil War were mainly deployed in the skirmishing role. They formed a screening force in an arc ahead of the main formation of troops. The commanders in-charge of "Berdan's Sharpshooters" used bugle calls to maneuver their units as many of the men would not be in sight of the commander.

Below left: *A Union sharpshooter in a tree, drawn for* Harper's Weekly *by war correspondent Winslow Homer in 1862, during the Peninsular Campaign in Virginia.*

Below right: *Berdan's 1st Sharpshooters. A few Federal units won special notice for their rifle skills, none more so than the 1st and 2nd Regiments of United States Sharpshooters, commonly known as "Berdan's Sharpshooters" after the colonel of the 1st Regiment, Hiram Berdan. Seeing their role as skirmishers and special marksmen, Berdan selected experienced men and armed them with the best weapons*

available, the Sharps Rifle in .52 caliber. Many also carried telescopic sights. With a view towards camouflage, Hiram Berdan clothed his sharpshooters in green kepis or hats and dark green uniform blouses. In keeping with the rest of the army, the soldiers' trousers were light blue, but these too were later changed to green. They were held to the boots with canvas or leather leggings. By 1864, losses in Hiram Berdan's outfits were such that the Sharpshooters almost ceased to exist. At the end of that year they were consolidated into a single unit, and by early 1865 they were dispersed into other regiments.

The Musician

❖

MUSIC QUICKLY CAME TO OCCUPY A special place of importance in the soldier's life. It was a musical era. In the absence of other entertainments, family song fests around the piano were a cultural norm in the middle class of both North and South, augmented by public concerts and participation in church hymns available to everyone. Their songs, like their times, were highly sentimental, maudlin, demonstrating extremes of emotion, but especially concerning romantic love, the sorrow of loss, and patriotism. Stirring national songs helped rally men to enlist all through the war, especially at its outset. Often they learned their march steps to the tune of snappy martial airs, and later moved off to battle with songs in their ears. Sales of sheet music and song books were at their highest level in American history, and except in the bitterest of weather or the depths of depression after defeat, every camp North and South gave rise to hummed and sung melodies every night.

Most regiments, especially from the

North, brought some kind of band with them to the Civil War.

By the mid-19th Century military bands played an important part in the popular militia system throughout the country. The military bands of the Civil War were composed almost entirely of brass and percussion instruments.

The instruments were often indifferent in quality, and their players little better, though time and practice made some quite proficient. Many regimental and brigade ensembles, however, simply made a lot of noise. One Texas band was described by a

Confederate Musicians' Equipment.

1: Typical example of Confederate First National Pattern Flag as carried by army bands
2: Typical style of forage cap as worn by musicians
3: Bugle with attachment points for carrying strap
4: Snare drum complete with carry strap and drum sticks
5: Snare drum and drum sticks
6: Typical design of frock coat as worn by Confederate musicians.
7: Clarinet used by Confederate bands

8: Alternative type of bugle as used by armies of the Confederacy
9: Alternative type of bugle used by armies of the Confederacy
10: Small horn insignia as worn on uniforms of some of the Confederate musicians
11: Militia waist belt plate
12: Fife as used by Confederate Army bands
13 and 14: Alternative type of fife used by musicians of the Confederacy

Most Southern instruments were either of prewar manufacture or imported although there was a major drum manufacturer in Richmond.

Left: *Pennsylvanian musicians. In armies on both sides, bands existed at regimental level and above. Not only did they provide music on the march and entertainment in camp, but drums and bugles provided the combat communication system of commands and calls during battle. Invariably, the bands marched at the front of the column to facilitate the use of the over-the-shoulder horns, enabling the music to flow back over the column. The instruments were primarily various brass horns and wood shell drums.*

Below: *Regulation drums from New York, Vermont, and Massachusetts regiments. Base and snare drums were the basic types and army records indicate that more than 3,200 were purchased during the Civil War. Associated accoutrements were slings, beaters, and sticks. Bands were played for parades, guard mount, morning colors, reviews, and funerals. During battle, the musicians sometimes served as stretcher-bearers and surgeons' assistants in hospitals. After the battle they gathered and buried the dead.*

Left: *A rare amateur photograph of two Yankee boy drummers taken by Lieutenant Henry Digby, an Ohio infantry officer, in 1861.*

dismayed auditor as "braying" while another listener described Confederate bands in general as so wretched that "their dismal noises are an intolerable nuisance." Discordance was hardly the exclusive realm of Rebel brass, however, for many would have argued that the 6th Wisconsin band was the worst of the war. It knew only one song, "The Village Quickstep." And even hearers who knew the song could never recognize it when the band played. It did not help that the regiment's colonel looked on his band as a punishment assignment.

Good or bad, still these bands were welcome in the camp as they brought relief from the tedium of daily life. Thousands did not wait to depend upon the bands, however, and instead made their own music. Every company, and indeed many messes, had one or more men who could saw out a few tunes on the fiddle, strum a guitar, play a flute, or even just twang a Jew's harp. Singly or in ensemble, they entertained themselves with "Hell Broke Loose in Georgia," the "Arkansas Traveler," or "Billy in the Low Grounds." Even more festive than this was the

occasional banjo picker, whose ringing strings could join with a good fiddler to provide a genuine hoedown for the troops to dance.

Cheerful instruments were necessary, too, because the natural bent of the individual was toward more sad and sentimental songs, reflecting his longing for home. They sang songs like "The Empty Chair," "All Quiet Along the Potomac," "When This Cruel War is Over," and "Just Before the Battle Mother." Ironically, a favorite on both sides was "Auld Lang Syne." "My Old

Kentucky Home" and other Stephen Foster tunes brought tears to blue eyes and gray, and looking forward to the day when peace would come, Yanks and Rebels alike sang of "When Johnny Comes Marching Home Again."

Just as their songs could serve to stir their martial ardor, so could the mournful melodies depress low spirits even further. "Home Sweet Home" was banned from the camps by commanders in the winter of 1862–63 after the Army of the Potomac had suffered the demoralizing defeat at Fredericksburg on December 13.

Below left: *Musicians from the 125th Ohio Volunteer Infantry, known as "Opdycke's Tigers." In 1862, Company A was mustered in at Camp Cleveland, Ohio. They were destined to go with the 105th Ohio, but the 105th had enough companies so the Governor ordered another regiment to be recruited from the Northeast corner of the state. Thus, the 125th Ohio Volunteer Infantry Regiment came into being.*

Below: *Drummer, Company F, 2nd Wisconsin Infantry, "Iron Brigade." Hardly any other unit of the Civil War would achieve such lasting fame as the so-called "Iron Brigade" of Wisconsin,*

Michigan, and Indiana. Its three Wisconsin and one Indiana regiments fought with a ferocity, and suffered losses hardly equalled. Indeed, so heavy were its casualties that the unit only existed for two years. It endured 33 per cent losses at 2nd Manassas in 1862, and nearly 60 per cent in that whole campaign. Going into Gettysburg the following year it numbered almost 1,800; after the battle only 600 were left. The battle in Pennsylvania virtually destroyed the original brigade. Men of the 2nd Wisonsin, like their drummer, wore dark blue trousers, with dark Hardee hat, their regimental number encircled by a brass bugle.

The Daily Life of the Soldier

❖❖

FOR EVERY DAY SPENT IN BATTLE, YANK and Reb passed weeks—even months—fighting other enemies: heat and cold, hunger, deprivation, bad sanitation, foolish officers, the allurements of the devil, and worst of all boredom.

Out of all came their most enduring memories of the days of their youth. Their pleasures were simple, but to the men in blue and gray they were triumphs in themselves, adversities conquered in the unending battle to make the campgrounds of North and South homes away from home. The new soldiers came ill-prepared for their lives in camp. Hometown oratory charged their emotions to expect an immediate rush headlong into glorious battle, fight day in and day out, and then, the war won, return home again in triumph. Their first scanty drill and training in the rendezvous camps gave little hint of what would really come once they joined the armies in the field. No one taught these men to cook, or pitch tents, or not to dig their latrines upstream of their camps.

The new soldier learned rather quickly that his only real place of refuge from the parade ground was his tent, his home for three seasons of the year. As with his weapons, a considerable variety of shelters first appeared in the summer of 1861. Some units like the Washington Artillery of New Orleans came with candy-striped tents. Others showed up with nothing at all, and the governments had to cast about for what would suit their regiments the best. Wall tents were initially popular, canvas dwellings shaped like a small house. But they proved too expensive to produce, too cumbersome to pitch and carry, and eventually found themselves inhabited only by those too weak or too exalted to do the work of erecting them—hospital patients and officers.

Much more popular and efficient was the Sibley tent, named for its inventor Henry H. Sibley who became a Confederate brigadier general. It resembled nothing so much as an Indian teepee, a tall cone of canvas supported by a center pole. Flaps on the sides could be opened for ventilation, and an iron replica of the tent cone called a Sibley stove heated the interior. Often more than 20 men inhabited a single tent, spread out like spokes of a wheel, their heads at the outer rim and their feet at the center pole. When cold or rain forced the men to keep the tent flaps closed overnight, the air inside became unbearable. Eventually, Sibleys also proved too cumbersome for extensive field operations.

Rapidly the tents became simpler, lighter, and as a rule less comfortable. For

Below left: *A Union camp where the troops have pitched their Sibley tents off the ground.*

a time Billy Yank tried sleeping in the wedge tent. Exceedingly simple, it was little more than a length of canvas that its four to six occupants draped over a center pole. Stakes held its sides to the ground and end flaps closed the openings, allowing some privacy, but absolutely no comfort for the men.

If that were not bad enough, by the latter part of 1862, and for the balance of the war to follow, an even smaller soldier shelter came into use. It differed little in nature or name from the pup tent of later wars. Two men shared it, and it took two to make it, each one carrying with him a half of the canvas. They buttoned their halves together, slung it over a center pole, and then laid down side-by-side in the cramped interior to contemplate what little impediment, if any, their shelter offered to the elements since it had no end flaps to hinder cold and wind.

Confederates suffered continually from want of proper shelters, as they suffered with a shortage of just about everything else. Captured Yankee tents were often all they had, for wartime shortages affected canvas as well as weapons and ammunition. Lacking tents, the Southerners improvised crude shelters as best they could, often piling brush or stretching oil clothes over fence-rail frameworks to make so-called "shoebangs". However crude, still inhabitants pronounced them "very comfortable in warm weather."

However, it was that fourth season of the year, with winter's chill, that most challenged the Reb's and Yank's ability and imagination. When the leaves began to turn and the north winds freshened, the men in the tents took their axes and saws

out into the neighbouring woods and virtually mowed them down. If timber was in sufficient abundance, whole log cabins rose up. More often, however, the soldiers blended earth and trees, their tents, even scavenged portions of local buildings, to produce their winter quarters. Before the ground froze, they dug their log walls another four or five above the pit, capping them with flat roofs of brush or boards, or even tents slung over a center pole. They waterproofed their roofs by spreading their own ponchos or rubberized blankets over the canvas, and kept the wind and

Confederate Personal Artifacts.

1, 2, 4, and 5: Pocket bibles and hymnals
3: Eye glasses
6: Personal effects bag
7: Photograph album
8: Water bottle
9: Bullet molds
10: Gunpowder can
11: Percussion cap tin
12: Pocket watch
13: Case for eye glasses
14: Wallet
15: Carved spoon

16: Carved pin
17: Percussion cap tin
18: Chess board and set
19: Paint box
20: Pocket knife
21: Hammer
22: Housewife
23: Miniature shoe ornament
24: Flute
25: Change purse
26: Deck of playing cards
27: Guitar
28: Powder horn

rain from whistling through the walls by packing the chinks between the logs with mud. Every winter hut was as individual as the men who built it.

Making matters even more difficult for the men, winter or summer, was that they were left entirely on their own to fill their idle time, and as the war went on, they had more and more of it to fill as drill was relaxed. Neither government made a concerted effort to provide systematic recreation or diversion. Worse, furloughs or brief releases from camp to return home for a visit were extremely limited. Men

from the North were too far away from home to get much use from a furlough, and Confederates were too few in the first place to allow them to go to the rear.

While they were required to remain in camp, almost like prisoners, the soldiers had to contend with the ever-present mud in winter and dust in summer. In the latter season of 1864 one Connecticut soldier likened a walk through a camp to a stroll through an ash heap. Relief societies like the United States' Christian Commission and several state societies, North and South, did what they could to bring a little

comfort to the soldiers' lot, but it was an ever-losing battle.

Filling in all those countless thousands of hours of unoccupied time proved to be the greatest challenge facing Yank and Reb alike. Not surprisingly, so many men being away from home for prolonged periods for the first time in their lives, it was the common soldiers' preoccupation with the folks at home which afforded the most popular camp pastime. Never before had such a massive number of Americans been away from home for a prolonged period. Instinctively, they sensed that they were

living through something unusual, an epoch worth remembering and reporting to their families. Letter writing, too, was the only contact that many could have with their loved ones, given the restrictions on furloughs. As a result, they sent letters back and forth that taxed the Postal Department as never before.

There was a remarkable sameness to what men in blue and gray wrote home about. They talked of their battles, to be sure, but those were few and infrequent. More often they told of their friends, their day in camp, the marches, the heat, the weather, sickness—virtually anything that came to mind—as if the very act of writing was the bond with their loved ones, and not what was written. They used ink and pencil, even crayons. They wrote on foolscap and parchment, in the margins of newspapers and on the back of wallpaper. When a precious sheet of paper was filled, if there was more to say they gave the sheet a quarter turn and cross-wrote over what they had already written.

Newspapers proved ever in demand, especially the illustrated press of the day. The *New York Illustrated News*, *Frank* *Leslie's Illustrated Newspaper*, *Harper's Weekly*, and for a brief time the

Below left: *A newspaperman. Illustrated newspapers, containing woodcuts portraying recent major events, were always in demand as soldiers on both sides were keen to follow the course of the war.*

Below: *A big reason for writing all those letters was the hope of receiving some in reply. The day when the mail wagon arrived, like this one of the II Corps Army of the Potomac, was a blessed one.*

Confederate *Southern Illustrated News*, provided the men with weekly accounts of the course of the war and events at home, illustrated with crude and often very inaccurate woodcuts. Literary magazines also came to the camps, but far more popular were booklets created especially for soldier consumption, the "dime" novels and paperback "penny dreadfuls" that the sutlers sold. Thousands of copies circulated among the soldiers. In the end, the men simply read or looked at whatever they could find, and if that was not sufficient, they sometimes created their

own reading material. Scores of regiments edited and printed their own newspapers.

Teasing was a chronic release, with practical jokes as commonplace as drill. In winter quarters someone could always count on a soldier dropping a handful of gunpowder down a chimney for some explosive fun, or else covering the chimney over with a blanket or boards to smoke the inhabitants out into the cold. If a new recruit went out on his first sentry duty, veterans would sneak up upon him in the dark. When he challenged their approach with "Who goes there?" the reply could

prove to be anything from a blue streak of oaths, to "a flock of sheep!"

Soldier fun took a more stately, ceremonious turn in some of the camps, especially those which were more permanently established. Fraternal orders and secret societies enjoyed a popular wave in the 1850s before the war, and many of their members brought their lodge ritual and dogma with them to the army. Masonic lodges thrived in many of the camps, North and South, with more than one recorded case of combatants ceasing hostilities temporarily in order to

join in some fraternal ceremony.

Several camps were entertained by literary and debating societies. The 50th New York Engineers built their own theater out of timbers at Petersburg in 1864, in order that their dramatic club, "Essayons", might perform.

Perhaps the soldiers' way of finding fun were the more inventive because more conventional entertainments cost money, and the boys of 1861–65 were not very well financed. Indeed, even pay day itself was one of the happier diversions in camp, though rarely for long.

It is no wonder that the frustration of poor pay and harsh living environments often produced a ruggedness in soldier fun that sometimes had its roots in anger and frustration. Every winter saw snowball fights, usually on a small inter-personal scale. But occasionally a little good-humored—or not-so-friendly—contest could expand rapidly into a small-scale battle of its own. Many units felt strong rivalry, especially when well-equipped and supplied regiments were bivouacked near outfits from some poorer locale. Jealousies smoldered until some vent for release

presented itself, and a snowball fight proved idea. Most famous of all was the Great Snowball Battle of March 1864, when the Confederate Army of Tennessee in winter quarters at Dalton, Georgia, began an impromptu contest that eventually turned into a full-scale battle. Even generals joined in, personally

Below: *Union correspondence. In an era when hundreds of thousands of Americans were illiterate, the number of soldiers who either wrote letters themselves or else had literate friends write home for them is truly remarkable.*

leading whole regiments in charges, taking prisoners, and giving no quarter.

Soldiers raced with wheelbarrows, wrestled, boxed, leaped hurdles, and more, but probably their favorite sport proved to be the infant game of baseball. The game used a soft ball, and the base runner was only put out when actually hit by a batted or thrown ball.

As much as anything, the men, as soldiers of all times and places, simply sat and talked. Politics, philosophy, the progress of the war, reminiscences of home and family, any topic could draw a conversation to pass an afternoon or evening. Camp gossip filled most of their talk; what officer was a coward, which one was overlooked because he did not have the right connections, where the next battle would be fought, when the war would end. Rumors flew like flies in such an environment. Others, however, did not appreciate the promiscuous spread of half-truths and gossip.

A number of leaders on both sides tried to do something about the language in the ranks. These were futile attempts. It was a soldier's form of release. He could not talk back to an officer but he could curse him back in the semi-privacy of his tent.

A good reason for a soldier's profanity might have been his losses at wagers, for gambling of every kind was common among the men. Both sides tried to put a stop to it but they might as well have tried to make the soldiers drink pink tea instead of coffee.

Theft in the camps was a common occurrence, and not too surprisingly, since it was an almost natural outgrowth of the "foraging" which they were encouraged to participate in along the march. When not

plundering the countryside, or their own messmates, many soldiers found sport in robbing the sutlers who followed the armies. Many regarded it as simply tit for tat, assuming that the sutlers were gouging them heavily by selling shoddy products at inflated prices.

Every kind of bad conduct had causes that were legion, but the most common of all was simple drunkeness. Given the opportunity, the men sometimes made their own drink, fermenting anything they could find, even pine boughs.

Neither side in the war ever completely accomplished the task of turning raw civilians into soldiers. In battle the men looked to their officers for leadership, but when it came to the ways they used—and misused—their leisure time, it was no one's business but their own.

These men were the products of the days of Jacksonian America, highly individualistic, independent, deeply imbued with the American ideal that one man was as good as another. They would not be ordered about like cattle, and such discipline as officers were able to maintain came at the enlisted men's sufferance, and

Below: *Except in permanent camps, shelter space was almost always scarce. This "A" tent was designed to hold four men, but it appears to have been the temporary home of at least seven soldiers of the 22nd New York. It is highly improbable that the two black servants at the rear right in the photograph were permitted to sleep in this or any other tent. Troops spent much of their spare time in camp where they could play games, gamble or make music. Whether they were on the Tennessee River or in Virginia, the men could, of course just, simply sit and talk; fight anew old battles, and boast of what they would do in the ones to come.*

only after the officers earned their respect. No wonder that at the war's outset, forseeing the problems ahead, Confederate General Joseph E. Johnston lamented that "I would not give one company of regulars for a whole regiment of volunteers."

As a consequence, discipline in this war would never reach a point at which it could predictably deter the men from doing what they pleased, whether it be gambling, drinking, and thievery. They had no use for the pomp and ceremony of soldiering, nor for its artificial etiquette.

The guardhouse was the most common

punishment, the number of days inside determined by the severity of the offense, from only a few hours to a month or more. Whatever the sentence, the guardhouse— often just an open field marked by ropes and watched by sentries—was hardly a hardship. Bread and water could make it less bearable, but in fact many offenders looked upon it as a respite from guard duty. Commanders used their imagination a bit more when it seemed necessary for the punishment to fit the crime. A cavalryman carried a saddle on his back around his camp after attempting to steal

it. Insubordination could bring several hours of the ball and chain, usually a 30-pound cannon ball on a few feet of heavy chain attached to the man's leg.

Certain special crimes such as cowardice, desertion, insubordination, rape, murder, or treason, were regarded almost uniformly by all officers, and nearly all shared the same notions of proper punishment. The lucky man was often simply discharged from the service dishonorably. His head shaved, his uniform stripped of its buttons and insignia, he was drummed out of camp in

sight of his comrades while the regimental band played the "Rogue's March". When this punishment seemed insufficient a man could be branded to carry his shame with him for life.

From the start, military law provided the death sentence to deal with deserters when caught. However, commanders were reluctant to impose capital punishment early in the war, not realizing the necessity of the example, and still feeling the personal sympathy for the volunteer soldier which several years of war would eventually replace with a more strictly professional military attitude. When the sentence of death was imposed, it was often commuted to life imprisonment, or incarceration for the duration of the war. But finally, in cases of rape, murder, spying, severe theft, and desertion, the death penalty was more frequently imposed. Occasionally the sentence had to be carried out, publicly, usually by firing squad, though hanging was sometimes employed for specially unsavory offenses such as rape. Capital punishment was meted out to 500 Yanks and Rebs in the war, more than in all other American war combined, and two thirds of them for desertion. The offenses that led to these punishments were, however, the exception in the life of a soldier.

Below left: *Beaufort, South Carolina, became a Union military center. Note the grave slabs resting against the building on the extreme left.*

Below: *A church built by the 50th New York Engineers in front of Petersburg. Troops, both North and South, often carried bibles or prayer books. Many men were sustained by their faith during the Civil War.*

The Wounded

❖

DURING THE CIVIL WAR THE SURGEONS were heavily outnumbered by the sick and injured. In the North there was but one doctor for every 133 men in the ranks, and in the South it was worse—one for every 324. These massive case loads could be death-dealing, and it is no wonder that alcoholism was a common complaint lodged against the doctors. Drink was their only relief, yet it also led to harmful myths that eroded the soldiers' confidence, such as the story of the drunken surgeon who went to set a broken leg, but performed his operation on the wrong limb, leaving the patient to die of shock.

No wonder the soldiers coined a host of epithets for their doctors, from "sawbones" and "Old Quinine," to "Loose Bowels." Yet when a man felt that he needed a physician, when he was wounded and bleeding in pain, he wanted whatever treatment was available, and quickly. It was a veritable bedlam. Every building and tent available became a hospital. Wounded and screaming men were lying everywhere in their own blood

and filth. Doctors were in short supply, medicines and opiates were often the same, and even water to cool the parched tongues of the wounded and dying might be contaminated and so offensive that men retched at the smell of it.

Rifle bullets caused more than 90 per cent of all Civil War wounds, and artillery accounted for most of the rest. Whatever the agent of his injury, the Civil War soldier at first felt little pain on being struck—just a staggering impact that frequently sent him sprawling on the ground in a momentary daze. Then began

an ordeal of one crisis after another.

Those fortunate enough not to fall between the lines, where they might lie for the duration of the battle or be overlooked in the confused aftermath, were carried from the field either by their friends or litter-bearers. Their feeling was returning by then, and the pain could quickly escalate into agony. Clumsy bearers could make it worse as they jolted and often dropped their litters, on top of which all too many of the bearers were practised thieves whose first interest was in rifling the pockets of the helpless wounded on

their stretchers. Ambulances were little better, with inadequate springs and uncaring drivers; the excruciating pain exacted by a rough ride could itself send a soldier out of his pain and on his way to the next life.

Below: *A Union repair shop for ambulances in Washington, April 1865. These men were part of an army of unsung heroes who kept the locomotives moving, the paddle wheels churning, and factory machines running. Little more than a two- or four-wheeled open wagon, the battlefield ambulance came into its own in the Civil War.*

At the field hospital itself, a sort of triage separated the slightly wounded from those needing immediate attention, and from those beyond help. The first and last were placed aside, the former to wait, the latter to be made as comfortable as possible as they died. These men were given opium or whiskey if available and then ignored while the surgeons went to work with their probes, their knives, and their saws.

The size of the bullets that struck men in the war, ranging from .36 caliber all the way up to a massive .75, ironically made some of the surgeon's work simple, insuring that any abdominal or chest wound was almost invariably fatal. Men with head or serious body wounds were usually set aside. Amazingly, about a quarter of these men actually recovered, very likely a better result than if the physicians had actually tried to save them. For the rest, any limb wound that did not shatter the bone had probably done irreparable damage to the nerves, tendons, or arteries, leaving the surgeon only to find the bullet and stop the bleeding, and three times out of four, amputate the limb.

The lucky soldier received some anaesthesia before the knife sliced into him. Doctors preferred chloroform when they could get it, putting a soaked sponge or cloth over the patient's nose until he went limp and limber. Ether, too, saw use, as well as laudanum. But all anaesthetics, especially in the Confederacy, could suddenly fall into short supply if the surgeons were not prepared for a major battle and its attendant casualties. Meanwhile, outside the operating tent, casualties awaiting amputations of their own could only lie and listen to the

screams of those not fully anaesthetized, and watch the results of the knives' work accumulate. After Gettysburg some men told of seeing piles of severed limbs.

"The surgeons and their assistants, stripped to the waist and bespattered with blood, stood around, some holding the poor fellows while others, armed with long bloody knives and saws, cut and sawed away with frightful rapidity, throwing the mangled limbs on a pile nearby as soon as removed," wrote a Confederate cavalryman. The sight was too much for many of his soldiers, who vomited in their saddles when they passed by the scene.

The surgeons had little time, and often no inclination, to clean either their hands or their instruments, unknowingly spreading a host of diseases from one man to another. With hideously contaminated hands, they handled the raw flesh of new wounds, probing deep with their fingers. After the Battle of Perryville, Kentucky, in October 1862, one whole Yankee hospital was filled with cases of meningitis, osteomyelitis, and peritonitis, almost certainly all caused by the surgeons' filthy

Below: *Confederate medical equipment, including a medical chest, a pocket drug kit, medicine bottles, and a stretcher. The surgical kit for major amputations contains several large scalpels, a bone saw, several tourniquets, probes, and bone-cutting pliers. Fighting for a cause in which everything was in short supply, the Confederate surgeon's collection of instruments, medicines, and accessories was always limited. Most of it was imported, and all of it was precious. Needles and scalpels could mean men's lives in surgery. And primitive though that equipment may seem, it was all that stood between the soldier and the grave.*

hands. Their diagnosis, however, was "poisonous vapors" once again, and their treatment was simply to open the hospital windows for fresh airs.

"Oh it is awful," a surgeon cried after the fighting in the Wilderness in Virginia in May 1864. "It does not seem as though I could take a knife in my hand today, yet there are a hundred cases of amputation awaiting for me. Poor fellows come and beg almost on their knees for the first chance to have an arm taken off. It is a scene of horror such as I have never saw. God forbid that I should see another."

Most surgeons, despite their ignorance, tried their best for their men, and the pressure and the overwork took its toll on their own wellbeing. They could not rest so long as there were wounded, and after a battle like Gettysburg or the Wilderness, the men needing medial attention could number in the tens of thousands.

Even if they survived the field hospitals, the wounded had another ordeal to endure as they were taken to the rear to the hundreds of general hospitals that grew up in most cities of the North and South. Here, where the fatal infections and

gangrene most often surfaced, they might spend months, even years, slowly recuperating. Richmond was a city of hospitals, with 34 of them in operation. In Washington there were 25 military hospitals in the Yankee capital, and even more in its environs.

The doctors running these established hospitals ranged from those too old for field service, to those too inexperienced. The nursing staffs were little better. Volunteer women helped, especially in the Confederacy, but in the North a gradually developing professional nursing corps

took over those duties left to them. With men in short supply, and needed in the armies, women came forward to help treat the wounded and ill. While most went through the war unnoticed, some like Dorothea Dix and Clara Barton achieved considerable fame, and began careers which led to great strides in health care after the war. Mostly they were volunteers, though Clara Barton organized a corps of nurses to her exacting standards, which included the stricture that no nurse should be too pretty.

The situation in Richmond remained

Below left: *Union Ambulance Corpsman and Hospital Steward. Circumstances very quickly dictated that a large number of special support services be created to help the enormous number of sick and injured. Out on the battlefield an ambulance corps was organized in an attempt to get the wounded speedily to the surgeons in the rear. Men too short or otherwise unfit for active duty became ambulance corpsmen, like the boy on the left. Their uniforms differed little from those of the regular soldiers except for an occasional badge. More specialized training was required for the hospital stewards like the man on the right. Given at least a smattering of medical education, their*

tasks were to tend the wounded, assist the surgeons, and perform a number of other necessary functions, several of which would later be taken by female nurses in the bigger general hospitals. Only the medical chevrons on his uniform denote his branch of service.

Below: *A field hospital in Virginia. Besides bullets, it was diarrhea, measles, smallpox, pneumonia, scurvy, and a host of other diseases and afflictions that might land a fellow in the hospital. Indeed, more soldiers went under the sod from disease than from death or mortal wounding in battle.*

less formal throughout the war, and the male opposition to female nurses was harder to overcome. A middle-aged Jewish widow named Phoebe Pember was not to be deterred, however. Refusing to take no for an answer, she was appointed Chimborazo Hospital's first female hospital matron and worked there for the rest of the war. She found herself, "in the midst of suffering and death, hoping with those almost beyond hope in this world; praying by the bedside of the lonely and heart-stricken; closing the eyes of boys hardly old enough to realize a man's

sorrows." Phoebe Pember's story was typical of those who tried to care for the suffering and relieve their pain.

Lurking in the shadows behind the parade grounds and campfires were enemies more dread and sinister than all the bullets on the battlefields. Ignorance and disease lay in store for everyone. Epidemics swept through the armies. Never before in American history had so many men congregated in so confined an area. Tens of thousands of rural boys had grown up without ever being exposed to ordinary childhood diseases. As a result,

measles, mumps, chickenpox, scarlet fever, and more, killed thousands in the early months of the war. Typhoid and diptheria, thanks to contaminated water, swept through whole regiments.

Just a short time after organization, many regiments began to suffer a high rate of attrition from sickness. Most units started the war around 1,000 strong. But by the time the 1st Connecticut went to its first battle, a few months later, it counted only 600 fit for duty. And the 128th New York suffered even more, numbering barely 350 after only a year of active

service. Some 200,000 men, over 20 per cent of those enlisted in 1861 and 1862, had to be dismissed and sent home after their illnesses and handicaps manifested themselves in the field. Even then, the state of sophistication in dealing with unsound bodies was such that the best authorities hardly knew what to look for. In the South, always hard-pressed for manpower after the first year of the war, instructions governing who should serve and who should be rejected cautioned doctors to "exercise a sound and firm discretion and not yield your judgement in favor of every

Confederate Medical Officers' Uniforms and Equipment.

1: Frock coat of surgeon Lieutenant Colonel Samuel Bemiss
2: Epaulettes of Dr. G. Charter, 53rd Va. Inf.
3: Civilian cape of Dr. A. Garnett, physician to President Davis and at Robertson Hospital
4: Forage cap of Dr. W. Wise
5: Surgeon's frock coat of assistant surgeon Captain R. Parker
6: Spurs of Dr. T. Berry
7: Field plate of Dr. O. Fairfax
8: Tourniquet

9: Brass bell from Jackson Hospital, Richmond
10 and 11: Case of surgeon Samuel Hollingsworth Stout
12: Roll of lint bandages
13: Phlebotomy knife found at Gettysburg and carved "Dr. F. Kempt, 17th Va. Vols."
14: Officer's sword c. 1820 of surgeon I. Habersham
15: Medical officer's sash
16 and 17: Scalpels from 20
18 and 19: Knives from 20
20: Amputation kit captured at Manassas and used by Dr. James Evans
21: Captain Parker's sash

complaint of trivial disability." Wisdom suggested that an active outdoor life in the army might even be a curative, and that many ailments were "strengthened and improved by the exposure incident to the life of the soldier." If a man had a short leg, a weak heart, bladder trouble, haemorrhoids, a hernia, even a missing eye or absent finger, still however interesting his case might be to the doctor's "professional" curiosity, so far as the army was concerned he was fit for service.

By the end of the war, Yankee surgeons determined that more than 6 million cases of illness had been treated, and those were just the ones that were reported. With something over a quarter million soldiers wearing the blue, that meant that every soldier, on average went before a physician at least twice, and some repeatedly. They complained of loose bowels, scurvy, smallpox, pneumonia, rheumatism, and more. Typhoid killed at least 100,000, while dysentery accounted for even more of the 400,000 in blue and gray who died from germs rather than bullets.

The fact is, when they went into battle, their likelihood of being wounded was high. When they were in camp, their odds of contracting some disease were even higher. The bullets that struck them hit with new and powerful impact. The organisms that attacked them were unknown and untreatable as yet. Wherever they went, Johnny Reb and Billy Yank stood in harm's way, and the treatments available to them afterwards were sometimes as dangerous as the enemies that sent them to the infirmaries.

For all their suffering, little in the way of medical advancement came as a result to temper the cost paid. More efficient

hospital organization, and the advent of female nursing did evolve, as did some rudimentary understanding of the role of cleanliness in preventing disease. Evacuation of the wounded took a giant leap forward in speed and efficiency thanks to a reorganized ambulance corps in the North. But these were modest gains when measured against the price. The real medical lessons of this war would not be learned for decades, long after it was too late for those who perished in the "seething hell and black infernal background" of this conflict.

Below left: *Dr. Mary Edwards Walker was given the Congressional Medal of Honor for her service during the Civil War. When war broke out, she went to Washington and tried to join the Union Army. Denied a commission as a medical officer, she volunteered anyway, serving as an acting assistant surgeon—the first female surgeon in the US Army. In September 1863, Walker was finally appointed assistant surgeon in the Army of the Cumberland. Walker then became assistant surgeon of the 52nd Ohio Infantry and served as a spy. She was taken prisoner in 1864 for four months until she was exchanged with two dozen other Union doctors.*

Below: *Ward 4 of the Lincoln Hospital, Washington D.C. Each bunk had movable fans that could be worked by the patient themselves. In every major city North and South hastily converted buildings soon became hospitals. Sometimes whole regiments could find themselves hospitalized, or so it seemed. Those too seriously ill to be treated and released near the front went to general hospitals. The Rebels had the same hospital experiences as Yanks, except that the scarcity of medicines made their ordeal much worse. These Confederate hospitals suffered a want of everything but patients.*

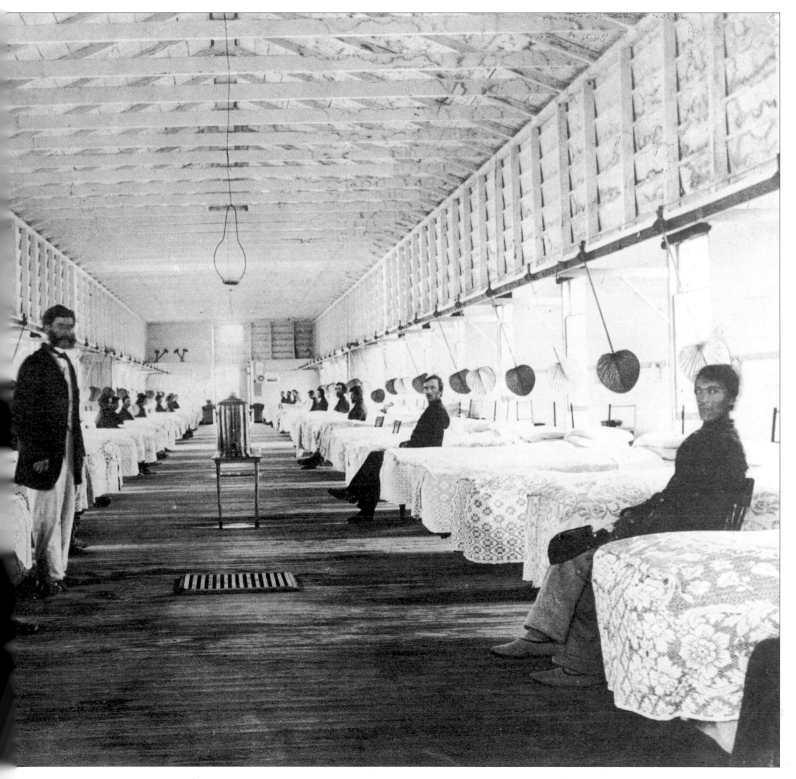

The Prisoner

JOHNNY REBS AND BILLY YANKS WENT OFF to war with a host of naive hopes and genuine fears: new friends, novel sights, camp life, hard marches, battle, martial glory, perhaps even wounds and death. But none of them went expecting capture or the nightmarish lot of the prisoner of war. None who went through that experience would ever forget it.

As so often in this war which everyone had been predicting for years, North and South were entirely unprepared to deal with captured enemies. As was so often the case, that lack of foresight led to tragedy. When 1861 dawned, not a single military prison existed in the United States capable of holding more than a few ill-behaved enlisted men. Even when the guns spoke at Fort Sumter, both sides immediately expected the conflict to last barely through the summer, and thus no preparations for prisoners were made.

It is indeed fortunate that the balance of 1861 saw so little action. With no major battles other than First Bull Run in the East and Wilson's Creek out in Missouri,

Union and Confederate authorities did not immediately face massive numbers of prisoners. Alas, even with this breathing space, neither side moved with dispatch.

In fact, it took some time before Lincoln even recognized Confederate prisoners. He believed the South was in a state of insurrection, there was therefore no "war", and only in war could there be prisoners accorded the standard treatment for captured enemies. During this period of blustering the numbers of captives languishing in hastily improvised prisons was increasing.

When soldiers were captured they found themselves standing for hours in holding pens, or in a gully surrounded by armed guards, while officers recorded their names and units. Provost marshals issued orders for sending the prisoners to established compounds far behind the lines, and then the prisoners were off. More often than not the prisoners walked into captivity.

After leaving the front, many arrived first at depot prisons like Point Lookout, Maryland, or Richmond's later infamous Libby Prison. From these points they were

Below left: *Brigadier General Joseph William Hoffman, the Union commander of prison camp organization. For Hoffman, prison management was a matter of efficiency, reducing the human component of men behind bars and walls, to an accountant's sort of calculation on food and fuel per man ratios. He saved a great deal of money at the expense of the health and nourishment of his prisoners. Hoffman was a brigadier general in the volunteer service, and wore the standard uniform of his rank.*

Below: *Confederate prisoners of war at Camp Douglas, Chicago, Illinois.*

sent deep into the interior, where they were to spend the balance of their prison days. And once at their ultimate destinations, the men's names were once again checked against a list.

The practice up to Bull Run had been to release prisoners on their parole, that is, to send them home under an agreement not to take up arms once again until properly "exchanged". Paroled prisoners remained free at home, though still members of the military and subject to its orders. However, they could not fight again until formally traded for a like number of

paroled prisoners on the other side. A paroled man who fought again before being exchanged was subject to harsh punishment if discovered.

The system did not work as neither side was ready for the overwhelming load of record-keeping required, nor for the scale and pace which the war would quickly assume. Some generals even believed the system encouraged men to get captured in order to be paroled home with slim prospect of exchange. The system broke down after the first few months. When black soldiers entered the equation after

1863, the Confederates refused to treat them on an equal basis with whites in exchange. That same year the whole agreement fell apart.

In 1861 Colonel William H. Hoffman was appointed commissary general of prisoners of the Union Army. His initial task was to establish the first specially created prison at Johnson's Island on Lake Erie. He did it with something that characterized all his operations—spartan thrift. Intended solely for the sake of wartime economy, Hoffman's stinginess would unintentionally lead to considerable

hardship and suffering for many Rebels. Hoffman was also never entirely able to keep up with the rapid influx of prisoners.

The story was even worse south of the Potomac. Management of Confederate prisons was put in the hands of Brigadier General John H. Winder. Where Hoffman's economy was self-induced, Winder had no choice but to cut corners. He established a few new camps, notably Camp Sumter near Andersonville, Georgia, but most Yankee prisoners were stuffed wherever he could find room, whether on a barren island in the James River, or in Libby's tobacco warehouse in Richmond. Winder never intentionally set out to mistreat or harm the prisoners entrusted to him, but suffer they did.

Filthy, unsanitary, riddled with vermin, the prisons of the Civil War were all, in varying degrees, hells on earth. Bedbugs inhabited every mattress and dark place. Perhaps worst of all were the fleas. The constant scratching helped make a shambles of the prisoner's already tattered clothing. Many, and particularly Confederates who were hardly well clad to start, often wore little more than rags when they first reached the prisons. Their clothes were often made rotten by mildew and they were often reduced to the humiliation of scavenging rags from the bodies of their dead comrades.

Below: *Confederate prisoner of war handicrafts. Rebel prisoners had little to occupy their time, so many of them began to carve unique objects for loved ones at home, serviceable items for survivors, and games with which to pass the time. A number were competent craftsmen and the surviving pieces provide wonderful examples of prison folk art.*

Prisoners in the South faced winters less harsh than the Rebels incarcerated in the north. The gales of winter tore through open stockades and drafty barracks. Hoffman recognized the problem, but dealt with it in his usual miserly fashion by acquiring ill-made or wrong sized Federal uniforms which had been rejected for field service. With these he equipped as many Confederate prisoners as possible, in the process also managing to find blankets for most of them.

On both sides of Mason's and Dixon's lines, with little else to occupy their day, prisoners spent most of their time thinking about their rations. Eating them, such as they were, provided the only break in the monotony of the day. What they ate matched their surroundings for miserliness and contamination. Meat rations came spoiled and fly-and-worm infested, while bread was moldy and full of maggots. Drinking water matched the food, coming from polluted wells, or camp streams fouled by prison waste.

There were also genuine atrocities, most often as a result of the incompetence of the men put in charge of the prisons. It was not, after all, the kind of position which tended to attract either the most gallant or most able of officers.

It is hardly surprising that, with all he faced from unintentional neglect to wilful mistreatment, many a prisoner decided not to wait for exchange. Many men escaped soon after their capture and before reaching prisons. Once in the pen, thousands were not deterred from making the attempt.

Alone or in pairs, several hundred prisoners made good their departure, though often only to be recaptured. Some

RULES AND REGULATIONS
OF THE
C. S. MILITARY PRISONS.

I. All orders effecting prisoners of war and the general discipline of the entire command, will be issued only by the officer commanding; and orders proceeding from any other source will not be regarded by officers on duty at the prisons.

II. There will be roll-call daily of the prisoners at 7½ A. M., and at 5 P. M., and the officer of the guard must be present at each.

III. No prisoner, whatever his rank, will be allowed to leave the quarters to which he is assigned, under any pretext whatever, without special permission from the officer commanding; nor shall any prisoner be fired upon by a sentinel or other person, except in case of revolt or attempted escape.

IV. No letters, packages, or parcels of any kind, can be passed into the prison or hospital, without first being examined by the officer commanding, or the Surgeon of the post.

V. Prisoners are not allowed to have any communication with persons outside of the prison, and no visitor will be allowed an interview with a prisoner without permission from the Brigadier General commanding the Department of Henrico from Md. 9th.

VI. Prisoners are not allowed to converse with the sentinels; nor must they congregate about the windows after dark.

VII. The firing of one gun at night, or two during the day, will be the signal for the immediate assembling of the guard.

VIII. Under no circumstances will the sentinel be allowed to sit down upon post, or to rest their guns on the ground.

IX. At 9 o'clock P. M., the lights throughout the prison, except in the hospital and officers' quarters, must be immediately extinguished; and it shall be the duty of the Officer of the Guard to inspect the prison at that hour, to see that the lights are put out, fire secured, and that everything is quiet.

X. No conversation, intercourse, or trading with the prisoners, *in any manner whatever*, will be allowed.

XI. The Officer of the Guard must not be absent at any one time from his post for a period exceeding one hour.

XII. The guard off post must remain constantly at the guard-house ready for instant service, and their guns must be kept on the rack.

XIII. Every guard room must be policed each morning by the old guard, and will not be received by the officer of the new guard unless in good order. Both the officers of the old and new guard will be held responsible for the execution of this order, and also for the safe keeping of all articles left in the guard house.

XIV. These rules and regulations must be read to the new guard every morning before posting the first relief.

(Signed,)

TH. P. TURNER,
Major Comd'g.

Approved,
JOHN H. WINDER,
Brig. Gen. Comd'g Dept. Henrico.

attempts were successful, such as Confederate General John Hunt Morgan's break from the Ohio State Penitentiary with several of his cavalrymen.

Most prisoners never attempted to escape. Their conditions simply wore them down mentally and physically to the point where they simply languished away in places little heard of before the war, but which rapidly became storied scenes of hardship and suffering. Probably the worst of all in the North was the prison camp located outside Elmira, New York, on the Chemung River. One man in five had scurvy, and men died at the rate of 10 per day. Before it closed at the war's end, a quarter of all of Elmira's prisoners died within its confines. The prison had been built for half the numbers Hoffman had been told to expect. As a result some prisoners had to sleep out in the open. When winter came there was but one stove for every 100 prisoners.

The most infamous prison was in the South. Camp Sumter, it was called, but it quickly came to be known generally by its proximity to Andersonville. Poorly located and hastily built, it afforded to its inmates only such shelter as they could themselves build out of scanty materials. Its only water came from a sluggish stream which served as a latrine, garbage dump, and provided drinking water for over 33,000

Below left: *A poster detailing the rules and regulations governing Union prisoners held in Confederate military prisons.*

Below right: *Former warehouses converted into a Union prison for Confederate captives. The war's first prisons were nothing more than hastily converted warehouses like this one.*

prisoners. In population, it would have ranked as the fifth largest city in the Confederacy. Its "citizens", however, were crammed into a 26-acre space that allowed each man only a small amount of space to live on.

At last the suffering came to an end. Federal authorities recommended the exchange system early in 1865, even while advancing Yankee armies were taking whole states from the Confederates and thereby freeing prisoners by the thousands. Finally the Rebel government stopped trying to hold on to their

prisoners. Thousands were simply paroled where they were and released. After the surrenders of April and May, prison doors everywhere opened at last.

So many died. Over 211,000 Billy Yanks were captured during the war, and of them at least 194,000 went into Southern prisons. Of their number, 30,218 never came home again: more than 15 per cent. About 214,000 Confederates were sent north to Union prisons, and there 25,976 were to die. Over 56,000 Americans, thus, had expired painfully, isolated, cut off from the comfort of friends and family,

locked away in the cold and festering prison hells of North and South.

For the winners came the opportunity for justice against their tormentors. Hysteria of prison excesses in the South soon swept Yankee press and pulpit. Someone had to pay for the horrors. Winder was dead but Major Henry Wirz, commander of Andersonville, was still alive. He was arrested in May 1865 and taken to Washington where he was subjected to a sham of a trial before a military tribunal. Admittedly an unsympathetic man, probably not an able

administrator, Wirz became the classic victim of circumstances. Protesting that he had been simply a soldier following orders, he was convicted of "murder in violation of the laws and customs of war".

There had never been any doubt of the verdict, or of the sentence. On November 10, 1865, Wirz mounted a scaffold at Old Capitol Prison and became the last victim of Andersonville.

Unfair as it was, the death Major Henry Wirz was symbolic of the unbelievable restraint on the part of the North, for he was the only Confederate to be executed after the four years of bloody, bitter war. Some 40 years later Major Henry Wirz became the second Civil War prison commander—along with Richard Owen— to be memorialized. A simple marker went up to his memory just outside the site of the infamous Andersonville prison camp, commemorating his innocence of the crimes charged against him by the Union authorities. Ironically, today, over the spot where Major Henry Wirz died, symbolic of the justice which he was denied, stands the imposing Supreme Court of the United States of America.

Below left: *The tattered uniforms and weary demeanor of these Yankees, newly-released from Confederate prisons in Texas in 1865, shows clearly how the privations of prison could debilitate a once healthy soldier.*

Below: *Brigadier General John H. Winder oversaw all prisons for Federal captives, he was also chief provost for Richmond. As chief provost he was responsible for controlling the issuing of passes into and out of Rebel lines. While Winder's management of the prisons was never willfully cruel, it still led to untold hardships for his prisoners.*

THE CAVALRY

NO SOLDIER OF THE CIVIL WAR CAUGHT MORE OF THE DASH and the flair of the era than the cavalrymen, and especially the Confederate trooper. His exploits were celebrated in both song and legend, he became in the hearts of his people the *beau sabreur*, the knightly paladin riding through the smoke of battle in daring raids against hopeless odds, to defend his country, home, hearth and honor.

Above: Sheridan's Cavalry Corps badge of Major John Cassals.

Right: Often the cavalryman's duty included garrison or guard duty along vulnerable railroad supply lines. This is a group of cavalry and infantry at a blockhouse on the Orange & Alexandria Railroad in 1864.

Cavalry Commanders

◆

EVEN THE BOLDEST OF THE BOLD, LIKE THE Civil War hero Winfield Scott Hancock, were eclipsed in the public mind, and in the memory of posterity, by a special few who so captured the imagination of the era and posterity that their fame often exceeds the real worth of their exploits. Nothing so appealed to the romantic mind then and later as a man on a horse. The very thought conjured images of cavaliers bedecked in plumes, atop fire-breathing steeds. It is no wonder that the cavalry in both armies during the Civil War, especially in the romance-ridden Confederate service, was self-consciously flamboyant. No wonder that the generals who led that mounted arm, North and South, quickly earned a special place in their people's hearts.

Of them all, none would exceed in romance and dash the incomparable cavalier in gray, James Ewell Brown "Jeb" Stuart. He began the war as a colonel in the 1st Virginia Cavalry, but even that took a romantic turn when some dubbed his outfit the "Black Horse Cavalry",

giving it a sinister, almost brigandish flavor. He was an accomplished cavalry commander but revealed a theatrical bent that at times lessened his effectiveness. He also could not resist the temptation to plunder, to bring his captures back with him, and to take unnecessary risks for the sake of the adventure, even when they impeded the performance of his actual task. Stuart, however was universally regarded as without a peer in the East, blue or gray.

Stuart's replacement, following his death at the Battle of Yellow Tavern on May 11,

Below left: *8th Texas Cavalry, "Terry's Texas Rangers" of the Confederate States' Army. One of the toughest mounted outfits in the South was made up of the rugged plainsmen of Texas, men for whom the Civil War was little more than the continuation of a struggle they had been waging for years anyhow, either with the Indians, Mexicans, or Free-Staters. They went into battle under their distinctive "Wigfall" flag, named for a leading Texas politican, Louis T. Wigfall. "God Defend the Right", it proclaimed. To help in that defense, the sergeant in the foreground carries a rare Dance revolver, a Confederate-made copy of the Colt .44 Dragoon. Indicative*

of the disdain with which most cavalrymen regarded the saber as a weapon, these two do not even carry them. They sit on Hope saddles, and carry the minimum of gear, adhering to the dictum to travel light and fast. Several men, like the one in the background, wore a silver star on their headgear, symbolizing Texas.

Below: *Helped considerably by his frightening blade, even this innocent-looking young man in blue quickly came to adopt a warlike posture. Confederate edged weapons, like their longarms and handguns, were usually inferior copies of existing Federal arms.*

1864, was a different sort of commander entirely. Wade Hampton was a South Carolinian, too genteel to affect the gaudy plumage and flamboyant garb of Stuart. But that did not mean he did not answer the same impulses of gallantry and daring. At the Battle of Gettysburg he found himself isolated from his command and facing a Yankee cavalryman at some distance. While the soldier fired his Spencer repeating carbine, Hampton sat his saddle and returned fire with his pistol. Then, when the Federal's weapon jammed, Hampton held his own fire until the jam

was cleared, whereupon the two resumed firing, both taking wounds. A year later, now in command of the cavalry corps of the Army of Northern Virginia, Hampton planned the daring "Beefsteak Raid" in which a herd of 3,000 beeves was captured behind Yankee lines and driven halfway around the Federal army besieging Petersburg, to reach the hungry mouths of Lee's army.

The Federals, too, had their dashing cavaliers. When Phil Sheridan led a small army in the Shenandoah in 1864, he seemed to have a constellation of colorful

horse generals under him: Alfred Torbert, Thomas Davies, David McMurtrie Gregg, and, most notorious of all, George A. Custer, a man with a positive instinct for battle, and a single-minded determination to throw himself and his men into the thickest of a fight and trust to "Custer's luck" to see them through. Vain, egotistical, prone to the role of martinet, still Custer was one of the ablest subordinate cavalrymen of the Civil War.

But others achieved greater things, if not greater glory. Colonel Benjamin Grierson, though he led only one cavalry raid, it

was, perhaps, the most effective of the war. His drive through the heart of Mississippi during April 17–May 3, 1863, proved to be the greatest—and most dangerous—diversionary action of the war. The plan grew in the mind of Ulysees Grant, who wanted something to distract the attention of the defenders of Vicksburg away from his attempt to move his army below the city on the west bank of the Mississippi, then cross the river below Vicksburg and move against it from the rear. He needed to cut the rail line connecting the city with the rest of

Confederate Cavalry Officers' Uniforms and Equipment.

1: Uniform trousers of Capt. W.H. Cleaver, Steele's Texas Regiment
2: Cleaver's frock coat
3: Frock coat of Major James B. Ferguson
4: Militia pattern hat, 6th Btn. Tennessee Cav.
5: Captain's frock coat of Lt. Col. R. Randolph; killed May 1864
6: Randolph's trousers
7: Sword of Lt. Gen. Wade Hampton
8: 1851 Federal saber belt
9 and 10: Officers' maroon silk sashes
11: Belt with Virginia plate
12: Model 1851 Federal sword belt and plate
13: Officer's holster
14: Officer's silk sash
15: Saber of Maj. Heros von Borke, member of Major General "Jeb" Stuart's staff
16: Jacket of Captain W. Cleaver
17: Folding dagger owned by Col. J. Mosby
18: Saber made by Boyle, Gamble and Macfee
19: Spurs of Capt. William Rasin
20: Haversack of Capt. J. Hobson
21: Hobson's tin canteen
22: Hobson's revolver saddle holsters
23: Havelock of Lt. Richard Dobie
24: Havelock of Lewis Stern

Mississippi and the Confederacy, and sufficiently confuse the foe as to what was going on to buy time to move his army. Already Grant had seen promise in Grierson, and on February 13, 1863, Grant suggested that the colonel and 500 picked men might make a raid against the railroad east of Vicksburg. "The undertaking would be a hazardous one," said Grant, "I do not direct that this shall be done, but leave it for a volunteer enterprise." Grant's friend Sherman had already recommended Grierson as "the best cavalry officer I have yet had," and

Grant would come to agree. The plan evolved considerably before it actually went into action. For one thing, Grant suggested that instead of returning from the railroad raid, Grierson should push on toward the south and east, into Alabama, but in the end left it to Grierson's discretion. That showed the greatest trust of all, for only the raiding commander on the scene could decide what was best; no one could predict all the variables that might combine against him, and he had to have the latitude to adjust his plans.

Poor Grierson, away on furlough, only

reached his command three hours before they departed on April 17. There was no time to rest.

Before dawn Grierson led his command, now 1,700 strong, out of their camp at La Grange, Tennessee, and soon crossed the border into Rebel-held Mississippi. For the next 16 days they would see no friendly faces, have no support to look to, and nothing but the enemy behind and ahead of them. Daring in the face of a daunting situation, Grierson reduced his command the third day out by sending some 175 men who were unfit for the rest of the

expedition back to La Grange, instructing their leader to be as ostentatious as possible, hoping that this party might distract Confederate attention from the main column.

A day later the Confederates had gotten Grierson's trail and were after him. Thereafter it was a chase through Mississippi, with the Federals sending out decoy parties to fool the enemy as to his destination, while the Confederates slowly brought more and more troops to bear on bringing Grierson to bay.

On the eighth day out, the raiders took

Below left: Trooper, 1st Virginia Cavalry Regiment of the Confederate State Army. This regiment began the war as a group of independent companies of horse from the Shenandoah Valley, organized into a regiment by James Ewell Brown Stuart, later of course to become a famous commander with the rank of major general. In the First Battle of Bull Run in July 1861 they achieved renown as the dreaded "Black Horse Cavalry", though the origin of the sobriquet is obscure. For the remainder of the Civil War they performed outstanding service with the Cavalry Corps of the Army of Northern Virginia. Stuart's horsemen wore chiefly homespun *clothing of plain gray or butternut, with black facings on their light-gray short jackets and trousers. They were well armed and carried Sharps carbines by leather shoulder belts, the standard U.S. cavalry saber of the time, and Colt Navy .36 pistols. Many of their weapons were captured from Federal cavalry units. Broad-brimmed hats with plumes completed their attire.*

Below: Members of the 7th Kansas Cavalry. The regiment was organized in October 1861, at Fort Leavenworth, Kansas, under the command of Colonel Charles R. Jennison.

Newton Station, on the railroad to Vicksburg, and effectively cut the line. They burned bridges, tore up rails, and destroyed two locomotives and large stores of ammunition. Then they were off that same afternoon to the southwest towards Natchez.

Ahead of them the Rebels were telegraphing to all points to gather troops to cut off any avenue of escape. Traps were laid at most of the major roads.

By April 30, Grierson and his men had been in the saddle day and night for two weeks without more than a few hours' rest at a time. Bone weary, they kept on until May 1, their 15th day out, when they came up against a roadblock in their path.

At Wall's Bridge, on the Tickfaw River, an ambush had been laid. They had to cross that river or else lose valuable time, time that would allow the converging Confederates in their rear to trap them.

With nothing else to be done, Grierson and his exhausted troopers attacked across the bridge and drove its defenders away in the biggest fight of the raid. But then they had to cross Williams' Bridge on the Amite River a few miles further southwest. The Confederate forces knew it too, and began ordering troops there for another trap. But in a frustrating misadventure, the Rebels stopped for another party on the way. This delayed them enabled Grierson's column to cross the bridge two hours before their would-be ambushers arrived. From that point onward, the raiders rode as if possessed. For 12 straight hours through the night of May 1–2, they rode without stopping, racing toward Federal lines at Baton Rouge, Louisiana. With 30 miles to still to go, they pressed on again, finally reaching safety late on May 2.

What Grierson had done was phenomenal. In 16 days Grierson had led his small force on a back-breaking march south through the entire length of Mississippi in the rear of the Confederate lines. The diversion he created allowed Grant to make his successful envelopment of the Rebel position at Vicksburg.

During this time Grierson's troops had also killed over 100 Confederates, captured and paroled 500 more, torn up railroads, destroyed 3,000 stands of arms and stores, and captured 1,000 horses and mules. It was probably the most brilliant

raid of the American Civil War.

More devastating still was the raid led by General James H. Wilson. Once a lowly staff officer with Grant, he caught the great general's attention during the Vicksburg campaign. In October 1863 he was promoted to brigadier general of volunteers and in 1864 took command of the Cavalry Bureau.

Wilson was then given command of the Third Cavalry Divison and finally chief of cavalry for Sherman's Military District of the Mississippi. He molded the western theater's mounted forces into an effective

Below: *Union cavalry officers' uniforms and equipment. These include a pair of officer's high boots, dress epaulettes, shell jackets and sabers. The cavalry branch of the service color was used as background for shoulder straps, piping for coats and trousers. A predecessor branch, dragoons, utilized the color orange in the same manner until discontinued in favor of cavalry in 1861. The dragoons were formations of light infantry soldiers, who rode instead of walked from one part of the battlefield to another. Regardless of the name, however, Rebel and Union cavalry units often acted like dragoons and mounted infantry.*

combat force. He led the cavalry in the field against General John Hood at Franklin and Nashville at the end of 1864. In 1865 led a small army of cavalry through Alabama in a lightning raid almost unparalleled for destruction by any similar exploit of the Civil War.

It was also Wilson, in the end, who was the only Yankee cavalryman to best substantially the undoubted master horseman of the entire war, Nathan Bedford Forrest. Literally an untutored genius of war—he was marginally literate, though extremely intelligent—Forrest began the war a private in the 7th Tennessee Cavalry. By 1865 he was a lieutenant general commanding a small army of cavalry, and behind him lay a series of the most stunning defeats ever suffered by Yankee horsemen during the Civil War.

Time after time he appeared where it seemed he could not possibly be, defeated numbers considerably superior to his own, then reappeared somewhere else to wreak more havoc. "That devil Forrest," he was called by his foes, and in 1864 Sherman detached inordinate men and means to try to stop—unsuccessfully—his depredations on Union supply and communications.

Frighteningly fearless himself, Forrest personally killed more of his foes than any other general on either side, and even killed one of his own officers in a fight—after the officer had already shot him in the abdomen. There was no dash, no dress parade finery about Forrest, and his command; just cold, calculated, ruthless daring, and efficiency. Opinions will always vary, but many would argue that he was, taken all in all, the greatest cavalryman who ever lived.

Thus these amazing men on horseback are remembered as the greatest, the boldest, the most colorful, and so on. These legendary cavalrymen, blue and gray alike, have never released their grip on the human imagination, and probably never will.

The Union cavalry did not win the war, and Confederate cavalry did not lose it. Both cavalry forces played their part along with the other services, and to the degree that their efforts integrated systematically into the entire scope of their nation's war efforts, they made their contribution.

Below left: *Colonel John Singleton Mosby. Few raiders of the war could even attempt to approach the record of the "Gray Ghost" of Virginia. He seemed invincible and unstoppable, and indeed he was. In 1863 Mosby was given permission to organize his Partisan Rangers. Mosby became an expert in guerrilla warfare tactics and his small unit of a hundred soldiers were very active during the Union Army during the Wilderness campaign. Mosby undermined the enemy's transport system by destroying rail lines and bridges. In 1865 General Philip Sheridan sent out a hundred men to hunt down Mosby but they failed to catch him.*

Below: *1859 Officer's McClellan saddle of Major General John Sedgwick. This cavalry commander began his Civil War career during the 1862 Peninsula Campaign. Promoted to major general the same year, he was wounded at Antietam, but was fit enough later to command the VI Corps during the Fredericksburg Campaign. John Sedgwick's command was in reserve during the Battle of Gettysburg but fought later at Rappahannock Bridge. In 1864 Sedgwick led his corps at the Wilderness and Spotsylvania, where he was killed. His saddle was presented to him by the officers of the 2nd Division of the 2nd Army Corps.*

The Cavalryman

❖

OUT OF THE TENS OF THOUSANDS OF young men who flocked to the recruitment centers in the first days of the war, many went with a special branch of the service in mind. Lured by the romantic notions of gay cavaliers, bedecked with plumes and flashing sabers, riding merrily through the countryside, and cutting a dashing picture before the ladies, a host of enlistees chose the newly forming cavalry regiments for their service. Inevitably these and other preconceived notions about cavalry service would be proven false, as they would be in every aspect of the war. Indeed, in the spring of 1861, the role, if any, of the mounted arm in the coming fray was entirely uncertain.

If any of those confused and faintly frightened young men could have looked ahead, however, they would have seen that the cavalry as it was at the war's outset, and as it would become by war's close, was destined to play an integral part in the national tragedy.

In 1861, cavalry doctrine North and South, preached at the military academies

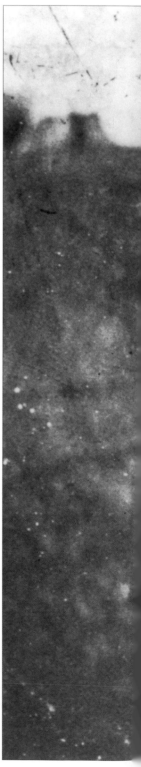

and in the tactical manuals widely circulated, showed little development since the days of Napoleon. The army's standard text, *System of Cavalry Tactics*, was 20 years old, and was borrowed almost in its entirety from a French book. It still reflected the Napoleonic ideal of using cavalry masses—up to 12,000 in some of the Emperor's battles—to thunder down upon, intimidate, and plunge through enemy infantry lines. The value of cavalry, read a West Point text, "resides in its shock". Furthermore, despite some Napoleonic examples of horsemen riding

Below left: *Sergeant, 6th Pennsylvania Cavalry "Rush's Lancers". Oddly enough, Pennsylvania became known during the war for some of its unruly cavalry regiments. Arguably the worst disciplined regiment in the Union army was the 3rd Pennsylvania Cavalry, with more than its full complement of courts martial, desertions, insubordinate enlisted men, and incompetent officers. Perhaps it was in reaction to such a poor reputation that the 6th Pennsylvania Cavalry strove so hard to create a distinguished record with the Army of the Potomac. Of course, part of its reputation derived from its distinctive—indeed, in the Union Army,*

unique—weaponry. Originally uniformed and equipped like any other cavalry regiment in the army, the 6th Pennsylvania Cavalry—called "Rush's Lancers" after its colonel, Richard Rush— later adopted to fight with lances. These wonderful weapons were quite useless against the poorest Confederate firearm, and were discarded.

Below: *The cavalryman's most valuable piece of equipment was his horse. In the first year of the war many an unfortunate man was given an unsound mount, but Union agents soon found better animals.*

to battle, then fighting dismounted very effectively, the prevailing notion remained that, in the words of Captain George McClellan, "The strength of cavalry is in the spurs and sabre." And this is what he wrote in an all-new cavalry manual published in 1861, just as the Civil War was commencing.

In other words, cavalrymen in this new war were expected to behave as in wars more than a century before—to ride to battle, then dash into the fray in the overwhelming mounted saber charge. Very few, though McClellan and General Winfield Scott were among them, seemed to suspect that the wooded ground and narrow roads of America might make inoperable the cavalry tactics used in Europe decades before, and that the new ideas would be needed. Almost everyone who gave the branch of the service any thought, continued to regard it first and foremost as the real of dashing gallants in resplendent garb, the *beau sabreurs* of the military. No one had quite escaped the notion of one of Napoleon's marshals who said that cavalry, in the last analysis, served best to add a bit of class and style to battles which were, otherwise, just tawdry brawls.

Lincoln and his administration blundered badly at first by entirely ignoring the mounted arm, probably because, like most, he failed to grasp its necessity in the war to come. Incredibly, only a few more immediately available companies of the existing regiments were called east in the days after Fort Sumter, and no plans went forward to raise new regiments. In his first call for volunteers, Lincoln said nothing about cavalry, and when Northern governors offered to send

mounted units, the War Department issued orders to accept no cavalry. Expecting a short summer's campaign before the rebellion was put down, the government in Washington continued under the influence which had always kept the cavalry small—economy. Horses were expensive to maintain.

Then came the disaster at First Manassas or Bull Run. General Irvin McDowell, with an army numbering close to 37,000, marched into Virginia with just seven companies, fewer than 700 horsemen, riding along. As a result, he

moved almost completely in the dark, with no useful reconnaissance, no scouting reports, and in the battle itself, no substantial mobile force to exploit a breakthrough or guard his flanks. Worst of all, he had nothing with which to neutralize the enemy cavalry, which itself consisted only of the 1st Virginia Cavalry commanded by Colonel "Jeb" Stuart. Filled in advance with dread of the so-called "Black Horse Cavalry", Federal infantrymen panicked when Stuart rode out of some woods against them. Later, at the critical moment of the battle when

McDowell's shaky flank was wavering, Stuart with infantry support put the flank into a flight which soon became a general rout. McDowell's lack of cavalry, and Stuart's presence, did not alone account

Below left: *A detachment of the 1st United States Cavalry at Brandy Station in Virginia, where the North's horsemen had come of age in the greatest cavalry battle of the war some eight months earlier.*

Below: *Union overcoat for enlisted mounted man, front and rear.*

for the Yankee disaster, but they did reveal that cavalry could not be over-looked. Furthermore, as McDowell himself would point out after the fact, cavalry was most needed for gathering information while operating in an enemy's country, and for shielding from an enemy one's own movements. Already, from bitter experience, men were beginning to sense glimmers of change.

But learning remained slow, especially in the Union, and old habits of economy at the price of innovation died hard. It cost nearly $500,000 to raise and fully equip a mounted regiment, and many professional soldiers doubted the point of it. Old General Scott, for instance, shared the disdain and suspicion of many infantrymen for their mounted compatriots.

It was also a question of time. Contemporary military wisdom maintained that it took three full years to train a cavalry officer adequately, and nearly as long for the men in the ranks to be trained and disciplined. Since this would be a short war, there was little point in raising such outfits. The conflict would end before they could render any useful service. Besides—and her came the early expressions of prejudice against volunteers that almost all professional soldiers repeated again and again—such work as the cavalry would be required to do was best left to the Regulars, and the five regiments in service would be enough. Small wonder, then that in Lincoln's call for 48 regiments for three years service that spring, only one of these regiments was to be of cavalry.

In the end, political pressure placed on Lincoln by his governors induced him, in

turn, to move the War Department into accepting the first volunteer cavalry regiments. And after the disaster at Bull Run, Washington's attitude changed dramatically. Within six weeks of the defeat, there were 33 mounted volunteer regiments in service, and 82 by December 31, more than 90,000 cavalrymen.

Across the lines, in the new Confederacy, the story was much different. It helped that President Jefferson Davis himself once served as a lieutenant in the 1st US Dragoons, and later as secretary of war for President Franklin Pierce he showed considerable interest in studying French cavalry technique. Even more important was the emotional attraction which the dashing mounted service had for the more high-spirited young men of the South. Accustomed since youth to riding, and inspired from childhood by stories of Revolutionary forebears like the "Swamp Fox" Francis Marion, "Light Horse" Harry Lee, and other cavalry heroes, sons of high-born and wealthy families were anxious to lead new regiments of heroes. Many a farmboy eagerly enlisted to serve them, especially after exaggerated stories of Stuart's "Black Horse Cavalry" at Manassas assured them that all the real glory would

Below: *Confederate Cavalry artifacts. At the beginning of the Civil War, Confederate cavalry was superior to its Union counterpart, primarily due to the Rebels familiarity with weapons, horses, and terrain. Much Southern equipment was captured Union material such as the Sharps carbine, Remington revolver, and Model 1840 cavalry saber. As with the Union cavalry, the branch designation color, as shown on the piping of the shell jacket is yellow.*

be had in the saddle.

North and South, the story of raising the volunteer regiments proved much the same. Once a governor authorized a new regiment, an appointment to its colonelcy went to the man who would raise it. He might be an officer from another branch of the service, a prominent politician who popularity could lure 1,200 or so to enlist, someone to whom the governor owed a favor, or from whom he sought one. There were as many considerations for appointment as there were men to commission; presidents and secretaries of

war also often got involved in designating new colonels. In short, it was American political democracy in action. However he got his appointment, once the colonel enlisted his men he equipped them with whatever the governor, or the Capital, provided. Few regiments on either side went off to war with everything their regular army regulations required, but almost every trooper had the basics—revolver, saber, carbine, saddle, and horse. Beyond that, equipment depended upon good fortune, and the whim of the quartermasters.

Not only did the Confederacy begin the war with the first victories—Fort Sumter, Big Bethel, and Bull Run—but from the first it enjoyed almost undisputed pre-eminence in the mounted arm. That came in part from having a head start in enlistments, and a more enlightened attitude towards cavalry. After all, Confederates knew the war would be fought on their own territory, and they knew best from riding all those fields and roads just how cavalry could use them. Moreover, it cannot be doubted that Southerners were by and large better

horsemen thanks to having more experience in a predominantly rural society. The Southern policy of men providing their own horses meant that a cavalryman did not need weeks or months to get accustomed to his mount. North of the Potomac, where all horses were issued by the government, a mount and rider met for the very first time when they started training together. Additionally, a Rebel rider went to war knowing he had a sound, healthy horse. In the Union, already suffering the abuses of contract frauds and dishonest traders, tens of thousands of unsound animals were bought and, through faulty inspection procedure, allowed to get into the hands of green recruits.

It hardly afforded cause for wonder, then, that for two years after the commencement of the war, the Confederate cavalry reigned supreme in every theater of war, the Southern mounted leaders quickly became national heroes. Even one of their foes, General William T. Sherman, would declare that Confederates were "splendid riders, first rate shots, and utterly reckless." He

Below: *Company I of the 6th Pennsylvania Cavalry, also known as "Rush's Lancers", in May 1863. At the time this company was serving as headquarters escort for Major General Joseph Hooker, the commander of the Army of the Potomac. The man in civilian clothing seated on the left side of the photograph is the famous war artist Alfred Waud. The men of this unit were the from elite of Philadelphia society. Many officers had previously served in the First Troop Philadelphia City Cavalry, a militia unit originally formed to serve as George Washington's personal bodyguard. The unit lost 172 officers and men in the Civil War.*

frankly termed them "the best cavalry in the world".

North and South, the life of the average mounted soldier was not markedly different, nor was it greatly varied from that of the other branches of the service. For all the glamor of youthful expectations, real soldiering turned out to be far from glorious battle. Drill, foraging for food, tending to animals and equipment, occupied an inordinate amount of time, and what time was left, the troopers took care of with gambling, prank-playing, and simply relaxing. Yet

for the cavalryman there was, at least, an added dimension of mobility thanks to his horse. The need for frequent scouts and reconnaissance, even when the armies sat in winter quarters, allowed the troopers to break the monotony of camp life.

Better yet, from the point of view of the cavalryman, that mobility allowed him a far greater opportunity to scavenge and, occasionally, to plunder. This, and the natural inter-service rivalry at arises in all armies, rather quickly led to the mounted arm being the most resented of all, in and out of the military.

Adding to the hostility was the fact that, with the evolution of cavalry doctrine slowly taking it away from participation in pitched battles, the big fights were almost exclusively the realm of infantry and artillery. As a result, men in those branches rarely saw horse soldiers actually engaged in combat. Inevitably this led to the taunt of "whoever saw a dead cavalryman?" When a mounted unit passed a marching column, the foot soldiers invariably hurled insults.

Ironically, it was in the Union Army, which seemed for so long to lag behind the

Confederates in leadership, experience, and everything else except manpower and supply, that the ideal role of Civil War cavalry first evolved. Perhaps it came thanks to Northerners being less hide-bound by a mounted tradition, less wedded to classical notions of cavalry doctrine. Whatever the case, Federal horsemen, though they started the war substantially behind their foes in experience and competence, gradually erased the difference. Only better leadership, more efficient organization, and actual field experience would raise the Federal cavalry to the level of the Confederates, but it was slow in coming. In the summer of 1862 a significant change did come when General John Pope, taking command of the Army of Virginia, directed that all cavalry units within each army corps be consolidated, to serve under a corps chief of cavalry. This paved the way for the Union horse would be consolidated into a single cavalry corps. Better leadership and superior equipment ensured the Union cavalry got the upper hand. The Spencer carbine was the principal weapon for the Union cavalry during the last two years of the war. With few exceptions, the usefulness of the saber was over, and repeating, rapid fire weapons dominated the battlefield.

Below: *Union cavalry artifacts, including a fine Model 1860 Spencer breechloading, repeating carbine. The saddle is a US Army Model 1859 McClellan saddle with blanket roll. The lance was used by the 6th Pennsylvania Cavalry, "Rush's Lancers", between 1861 and 1863. The Yankee cavalry had achieved the upper hand by mid-1863, with adequate leadership and far superior equipment.*

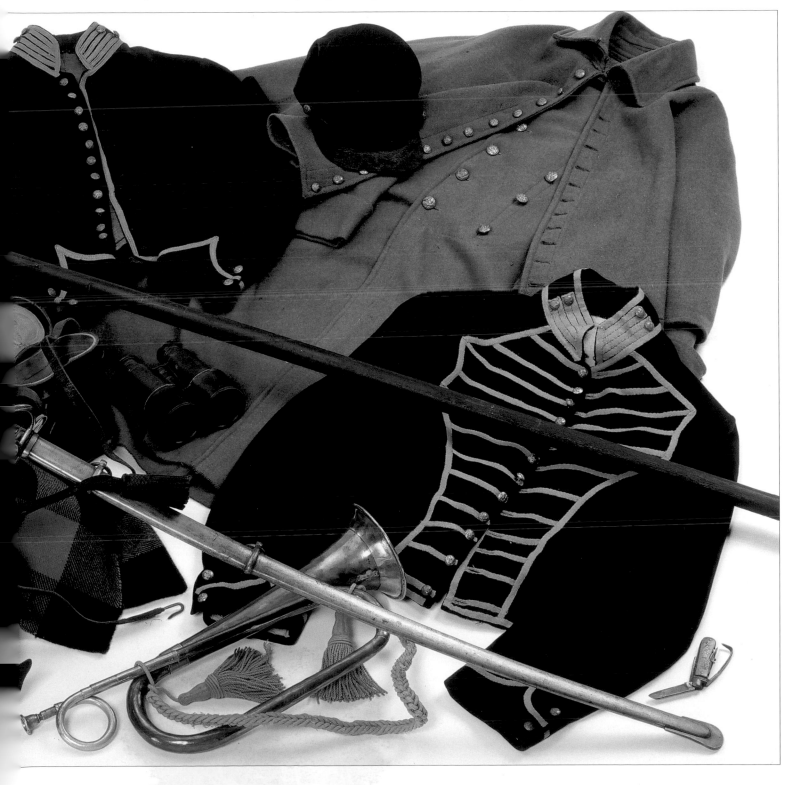

THE ARTILLERY

FEW ARTILLERY UNITS ON EITHER SIDE BEGAN THE WAR with much fanfare or good auspice. It was the forgotten branch of the service. In the first flush of enthusiasm, North and South, everyone rushed to get into the infantry. The foot soldier, with his gleaming rifle and bayonet, captured the American imagination. For those with an extra quotient of dash, the cavalry beckoned. The artillery, on the other hand, simply was not a romantic arm of the service.

Above: Artillery officer's insignia: Lt. G.W. Taylor, 4th MA Battery.

Right: The Union 13-inch mortar "Dictator" in operation during the siege of Petersburg. It was the most photographed cannon of the war.

The Gun Batteries

❖

DESPITE THE LACK OF ENTHUSIASM FOR the artillery arm, there had been a number of private artillery companies across the nation before the war, some state militia, and other well-funded and organized "fraternal" outfits both North and South. The most famous was undoubtedly the Washington Artillery of New Orleans, formed in 1838, and already blooded by service in the war with Mexico. The flower of New Orleans society joined its ranks. By 1857, however, its ranks had dwindled to 13 names on the rolls. Clearly, the rise of the infantry militia companies in the city had eroded its membership away to more popular forms of service. Elsewhere in the nation before 1861 there were other such organizations. Yet compared to the burgeoning number of infantry and cavalry companies in pre-war America, their ranks were few. The fact is, there was no sort of artillery tradition in the country.

Consequently when 1861 and war came there was no rush on either side to don the red stripes and facings of the artilleryman's

uniform. Additional obstacles existed as well. Artillery service required of its enlisted men a greater degree of technical skill, frequently some mathematics, and no small degree of brawn. On top of that, it offered seemingly greater dangers than the other services. After all, cannon were the targets for other cannon, and it took a serene indifference to death for a man to stand at his gun impervious to the fact that the other side was hurling 12.3-pound iron balls at him. Furthermore, while infantry and cavalry regiments could be raised and even equipped within a small area, artillery batteries had to rely upon the state or Federal government for equipment, and many simply could not be raised locally.

From these and other causes, the artillery was always the smallest branch of the service North and South. By the war's end, the Union would enlist 432 batteries, accounting for just 12 per cent of all units that served. In the Confederacy, 268 batteries, battalions, and regiments numbered somewhat more, almost 18 per cent, but clearly neither army nor people were enthralled with serving the big guns.

Below left: *Artillerymen from the Washington Artillery of New Orleans. This unit was among the oldest and proudest of the private or fraternal artillery companies. All told it comprised five companies, four of which went to Virginia in the first days of the war, and remained there thereafter. The fifth company served with the Army of Tennessee.*

Below: *A Union field gun crew. Each man has a role in serving the rifled piece. The most important one at the moment is the fellow who will yank the lanyard. This will create a spark which ignites the powder, and the gun fires.*

It is ironic, then, that once the new artillerymen were in their units, they often resisted strenuously the efforts of others to convert them to another branch. When the Washington Artillery of Augusta, Georgia, entered Confederate service and went to Pensacola, Florida, the commander, General Braxton Bragg, tried to switch them to infantry. The Georgians promptly arose in protest and requested transfer to another theater of war before Bragg backed down.

The gunners in blue and gray met with much the same experience as their

Left: *Thousands of cannon balls, neatly stacked, were stockpiled at the Washington Arsenal, pictured here in 1864. A haunting fear on the part of President Abraham Lincoln, practically amounting to an obsession, centered in the fact that Confederate raiders might swoop down on the capital. The president saw to it that Washington was never short of ammunition, and was ringed by forts that made it one of the most strongly fortified cities in the world. In addition President Lincoln also demanded that commanders station large bodies of troops at the capital, no matter how desperately they were needed elsewhere.*

Below: *Confederate artillery officers' uniforms and equipment. These include officers' frock coats, forage caps, leather gauntlets, a sash, a uniform vest, and shirt. The branch designating color for the artillery in both the Union and Confederate Armies during the Civil War was red. Red forage caps topped with gold braid added to the aura of the artilleryman on both sides. They were among the most colorful uniforms in the Confederate forces. The campaign chest belonged to Lieutenant William T. Mumford of Company G, Louisiana Artillery and the field glasses (far right) were used by Major General S. Jones.*

counterparts in the infantry and cavalry in their first days in the uniform. They had the same cheering send-offs from home, the same trips by water or rail to the training grounds, the same first encounters with camp life and also camp death through measles.

Batteries in the Union Army were, as a rule, issued their guns, teams, and attendant equipment soon after their initial training and indoctrination into the military were complete. Across the lines, on the other hand, equipping a battery was all too often a gradual process,

accomplished in unplanned stages. A Mississippi outfit left home with 65 horses but only one cannon, and had to wait many months before another three field pieces arrived. It was March 1862 before the final guns arrived, making up its full six-gun battery complement, along with caissons, limbers, traveling forage, and battery wagon.

Whatever they had when they began their service, the gunners looked forward to the same endless round of repetitive drills as their compatriots the foot and horse soldiers. Officers divided their

artillerymen into two groups, gunners and drivers, and drilled them accordingly. That exercise done, they might go through their full routine two or three times a day.

Wherever they served, whether in field or fort, the artillerymen of the Civil War were always in the thick of the action. It is no surprise that the very first shot of the war was an artilleryman's signal shell fired over Fort Sumter to commence the Confederate bombardment. If the account of one of General Robert E. Lee's officers may be accepted, the final shots fired by the Army of Northern Virginia came at

Appomattox from the guns of Captain Valentine C. Clutter's Virginia battery. Two days later, with the war in Virginia over, an old colonel and his battery were guarding a pass in the Blue Ridge mountains when approaching Federals first tried to drive them out, and then passed on the news of Lee's surrender.

When confirmation of the fact came to him, the old colonel formed his battery as if on parade. He ordered the men to run the guns up on to the bluff overlooking the Shenandoah River.

The sun was setting in the west, the embers of their campfires dying out, as the colonel gave the order to fire. There was no target. It was simply a parting shot to the way of life they had known for four years. When the roar had ceased to echo in the surrounding mountains, he ordered the battery to push their guns into the river. Over the edge the battery's guns went into the waters below.

All that remained were the men and the horses, and it is a fitting irony that, just as they had made war together, so now they would make peace. Federal terms allowed the men to take their horses home with them, and soon the animals that for four years had rushed their pieces to and fro in battle, were harnessed to the plow turn soil for the rebuilding of the nation.

Below: *Field artillery projectiles. There were great technological advances with artillery during this period. Smoothbore pieces were becoming obsolete with improvements in time and percussion fuses utilized by an array of rifled pieces of greatly increased range. Pity the artilleryman, however, working on big batteries who had to spend his war service carrying these heavy projectiles.*

The Artilleryman

❖

FOUR PRIME ATTRIBUTES WERE NECESSARY in a good gunner — intelligence, self-possession, comradeship, and loyalty to the gun. Of the first, little more need be said. As for self-possession, one need only consider the potentially terrifying effects of deafening explosions, torrents of flame shooting from the guns, and clouds of choking white smoke. A battery in action looked and felt like a scene from Dante's *Inferno*, and only men who could remain calm in the midst of that chaos could work the guns effectively. Comradeship was essential, for such a small group of men, six or seven on a gun crew at most, working tightly knit and vitally interdependent, had to get along with one another. A grudge, a hostile feeling between any two which might interfere with the efficiency of the battery as a whole, could endanger all their lives and lessen their effectiveness. Above all else loyalty to the gun was life to the gunner. Without his guns, an artilleryman was nothing, and nothing in the war would so wound the pride of a battery as the loss to the enemy of one or more of

its cannon. The men would give up their lives to save their beloved guns, and others seemed momentarily to forget even issues of loyalty and uniform in their devotion to a field piece.

Whatever guns they served, the artillerymen North and South went through some of the same evolution of organization that their comrades in the saddle endured. At the war's outset, the Confederate artillery batteries were attached to individual brigades, usually in one or two batteries each. It was a cumbersome arrangement, for one general could jealously hold on to his artillery even though a fellow brigade commander elsewhere might desperately need it. By the end of 1862, the batteries were reassigned to the supervision of division commanders, who would order them about as needed among their brigades. It was a step in the right direction, and by 1864 they were all at the direction of army corps commanders under chiefs of artillery. In the Union forces the batteries came to be brigaded together under the corps commanders as well, though with corps and army chiefs of artillery. Since the artillery, unlike the cavalry, was clearly and exclusively a support army for the

Below left: *A Union artilleryman's jacket, front and rear.*

Below: *This is believed to be the first actual photograph of the Union Army in combat. It was made under fire by Mathew Brady at the Battle of Fredericksburg, Virginia, in 1863. Toward the end of the 4-second exposure time, the cannon roared, causing Mathew Brady's camera stand to shake, such that blurring of the image occurred.*

infantry, such formal organization, better than simply parceling it out among the several brigades, was imperative.

There was another sort of artilleryman in the armies, one whose service and weapons differed considerably from the men with the field batteries. All along the Atlantic seaboard stood masonry fortifications, some dating back to the turn of the century, built to guard river outlets, bays, and harbors, and major cities like Charleston, Baltimore, and New Orleans. Several also guarded Boston, New York, and other Northern cities, and

manning them was usually the task of "heavy artillery" units. These oversized regiments were intended to operate siege and seacoast guns, but often in the Union Army were rearmed with rifles and used as infantry. In the Confederacy, its forts were more frequently manned by displaced infantrymen or members of mobile siege and garrison units called siege trains. In the North it was a soft life, for no Yankee fort ever came under attack, or even threat. The men spent their war in garrison, practising at their guns, decorating their barracks, making gravel

pathways around the parade grounds, and polishing their gear for the frequent inspection visits of dignitaries.

It was a different matter in the Confederacy, and especially at hot spots like Fort Sumter in Charleston Harbor, or Fort Pulaski near the mouth of Georgia's Savannah River. The constant object of Union attacks, these places afforded little enough rest to their occupants. Indeed, Pulaski was taken from the Confederates in 1862 when Union siege artillery simply battered a huge hole in one side of its massive masonry walls, and infantry

prepared to swarm through. Other forts, like Jackson and St. Philip guarding New Orleans, came under the bombardment of heavy naval guns from the Yankee fleets.

North and South, most artillerymen could have been interchanged, and they would have been able to function without a flaw. The routine was unvaried, unless the special nature of the gun required it. Gunner Number 2 was handed a "cartridge" of ball and powder, which he set inside the muzzle of the cannon. Gunner Number 1, who never let go of his rammer, shoved the cartridge down the

tube until it reached the bottom. Meanwhile Gunner Number 3 kept his thumb—sometimes protected by a leather sleeve—over the vent hole at the breech. Once the cartridge was in place, he jabbed a wire pick through the vent to open the cloth bag at the base of the cartridge, exposing the black powder within. Gunner Number 4, who sometimes wore a pouch on his belt which contained friction primers, rather like blasting caps, now placed a primer into the vent hole. A lanyard, several feet of braided cord, was attached to the primer and, at the proper

command, a jerk at the lanyard ignited the primer which, in turn, sent a blast of flame into the cartridge, discharging the piece. Immediately Number 1 reappeared this time with a soaked sponge which he

Below: *Confederate artillery artifacts. Red piping and facings on Confederate and Union uniforms indicated the artillery branch. As in other branches, much of the equipment used by Rebel artillery was captured, as indicated in this photograph by the Model 1851 Colt Navy revolver and Model 1833 US Foot Artillery short sword.*

rammed down the barrel to put out any remaining embers or glowing fragments of the cartridge which might accidentally set off the next round prematurely. Gunner Number 5 ran forward with another cartridge and handed it to Number 2, and the whole process repeated itself. If the round happened to be an exploding shot, or shell, then Gunners 6 and 7 who manned the ammunition chest and handed cartridges to Number 5, cut the fuses according to the anticipated time of flight to the target.

If it all went according to the numbers, a practised gun crew could get through the whole process twice in a minute, even given that many batteries had gun crews of only five or six men. A sergeant or corporal stood at the rear of the piece, in overall charge of the operation, including using the variety of generally inadequate tools then available to sight the gun on its target. "Indirect" fire, the technique of shooting over a hilltop or obstruction toward some unseen objective, was still almost unknown. Men could only shoot at what they could see. That, and the limits of range of most cannon, meant that the sergeant had to sight on a target no more than a mile distant. Much of it was intuition and guesswork, and after every shot the process had to be done over again because the recoil of a firing field piece could send the gun rolling backward several feet. Indeed, it was the resighting, and not the loading steps, which kept the rate of fire to only two rounds per minute.

While all of this took place, the other half of the battery, the drivers, were concerned with other duties. Ideally there were six horses drawing every cannon and its attached limber, or two-wheeled

ammunition chest. One driver managed each of the three pairs of horses, called lead, swing, and wheel teams. Similarly managed six horse teams pulled each of the four-wheeled caissons, carrying more ammunition chests. Thus a fully equipped six-gun battery could require 72 horses at least, not counting those needed to draw a forge and battery wagon, carry the officer and act as replacements. It is no wonder that a battery's full complement of 155 men including officers and non-commissioned officers, were 52 drivers. Another 70 served as gunners.

That considerable élan and self-confidence characterized many of the artillery batteries, no doubt aided by the fact that, on average, the more intelligent enlisted men seemed to serve the artillery branch. Although it was not the most popular branch its ranks were filled with graduates. The Richmond Howitzers, for instance, contained quite a number of college graduates, and many of the rest were businessmen and clerks. Even allowing for exaggeration, the Howitzers were quite a remarkable outfit, with their own Glee Club, and Law Club that

conducted mock trials. Units required good officers to make it all work, for the branch was easily the most technically demanding of the combat arms. Like soldiers of all times, the Civil War artillerymen often thought all too little of his leaders but many soon earned their respect once in the field.

Below: Union Artillery artifacts. Federal Artillery uniforms complied very closely to regulations. The branch color, red, is readily apparent. The short, shell jackets were worn by horse artillery, while the longer coats were used by foot artillery.

THE WEAPONRY

❖

NOTHING COULD HAVE BEEN MORE FORTUITOUS THAN THE timing of the war's coming, at least so far as the makers of weapons were concerned. For the men who had to use and suffer by those arms, of course, it was a different story. Because only now was the nation technologically "ready" for a civil war. Had the two sides come to blows 30 or even 20 years earlier, there would have been little contest.

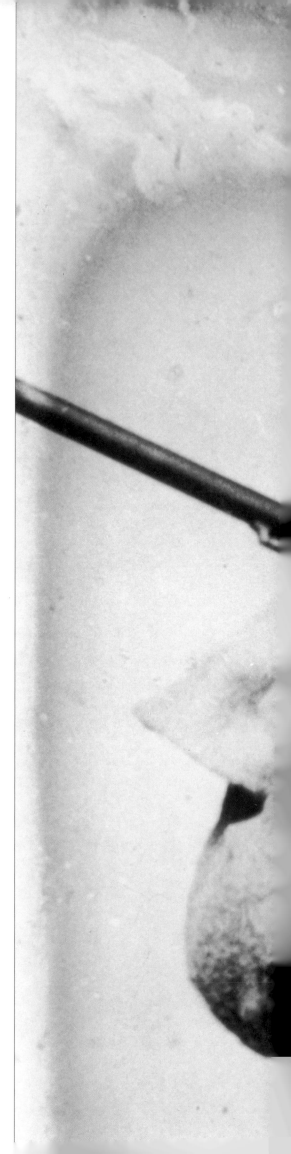

Above: Colt Model 1851 Navy Revolver, .36 caliber.

Right: Henry Kelly of the 1st Battalion, 1st Virginia Cavalry, poses with his Colt Revolving Carbine and Colt Navy .36 Revolver.

Cannon

IF ONE OF THE HOLDOVERS FROM Napoleonic tactics was the notion of the bayonet deciding battles, another was that artillery was second only to thunderbolts in effectiveness.

The truth of the matter was otherwise.

By the time of the Civil War, technology had advanced the big guns very little since the time of Napoleon. While a wonderful variety of designs was available, all but a few operated on the same principle of the first artillery pieces centuries before. A hollow tube, either of brass, bronze, or iron, was open at one end and closed at the other. A bag of black powder was rammed into the muzzle, the open end, then shoved to the back of the tube. The projectile was pushed in after it. Most of the tubes were smoothbores; a few had rifling. The piece was simply detonated either by the old fashioned method of applying a flame or lit fuze to touch-hole at the breech, or, more often, a copper priming fuze was inserted into the vent, and its spark set off by jerking a friction primer. The projectiles, too, differed little

from those of earlier generations, being only sometimes larger and a bit more reliable. There was the solid shot, literally a round ball of iron, and of little effect except when it hit an opposing artillery piece—and of course, any unfortunate man in his path. Other loads were designed to be more effective as anti-personnel weapons. The shell, either round or, occasionally, cylindro-conoidal, was hollow inside and contained a powder charge. A timed fuze in its base was theoretically ignited at firing, and when the interior charge went off, the shell flew

apart into a dozen or more pieces. Unfortunately, fuzes were notoriously unreliable, sometimes no more than one in 15 actually working. On top of that, the estimates of timing by gunners could be off, the trajectory of the gun faulty, and the shell might bury itself in the ground before going off, if it exploded at all, thus doing little or no harm.

More effective was spherical case shot, again a round ball, but this time hollow and containing up to 78 lead musket balls and an exploding charge.

When it went off in the midst of a line

of soldiers, this could be deadly, though many of the balls flew straight up into the air and others straight down into the ground, doing nothing while of the rest, only those at the forward and sides of the

Below left: *Cannon at Battery DeGolyer aimed at Great Redoubt in the Vicksburg National Military Park.*

Below: *Outside Washington a fort displays a stand of the massive cannon balls for the big guns, each equipped with special gripping holes for the tongs needed to hoist it.*

moving ball had any chance of being killed or injured. Of the 78 bullets, probably no more than a third had even the potential of putting men out of action. Grapeshot, large iron balls 2 inches in diameter and arranged in "stands" of a dozen or more, was not much used in the Civil War, but a cousin called canister was the most damaging of all artillery loads. On top of the powder charge in a smoothbore, the gunners would ram down a tin can filled with 27 cast iron balls, each nearly half a pound in weight. The load was used against attacking infantry when within 300 yards or less. On being fired, it turned the cannon into a huge shotgun.

The artillery of both sides in the war was dominated by a basic fieldpiece design little changed from the time of Napoleon and, in fact, named for him. The Model 1841 gun-howitzer in several variants, most especially the Model 1857 12-pounder Napoleon, was the workhorse of Union and Confederate artillery. It combined the longer range of the old standard gun with the lighter weight and somewhat higher trajectory of the howitzer. It took its nickname from the great exponent of artillery, and the 12-pounder reference derived from the 12.3 pound solid shot that it fired. It had a smooth bore of 4.62 inches, weighed 1,227 pounds exclusive of its two-wheeled wooden carriage, and twice a minute could fire a projectile out of its bronze tube, sending it up to 1,600 yards. It was simplicity itself, and indestructible. Its carriage generally wore out long before the gun tube. The Union manufactured over 1,100 Napoleons, at a cost of about $600 apiece. The foundries of the Confederacy made another 500 or more,

using everything from bronze, to brass, to cast iron.

Such smoothbore fieldpieces also came in smaller, 6-pounder, variants, and all the way up to 24- and even 32-pounder howitzer sizes. All were used essentially the same way and for the same purposes. Much larger smoothbores, monsters with bores up to 20 inches and more in diameter, and capable of firing projectiles weighing more than half a ton, were built for seacoast defense in the North and to protect large stationary fortifications. One Isaac Rodman smoothbore was capable of

hurling a ball nearly 5 miles out to sea—farther than anyone could see for aiming! These massive columbiads, as they were sometimes called, rarely fired in anger.

More often used were their short, stubby cousins, the mortars. Fat and squat, these weapons had a very specific purpose. They were designed to sit low to the ground, and to fire a heavy exploding ball high up into the air in an arching trajectory that could take it over and behind earthworks or masonry fortifications, to explode in their rear. Very few traveled with field armies, for they

were of no use in conventional battles. But when it came time for a siege, as at

Below: *Artillery pieces. The artillery of both combatants were quite similar. The more popular types were the Ordnance rifle (far left), Parrott rifle, and the smoothbore "Napoleon", fabricated by both sides in various configurations. The Confederate artillery also used many obsolete pieces updated by binding and rifling. The Model 1841 6-pounder field gun (far right) was used by the Union artillery while the 12-pounder Dahlgren boat howitzer (center) was issued to their navy.*

Vicksburg and Petersburg, then the mortar came into its own, and they, too, came in sizes up to 13 inches, some even being mounted on flatboats or railroad flat cars for greater speed and mobility.

Newer technological innovations vied for the attentions of the artillerists. The rifling revolution was not restricted just to shoulder arms. Many experimental models had been tested prior to the war, but when the conflict came, inventors and manufacturers rushed to get into production. Quickly the 3-inch bore, with deep rifling grooves, imparted a spin to its elongated shells that gave them greatly increased range and accuracy. It was lighter in weight than a Napoleon, and used a smaller charge, its wrought iron tube fitting the contours of the rifled projectile so closely that maximum efficiency was derived from the powder charge. Equally as popular was the 10-pounder Parrott rifle, named for its inventor Robert Parrott. It was a cast iron tube, with a wrought iron band around the breech, reinforcing it for large loads. This allowed it to use the same projectile and the same load as the ordnance rifle, while gaining nearly 100 extra yards in range, up to 1,900. The Parrotts were made in a number of sizes all the way up to massive 300-pounders. While the Confederates tried to copy the Parrott, they did not have sufficient facilities or machinery to do so in numbers. Indeed, for their rifled cannon the Rebels depended heavily upon British imports, especially Blakely and Armstrong guns, most of which used variations of the Parrott reinforcing principal.

The Armstrong also illustrated another innovation, the breechloader. Hoping to

allow for greater rate of fire, Armstrong designed a powerful hollow screw for the breech of his gun. When cranked back, it allowed a solid breechblock to be removed, the projectile and charge shoved in, and the breechblock replaced. Cranking the screw back tightly, the piece was ready to fire. Even more innovative was the Whitworth, whose threaded breechblock unscrewed and turned to the side for loading. The breechloaders proved to be temperamental and only a few were ever used. Lee did have two with the Army of Northern Virginia, each capable of

firing up to 6 miles—not much of an advantage when a gunner could rarely see more than half a mile in any direction.

A number of other military innovations also appeared. The "Steam Gun" attempted to use steam pressure instead of gunpowder. The "Wire Gun" sought to reinforce the barrel for heavy charges by using tightly-wrapped steel wire. An attempt was made to join solid shot with a length of chain which was expected to stretch upon firing, start spinning, and mow through the infantry. At least one double-barreled fieldpiece was tried but

failed. So too did attempts to make repeating cannon. The idea of a stationary, mounted repeater remained persistent, and if it could not be applied practically to large bores for cannon projectiles, still inventors found ways of making, in effect, precursors of machine guns. Confederates also experimented with land mines, called "torpedoes". The were, arguably, the first booby traps and could be deadly.

Below: *A Union battery at drill. Though clearly a "posed" photograph, it nevertheless shows the artillerymen in their positions.*

Shoulder Arms

WITH THE OUTBREAK OF HOSTILITIES IN 1861 there were about 525,000 obsolete Model 1816 and 1840 .69 caliber muskets stored in armories around the country. Most had been altered to the percussion system between 1855 and 1860, and some were even rifled and sighted, but a number were still flintlock. Confederate forces quickly took over all weapons in southern repositories. Those in the North were issued just as quickly to the volunteer army being assembled, particularly the western units. Also at the beginning of the war there were some 167,000 Model 1842 muskets, .69 caliber, in storage. Some of these were also rifled and sighted but some were veterans of the war with Mexico. All of these that had not been confiscated by Southern states were issued to volunteers.

Federal agents were immediately dispatched to the arms markets in Britain and other European countries to purchase available arms. Many of the Austrian, Belgian, and Prussian muskets acquired were as obsolete as the smoothbore

muskets available in North America. Nevertheless, they too usually went to the western troops.

The Model 1855 rifle-musket adopted was the first longarm of .58 caliber to fire the Minie bullet. Some 60,000 of these arms were fabricated at Springfield and Harpers Ferry Armories before the war but had already become obsolete by 1860. The most typical of all Civil War arms was the Model 1861 rifle-musket manufactured at Springfield Armory and by more than twenty contractors in the Northeast. Almost 1 million were

Union Longarms and Accoutrements.

1: US Model 1816 smoothbore musket alteration with bayonet in place
2: Scabbard for above bayonet
3: Cap box and waist belt
4: US Model 1842 smoothbore musket
5: Socket bayonet for 4
6: Cap box, waist belt and bayonet scabbard
7: US Model 1855 rifle-musket
8: Socket bayonet for 7
9: Rifle musket cartridge box with shoulder belt
10: US Model 1861 rifle-musket

11: Cap box
12: Socket bayonet and scabbard for 10
13: British Pattern 1853 muzzle-loading type Enfield rifle-musket
14: Tompion, plug for top of barrel
15: Socket-type bayonet, scabbard and frog for use with 13
16: Gun tools for use with rifle-musket
17: Justice muzzle-loading rifle-musket
18: Ramrod for 17
19: Non-commissioned officer's waist belt
20: Militia uniform waist belt with plate
21: .58 caliber paper cartridges

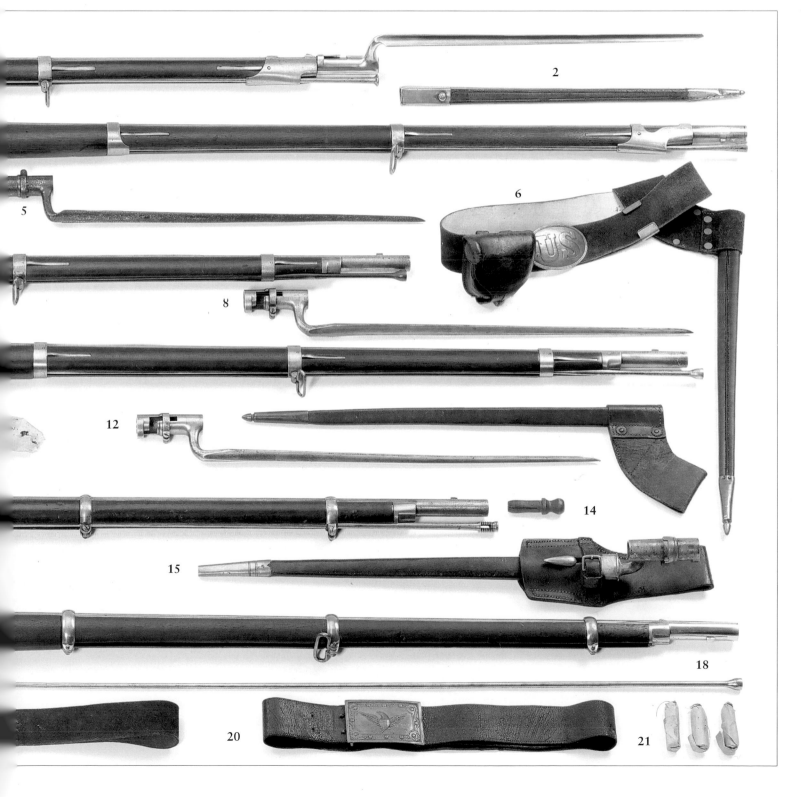

fabricated during the war, 265,129 being made at Springfield. This arm eliminated the troublesome Maynard tape priming system of the Model 1855 and became the epitome of the muzzle-loading percussion rifle-musket.

A Special Model 1861 rifle-musket was introduced, and over 156,000 of the type were made, many of them by the Colt Patent Firearms Company. Over 500,000 Model 1863 rifle-muskets were manufactured with two variations but most of these guns were received too late in the war to see much field service.

Federal arms agents did have some notable success in England. During the war years some 500,000 Pattern 1853 Enfield rifle-muskets, .577 caliber, were imported by the Ordnance Department, Northern states and Northern speculators. This weapon was second only to the Model 1861 rifle-musket in the hands of the soldiers and was well liked by all who carried one.

Rifles were originally issued to flank companies of infantry regiments, but in the Civil War whole Union regiments were issued the arms. The Model 1841 rifle was

manufactured at Harpers Ferry from 1846 until 1855.

Over 25,000 were manufactured there, and another 45,500 were made by E. Remington, of Herkimer, New York; Robbins, Kendall and Lawrence and later, Robbins and Lawrence, of Windsor, Vermont; and Tryon in Philadelphia. Many were altered and upgraded between 1855 and 1860 by re-rifling to .58 caliber, adding a long-range rear sight, bayonet adapters, and new steel ramrods. It was considered the most handsome of all US percussion rifles.

The Model 1855 rifle was made in limited quantities, with only 7,317 fabricated at Harpers Ferry. It had the distinction of being the last muzzle-loading rifle manufactured at a national armory. Confederates captured many late production rifles at the beginning of the Civil War.

Other American-made rifles were purchased and used in smaller quantities by the Union. The navy bought 1,000 Jenks Navy rifles before the war; these had a mule ear side hammer, the only such weapon purchased by the government. In addition, 10,000 .69 caliber Plymouth rifles were purchased for use on ships.

By far the most technologically advanced weapons were the Henry and Spencer rifles. Both were tube magazine-fed and lever-operated, a giant step forward. They fired self-contained waterproof rimfire cartridges. Of some 14,000 Henrys manufactured, the Ordnance Department bought about 1,700 and they were issued to the 1st Maine and 1st DC Cavalry Regiments. Many others were purchased privately at soldiers' own expense because of their

Below: *Soldiers of Company K of the 3rd New Hampshire with their longarms at Hilton Head, South Carolina in 1862. Although the rifle-musket was the primary shoulder weapon of the Union soldier, substantial numbers of rifles, both muzzle and breechloading were issued to troops in the field. Of primary importance in firearms development were the magazine-fed Spencer and Henry rifles. The Spencer rifle was personally tested and recommended by President Abraham Lincoln. The Henry, probably the most advanced weapon used in the Civil War, was the predecessor of the Winchester lever-action weapons.*

advanced design and firepower. The Union Army and Navy purchased over 12,000 Spencers. While neither rifle changed the course of history, both foretold the firepower of weapons of the future.

Both the Union Army and Navy purchased the Sharps rifle, Models 1859 and 1863. The army bought about 10,000 plus 2000 special set trigger rifles for the US Sharpshooters. The navy acquired at least 2,800. This breechloading rifle fired a prepared cartridge and was one of the most reliable and popular arms of the war.

More than 200,000 Austrian Lorenz Rifles, Model 1854 and 14,000 British Pattern 1856 and 1858 Short rifles accounted for the bulk of imported rifles, although small quantities of current and obsolescent Belgian and French rifles have been noted.

In the final analysis the Model 1861 rifle-musket, British Pattern 1853 rifle-musket and Austrian Model 1854 Lorenz rifle were the weapons most likely found in the hands of the Federal soldier.

All cavalry carbines that saw extensive service during the war were breechloading firearms using a specific cartridge. Unfortunately, the Union government adopted at least 17 different models. All fired non-interchangeable ammunition. Thus, a tactical advantage became an ordnance supply nightmare. Furthermore, even companies within a Union regiment were often armed with different-make carbines requiring specific ammunition. Standardization was never achieved during the war but the effect of overwhelming fire superiority was not lost on those who would fight later wars.

The Spencer carbine was a magazine-fed and lever-actuated breechloader of great

Confederate and Imported Cavalry Carbines and Artillery Musketoons.

1: Dickson, Nelson, and Company carbine with ramrod displayed in stowed position.
2: J. P. Murray carbine
3: Ramrod for use with J. P. Murray carbine depicted above
4: British Pattern 1853 Enfield musketoon with ramrod displayed in stowed position
5: British Terry's Pattern 1860 carbine with breech mechanism seen in open position for reloading
6: Ramrod for use with Terry's Pattern 1860

carbine depicted above
7: J. P. Mussry musketoon complete with ramrod in stowed position
8: British design of gun tool
9: British Pattern 1853 Enfield carbine with ramrod stowed in position
10: Tallahasee carbine with ramrod shown in stowed position
11: Branding iron with CS motif
12: Fabric-covered tin drum type of water canteen complete with strap
13: Spurs manufactured in Tennessee
14: Tarpley carbine with hammer cocked
15: Le Mat carbine

During the Civil War quite a few private contractors fabricated carbines and musketoons under contract to the Confederate Ordnance Department. J. P. Murray (Greenwood and Gray) produced substantial numbers (figs 2 and 7). Surviving specimens of Dickson, Nelson and Tarplay carbines (figs 1 and 14) are very rare. Most Confederate arms were either captured from the Union or imported. The Richmond Arsenal produced the largest number of carbines. Cook and Brother, the most prolific contractor, fabricated substantial numbers of carbines and musketoons patterned after the English Pattern 1853 Enfield.

ingenuity. The first Spencers were received in October 1863 and by the end of the war, large numbers of Federal cavalry were armed with them. Total Union government procurement was 95,181. The Sharps carbine was the most famous single-shot carbine of the war. It used a unique .52 caliber linen cartridge. The Ordnance Department purchased 77,330 New Model 1859 and Model 1863 carbines, and had few negative reports.

The Burnside carbine, 2nd, 3rd and 4th Models, used a peculiar .54 caliber ice cream cone shaped metallic cartridge. The

Ordnance Department purchased 53,031 of them and they were extensively used, and criticized by many to whom they were issued. "Buford's Cavalry" was armed with some Smith carbines the first day of the battle of Gettysburg. The Smith used a .50 caliber rubber cartridge later replaced by a foil round. The large spring at the breech tended to break in use. The government purchased 31,002, as well as 17,728 Gallagher percussion carbines, whose major drawback was the lack of an extractor to remove the fired cartridge.

In addition to these five types various

quantities of Starr, Maynard, Remington, Merrill, Joslyn, Gwyn and Campbell, Hall, Warner, Ballard, Sharps and Hankins, Gibbs, Lindner and Wesson carbines were purchased.

The story of longarm procurement in the Confederacy is very similar to that of revolvers and carbines. Without any existing native firearms industry to take the lead, the brand new Confederate Ordnance Department had to build from the ground up. There was no lack of enthusiastic and willing contractors who desperately wanted to fulfill government

contracts for patriotism and personal gain but there was an enormous lack of experience and reality as concerns production techniques, and particularly mass-production.

The South was blessed because of arms distributed under the Militia Act of 1808, and southern agents had been tireless and active in buying whatever arms were available to them in the north. The northern manufacturers' desire for profit, even as the war began, enabled these Confederate agents to buy current production arms and ship them south.

There were over 296,000 arms seized at Federal arsenals and installations. These arms were Model 1816 flintlock muskets, many altered to percussion, Hall's flintlock, breechloading rifles, Model 1841 rifles, Model 1842 muskets, Model 1855 rifle-muskets and rifles, and miscellaneous patterns. Only about 24,000 of these weapons were considered modern firearms.

An immediate effort was made to alter to percussion those arms that still operated by flintlock. This work was carried out at arsenals in Atlanta,

Knoxville, Memphis, and Nashville, Tennessee, and Columbus, Mississippi.

The capture of the US Arsenal at Harpers Ferry on April 19, 1861, was an

Below: *Captain A. Russell made this image of longarms and corpses along the stone wall and sunken road in front of Marye's Heights, Chancellorsville, only hours after the Confederates withdrew from this bloody action in May 1863. The dead and debris testify to the defense. Bullets caused more than 90 per cent of all Civil War wounds. Artillery accounted for most of the rest.*

incredible windfall. Besides the wagon-loads of finished firearms and partially finished parts, the gun-making machinery seized there facilitated the manufacture of arms at Richmond and Fayetteville.

The Richmond Armory was the most successful and productive Confederate ordnance facility during the war. Estimated production was just over 31,000 rifle-muskets and about 1,300 short rifles. In addition, the arsenal assembled over 1,200 Model 1842 muskets from parts and repaired nearly 25,000 arms. No other installation

achieved anywhere near this productivity.

The rifle-making machinery went to the arsenal at Fayetteville, North Carolina, and arms delivery began in 1862. By the time the armory was finally destroyed by General Sherman's 3rd Division, 14th Army Corps, on March 11, 1865, about 8,600 excellent brass-mounted, two-band .58 caliber rifles had been made there.

Cook and Brother had a private armory in New Orleans until Federal occupation, and then established another in Athens, Georgia. The Cooks produced rifles by August 1861, these being the first army

rifles manufactured in Louisiana. Cook products were brass-mounted copies of the English Pattern 1856 short rifle and other derivative English arms. The factory ceased production around July–August 1864 because the government had failed to pay for work completed. Cook and Brother manufactured nearly 7,800 firearms. Some of these were carbines and musketoons, but the bulk of them were short rifles. Cook and Brother production was easily the highest of any of the private contractors during the war.

A number of manufacturers tried to fill

the needs of the Ordnance Department. Most furnished longarms based on the popular Model 1841 rifle, usually omitting the patch box to simplify production and lower the cost. Mendenhall, Jones & Gardner fabricated just over 2,500 rifles but many companies produced fewer than 500 rifles and most did not approach 1,000.

Britain and Austria were vital to the Rebel war effort, as were the capture of so many Union guns. Rebel-made longarms probably made up less than 15 percent of the Southern arms.

Union Ammunition and Accoutrements.

1: Percussion cap box

2 and 3: Percussion caps as issued

4: Lawrence primers for the Sharps carbine

5: .58 caliber ball paper cartridge

6: Muzzle-loading .69 caliber ball paper cartridge

7: .50 caliber Smith cartridge

8: .52 caliber Sharps cartridge

9: .54 caliber metal cartridge for a Burnside carbine

10: .50 caliber metal cartridge for a Maynard carbine

11: .52 caliber Sharps and Hankins metal cartridge

12: .44 caliber metal cartridge for Henry repeating rifle

13: Tin of British-made Eley brand percussion caps for Colt pistols

14: Pistol bullet mold

15: Pistol tool

16: Packet of .31 caliber paper cartridges

17: Packet of .44 caliber paper cartridges

18: Open packet of .44 paper cartridges

Hand Guns

❖

THE FEDERAL GOVERNMENT PURCHASED just fewer than 400,000 handguns during the American Civil War for officers of all branches, cavalry troops, and mounted artillery personnel. The most popular calibers were .36 Navy and .44 Army. The total purchased officially did not include, of course, the private purchase of handguns by individual officers and enlisted men. However, the infantryman, after a long forced march, quickly realized he did not need the extra encumbrance of a handgun, no matter how small, and such weapons were promptly sold, sent home or discarded. Therefore, handguns were used in relatively limited numbers compared to the longarms of the infantrymen, who made up the great bulk of the army.

The predominant manufacturer of handguns at the beginning of the Civil War was the Colt Patent Firearms Company. Samuel Colt had carefully developed contacts within the Ordnance procurement bureaucracy to insure predominance of his products. Ordnance

Department and open market purchases of the Colt Model 1860 Army revolver amounted to 129,375 pieces.

Some 35,000 Colt Model 1851 Navy revolvers were bought by the Federal government and there were certainly other state purchases. Federal military units were issued nearly 165,000 Colt handguns. It has been estimated that 80 percent of Federal cavalry was armed with the Model 1860 Colt Army revolver at some point during service.

Second to Colt was E. Remington and Sons of New York. This company

Union and Confederate Officers' Handguns.

1 and 2: Pair of Colt Model 1851 Navy revolvers, .36 caliber; of Major General John Schofield

3: Butterfield Percussion Army revolver, .41 cal

4: Colt Model 1849 Pocket revolver engraved; of Captain J. N. Derby

5: Pettengill Army revolver, .44 caliber

6: Joslyn Army revolver, .44 caliber

7: Starr Model 1858 Navy revolver, .36 caliber

8: Allen and Wheelock Lipfire Army revolver, .44 caliber

9: Le Mat 2nd Model revolver, .41/45 cal, of

Captain J. N. Maffatt of the Confederate Navy

10: Adams Patent revolver

11: Colt Model 1850 Army revolver, .44 caliber, engraved; of Major General George B. McClellan

12: Whitney Navy revolver, .36 caliber, of Colonel Julius W. Adams

13: Colt Model 1851 Navy revolver, .36 caliber

14: Savage-North Navy revolver, .36 caliber

15: Starr Model 1863 Army revolver, .44 caliber

16: Remington-Beals Army revolver, .44 caliber

17: Colt Model 1848 Army .44 revolver, 1st Model

18: Perrin and Company revolver, .45 caliber

furnished Beals-Remington, Remington Old Model and New Model Revolvers in .36 and .44 caliber.

It is estimated that the Federal government purchased about 137,500 Remington pieces, primarily after stopping orders with Colt in November 1863 because Remington and others were less expensive. These solid frame revolvers were rugged and reliable.

The Starr Arms Company was the third largest Union supplier of double action and single action revolvers in both calibers, with total sales to the Federal government of nearly 48,000 revolvers. The Model 1861 double action revolver was delicate and prone to malfunction in the field. The Model 1863 single action was simpler and more efficient but still not liked by troops that carried them.

The Union Ordnance Department acquired nearly 17,500 Whitney Navy revolvers. Over 11,000 were issued to western army units with nearly 6,300 used by the Federal Navy. About 12,000 of the Savage Navy Revolvers were purchased, despite the ungainly appearance and fragility of the weapon.

These five makers supplied almost 380,000 revolvers to the Union of almost 400,000 purchased. Other revolvers were in limited use and evidence exists indicating that soldiers were armed with Adams, Allen and Wheelock, Butterfield, Freeman, Joslyn, Manhattan, Pettengill, Prescott, and Smith and Wesson No. 2 Army Revolvers.

Foreign handguns, for example the LeFaucheux pinfire, Perrin, and Raphael played minor roles. Some of these revolvers have appeared in contemporary photography of the war.

Below left: *Rebel cavalrymen with their sidearms. Confederate handguns were fabricated in limited quantities, the most common being the Griswold and Gunnison of which only about 3,500 were produced. Confederate forces utilized all weapons available, which accounts for the diverse types in service. All Rebel handguns are considered rare. Surviving examples of Confederate small arms ammunition are also extremely scarce, even though millions of rounds were manufactured. Confederate arsenals were never able to master the manufacture of metallic cartridges, which hindered their war effort. The variety of handguns used by Federal forces was*

quite large. Most were government issue to which were added a number of private purchases. Different models of the Colt and Remington are most prevalent. Federal ordnance facilities had the capability to produce metallic cartridges. This was a tremendous advantage.

Below: *A captain of the 9th Texas Cavalry. This captain of the 9th Texas Cavalry ably depicts what many of the mounted men from the western Confederacy looked like. Even more than their eastern counterparts, they carried a wide variety of weaponry depending upon what was available, and not according to regulations.*

This officer holds an English-made percussion shotgun, double barrelled. In his other hand he wields a Confederate-made Dance revolver, a copy of the pre-war heavy Colt .44 caliber dragoon percussion revolver. Distinctive to several Texas regiments was the "lone star" inside a circle badge on his hat and belt plate, while the slouch hat, too, is of the type generally worn by western Rebel cavalrymen. His jacket is gray, trimmed in gold, over brown trousers and brown leather boots. On these last he wears a distinctive Mexican style of spur with spiked rowels. his war-making, like his uniform and weapons, was rough and ready.

There were about 42,000 obsolete Model 1842 single-shot pistols in Federal government storage. There were also an unknown number of Model 1836 pistols, some still in flint but most altered to percussion, and some saw limited use in the early months of the war.

Almost any handgun of the period might have been carried off to war by an enthusiastic volunteer. On the field of battle, however, the majority of handguns were Colt and Remington revolvers.

The Militia Act of 1808 provided for the periodic transfer of arms from the Federal government to the individual states. Many of these arms were obsolescent but some were current models then in use by the "Old Army".

To supplement these arms some of the southern states sent agents to northern firearms manufacturers such as the Colt Patent Firearms Manufacturing Company, Hartford, Connecticut, and the Whitney Arms Company, New Haven, Connecticut. These agents purchased arms for the prewar state militia in 1860 and the early part of 1861.

Confederate or state forces seized Federal installations within their respective borders at the beginning of the Civil War. These included a number of Federal arsenals within the southern states that contained sizeable numbers of arms of all types. It is with the arms thus received, seized and purchased, that the Confederate forces marched off to war.

Among these arms were a number of single-shot flintlock and percussion pistols, Models 1836 and 1842, and some even earlier patterns. A few flintlocks were issued to eager volunteers, but every effort was made to alter obsolete flints to the

percussion system. A number of southern contractors performed this work, among them Thomas J. Adams and S. C. Robinson of Richmond, Virginia. These single-shot .54 caliber pistols were inadequate at best when facing Federal opponents who was eventually armed with a breechloading carbine and a six-shot revolver.

Southern agents were relatively successful in securing Colt revolvers even after the beginning of the war. A number of Colt Model 1860 Army Revolvers with full fluted cylinders were sent south and

Union and Confederate Handguns.

1: Uhlinger pocket revolver used by Union forces
2: Starr Army revolver as used by Union forces
3: Remington-Beals Army revolver used by Union forces
4: Remington-Beals Navy revolver used by Union forces
5: Remington New Model Navy revolver used by Union forces
6: Manhattan Pocket Model revolver used by Union forces
7: Plant Third Model revolver used by Union forces
8: Smith and Wesson No. 1 Second Issue

revolver used by Union forces
9: Colt Model 1862 Police revolver used by Union forces
10: Model 1836 pistol alteration
11 and 13: Confederate holsters
12: Griswold and Gunnison late model revolver used by Confederate forces
14: Rigdon, Ansley revolver used by Confederate forces
15: Leech and Rigdon revolver used by Confederate forces
16: Spiller and Burr revolver used by Confederate
17: Revolver bullet mold

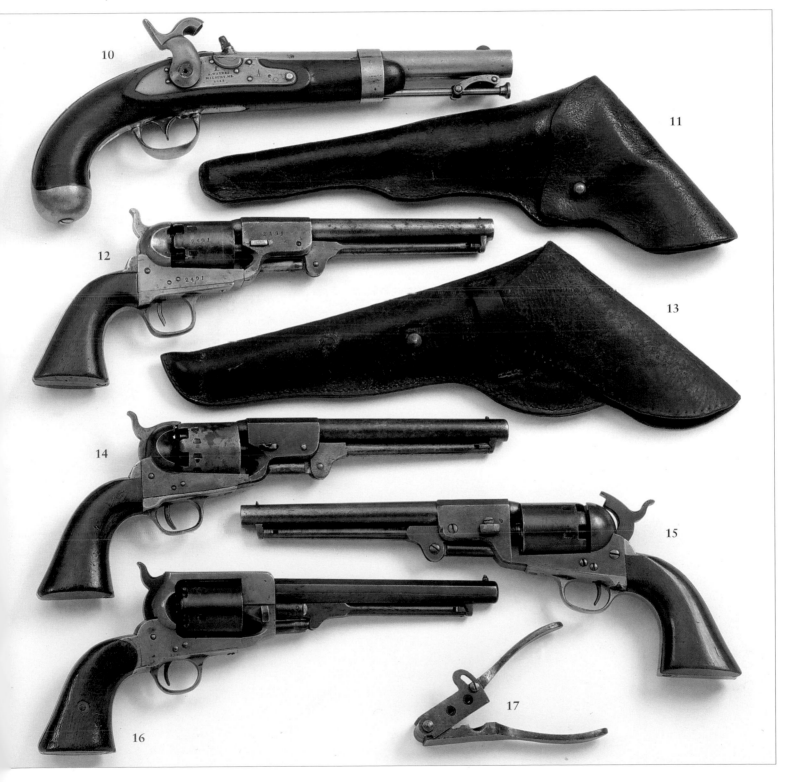

Colt was corresponding with Confederate authorities as late as June 1861, weeks after the first shot was fired at Fort Sumter in April 1861.

Throughout the war the Confederate forces were forced to utilize any weapon that was available, which accounts for the incredible variety of types in service. Battlefield captures and post-battle cleanup by Confederate ordnance personnel reaped great rewards.

Thousands of modern revolvers were acquired by the Confederacy in this manner. These were primarily current issue Colt Model 1851 and Model 1860 revolvers and Remington Old and New Model Navy and Army revolvers.

Handguns imported from abroad provided another source. Large numbers of small arms were imported from England, then one of the largest armament producers, but the Union Navy made strenuous efforts to prevent such warlike supplies reaching the South.

About 9,000 English Kerr revolvers were imported, in addition to smaller numbers of Webley, Beaumont-Adams, and Tranter revolvers. Kerr revolvers were well liked by those lucky enough to be issued this weapon.

Le Mat revolvers made in Belgium, France and then Britain totaled some 3,000 arms and French LeFaucheux pinfire revolvers were obtained in some numbers, although availability of ammunition was always a problem. Imported handguns equaled or exceeded revolver production within the Confederate states.

The least productive source of small arms for the Confederacy was the local ordnance industry. Despite all the patriotic

Confederate Pistols and Revolvers

1: Virginia Manufacture 1st Model
pistol alteration
2: Virginia Manufactory 2nd Model
flintlock pistol
3: Ramrod for above
4: Revolver holster
5: Palmetto Model 1842 pistol with integral
ramrod unstowed
6: J. and F. Garret pistol with integral
ramrod stowed
7: J. H. Dance & Brothers Navy revolver
8: J. H. Dance & Brothers Army revolver

9: Le Mat First Model revolver
10: Le Mat Second Model revolver
11: Columbus Fire Arms Mfg. Co. revolver
12: T. W. Cofer revolver
13: Tucker, Sherrard and Co. revolver
14: Griswold and Gunnison early model revolver
15: Clark, Sherrard and Co. revolver
16: Le Mat holster

In an era of enormous technical inventiveness,
manufacturers in the Confederacy played their
part, both by developing new pistol designs and
ingeniously copying those of their foes. Only
production limitations and the scarcity of

materials in the South restricted them. The
results of their labors varied enormously, from
flintlocks and crude percussion weapons to the
latest types of revolver. In an effort to furnish
arms to troops in the field, the Confederate
manufacturers utilized many obsolete arms of
earlier manufacture. Most flintlocks in the
Confederacy were altered to the percussion
system (fig 1), though in haste, some were not
(fig 2). Some Confederate revolvers were
fabricated in Texas (figs 7 and 8) and others
were manufactured abroad (figs 9 and 10).
All these Confederate weapons were produced in
limited quantities.

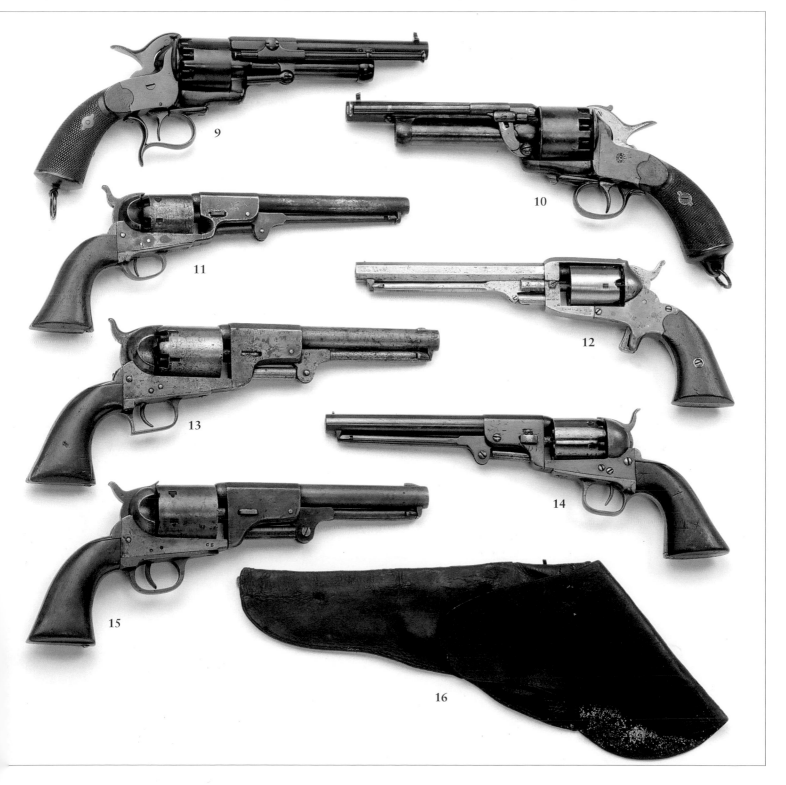

projections and Rebel government encouragement and funding, the fledgling arms industry suffered from terminal lack of experience.

None of the individuals or companies that secured Confederate government contracts had any prior experience in the manufacture of firearms. Confederate revolver manufacturing failed to achieve anywhere near projected production.

One of the greatest problems of this business was the dependence on untrained and unskilled labor. Even with Ordnance Inspecting Officers overseeing production there was a lack of quality control and early rejection rates were high.

Most of the Confederate revolvers were patterned after the Colt Model 1851 Navy or the Whitney Navy revolver. Griswold and Gunnison of Griswoldville, Georgia, managed to produce about 3,700 brass-framed .36 caliber arms, while Spiller and Burr produced about 1,500 brass-framed .36 caliber revolvers based upon the Whitney pattern.

Leech and Rigdon and Rigdon, Ansley & Company together produced another 3,000 revolvers. All the other makers,

Augusta Machine Works, Cofer, Columbus Firearms Manufacturing Company and J. H. Dance & Brothers, made so few revolvers that the sum total was less than 10,000 revolvers produced and delivered during the war, and some of these were of dubious quality.

In the final analysis, there were far more Colt and Remington revolvers in the hands of the Southern soldiers than the pitiful few Confederate revolvers manufactured. Very low survival rates have made these pistols extremely rare today. There have been more reproduction

Confederate revolvers of various models fabricated in Italy since the Civil War Centennial, 1961–65, than were ever made in the Confederacy during the actual conflict itself.

Captured Union Handguns as used by Confederate Forces.

1: Model 1841 flintlock type of percussion pistol
2: Unidentified type of underhammer pistol
3: Colt Model 1860 design of fluted Army revolver
4: Smith and Wesson No. 2 Army revolver

5: Unopened tin of percussion caps for use with revolvers
6: Packet of six paper cartridges incorporating bullet and charge suitable for use with Colt Navy pistol
7: Colt Model 1851 Navy revolver
8: Opened tin of percussion caps
9: Pistol bullet mold device
10: Remington New Model Army revolver
11: Whitney Navy revolver
12: Massachusetts Arms Company Adams Patent Navy revolver
13: Colt Model 1849 Pocket revolver
14: Colt Model 1860 Army revolver

15: Colt Model 1849 Pocket revolver
16: Pistol tool associated with Colt Model 1860 Army revolver
17: Pistol flask containing gunpowder used to charge individual chambers

As with Federal forces, the predominant sidearms in Confederate service were the Colt and Remington models. Either sidearm would normally have been captured or secured before the Civil War. Confederate forces imported more handguns than the Federal forces. These were primarily from Britain, although other nations like Austria also supplied arms to the Rebels.

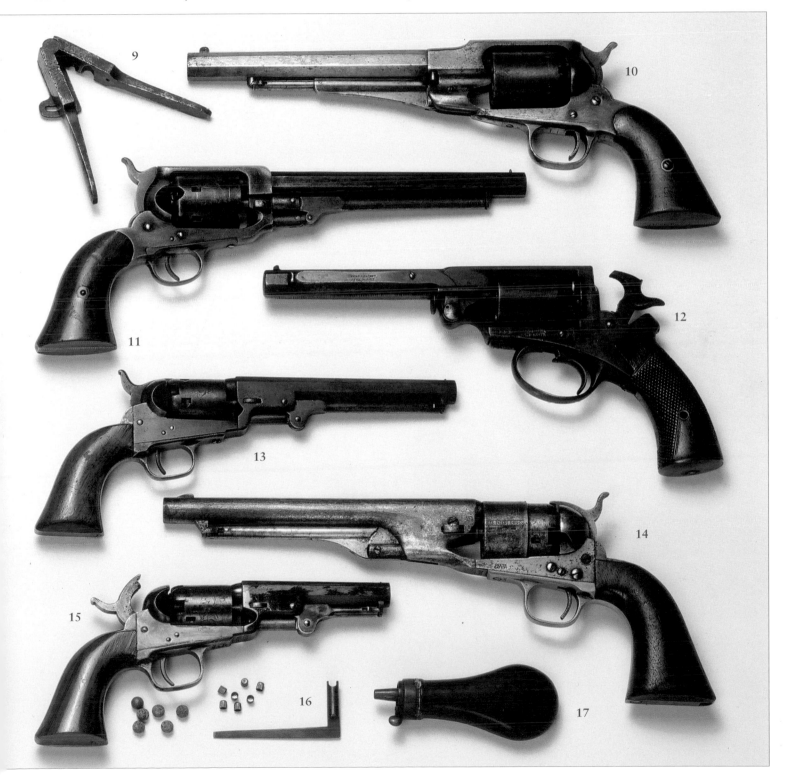

Edged Weapons

◆

THERE IS PROBABLY ONLY ONE WEAPON whose history goes back farther in time than the sword and the lance, and that would be the stone. To be sure, there were occasions during the Civil War when soldiers, out of ammunition, actually threw rocks at their foes, but no one every formally planned a role for such missiles in conflict. For edged weapons, however, the story was very much different.

For millenia soldiers had terrified their foes with sharp-edged, bright polished blades, gleaming in rank upon rank just before the attack, and promising painful, bloody battle. By the Middle Ages foot soldiers no longer carried swords, those being reserved for commanders and mounted forces. Instead, the man in the ranks carried a pike or lance, little more than a short sword at the end of a pole, literally extending the reach of his arm. Incredibly, centuries later, in 1861, some men still went to war with this, and nothing more.

In 1861, when the 6th Pennsylvania Cavalry enlisted under its colonel, Richard

Rush, the troopers were equipped with standard cavalry sabers, pistols and 9-ft-long Norway fir lances with triangular edged iron spikes at the tips. But for their uniforms and pistols, these Pennsylvanian troopers would not have looked out of place on the fields of Cannae or on the plains of Marathon.

A few other mounted regiments, especially Confederate units, also carried pikes. This was chiefly because the units could not obtain better weapons, but every unit that could, soon abandoned such medieval trappings for weapons more

in keeping with the war at hand.

"Rush's Lancers", as they were called, were only an extreme example of the backward-looking logic that dominated military thinking on both sides early in the war. Few high officials in Washington or Richmond fully appreciated the fact that the invention of the percussion lock, rifling in gun barrels, and the conical Minie bullet, made virtually all previous forms of weapons obsolete. This applied especially to edged weapons, which were only effective on a face-to-face, hand-to-hand basis, whereas the rifled bullet could

Below: Union infantrymen from the 107th US Colored regiment brandishing their shoulder arms with bayonets fixed. The bayonet dates back as long as shoulder arms, and is a vestige of pikes and spears. Innumerable illustrations from the American Civil War period showed people back home what war was supposed to look like, with soldiers in serried ranks advancing bravely with an iron line of gleaming bayonets before them. While the bayonet managed to instill some fear in a foe from time to time, the weapon rarely inflicted any wounds, being reserved for use as candlesticks and roasting spits.

deliver injury or death more than a quarter-mile from its sender. Unfortunately, it remained for soldiers in blue and gray to discover this for themselves, and to pay for the revelation with their blood.

While lances appeared only briefly, and disappeared quickly, a near cousin, in concept at least, remained on the battlefields throughout the war. The bayonet appeared more than a century earlier, at a time when flintlock muskets were cumbersome, slow in firing, and woefully inaccurate. Theory called for the

firing of a volley or two, then a spirited assault, trusting to the gleaming bayonets at the muzzles of the guns to do the real work, making the blade yet again just an extension of the infantryman's arm.

It was sound thinking given the state of shoulder arms in the 18th Century. Failing to appreciate the impact of the rifle on this, however, commanders going into the Civil War assumed that the same tactics should apply. Literally without exception, every properly equipped infantryman on both sides, perhaps as many as 2 million men in all, carried bayonets of varying size

and description. Their variety was almost bewildering. The average bayonet was 18 inches or more in length, trianglular in cross section, and tapering to a sharp point, with deep grooves between its edges. Some, however, were much shorter, little more than knives, while others stretched up to 2 ft from the muzzle of a rifle. Some, like the saber bayonet used with 1853 British Short rifles, were literally swords. The British Brunswick saber actually resembled an ancient Roman short sword more than anything else, as did a number of improvised

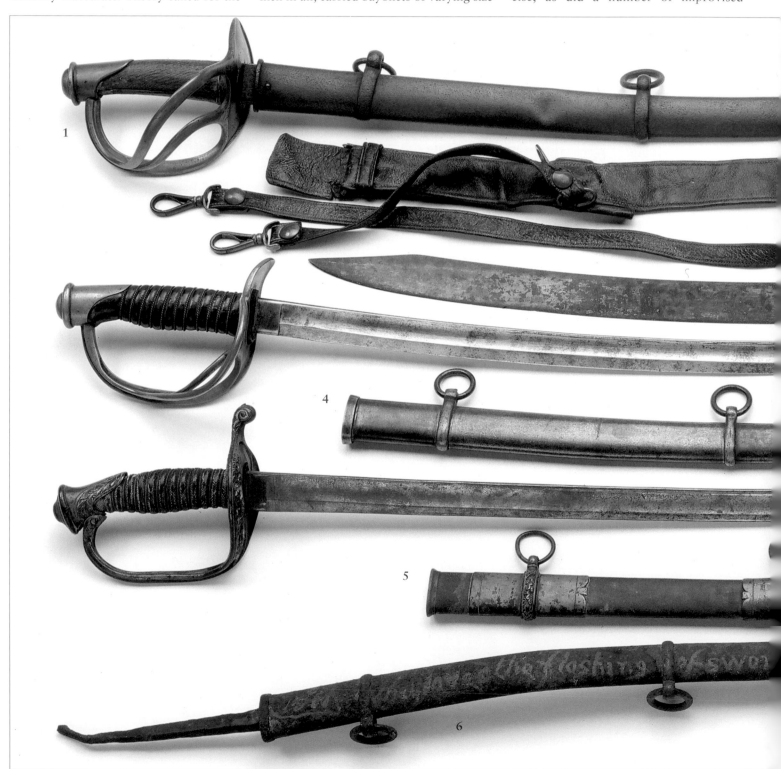

bayonets manufactured in the Confederacy. Union infantrymen carrying the Model 1855 saber bayonet wore a scabbard on their belts.

In the very first major engagement of the war, at Bull Run in 1861, commanders expected the bayonet, not the bullet, to win the day. General Thomas J. Jackson won his immortal sobriquet "Stonewall" on that field, only minutes after telling another Confederate officer, "Sir, we'll give them the bayonet" when the Federals were attacking. "Trust to the bayonet," Jackson said a little later as the

Union Swords used by Confederate Forces.

1: Model 1840 design of cavalry saber incorporating three-bar style of hand guard and housed in protective scabbard
2: Typical design of US officer's sword belt complete with straps and buckles for attachment to the sword's scabbard
3: Model 1812 design of Starr saber with simple stirrup style of hand guard
4: Model 1860 design of cavalry saber with variation in style of three-bar hand guard and complete with protective scabbard
5: Model 1850 design of Infantry Officer's sword

with decorative pommel and hand guard and complete with protective scabbard
6: Relic of Model 1860 design of cavalry saber housed in protective scabbard. Hilt, grip and hand guard are missing, exposing tang while the scabbard features a partly obscured inscription that may refer to a military unit and which appears to read "15th th. loved the flashing of swords that struggled to be free"

Like many other types of weapon, the Confederate forces had to rely on its enemy in the North to supply at least some of its swords and bayonets.

Confederate troops went into action.

Yet the men never did trust their bayonet, nor, with very few exceptions, did they ever have occasion to use them as intended. Bayonet practice during drill struck many as ludicrous, going through the manual of instructions, and looking, as one Yankee said, like "a line of beings made up about equally of the frog, the sand-hill crane, the sentinel crab, and the grasshopper: all of them rapidly jumping, thrusting, swinging, striking, jerking every which way, and all gone stark mad."

Despite all the intent and orders of their,

most Civil War soldiers never came to actual hand-to-hand fighting, and therefore never used their bayonets in combat. Instead, they jammed them in the ground at their bivouacs or into the walls of their winter huts, finding that the socket designed to attach the bayonet to the muzzle of a gun was ideal for holding a candle. More often still a bayonet, this time attached to the rifle, made a perfect spit for roasting some poor farmer's chicken or ham over an open camp fire.

If the bayonet proved ineffective, the sword, in all its varieties, was even less

useful in this war. With the exception of a few regiments, mostly Confederate, that carried Bowie knives, only cavalry units were issued with sabers.

Some artillery batteries equipped their cannoneers with weapons like the Roman-looking Model 1833 Foot Artillery short sword. And, of course, all officers were authorized to carry sabers at their belts.

The selection among such weapons was an even greater than with the bayonets. Some were ancient, like the Revolutionary War sword that Confederate General Joseph E. Johnston wore into battle. Other

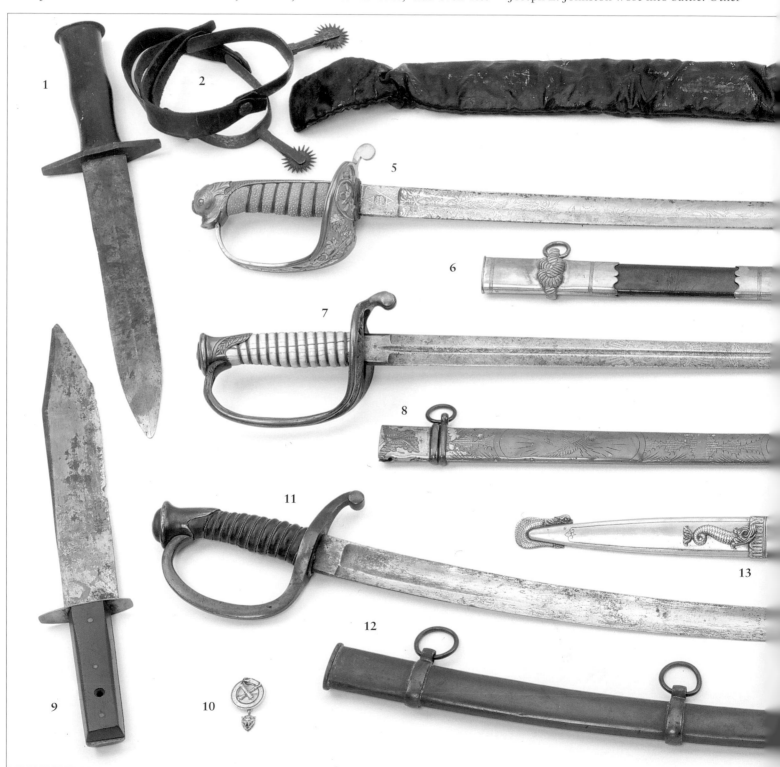

swords were massive, perhaps the largest being a 10-lb monster carried by Major Heros von Borke. Many, especially worn by non-combatant staff officers, were little more than ceremonial, and too lightweight for actual use.

The great majority of swords in use by both armies were based upon standard patterns issued in the old United States Army before the war. The Model 1840 and Model 1860 cavalry sabers predominated among bluecoat horsemen, and a great many Confederates carried them as well, after picking them up from

Confederate Officer's Edged Weapons and Memorabilia.

1: Spear-point side knife
2: Pair of iron spurs of the raker type
3: An oil cloth storage and carrying case for 5 and 6. The case is lined with chamois leather.
4 and 15: Burger Brothers side knife and scabbard. Inscription on the blade describes the weapon as a relic of the Battle of Williamsburg
5 and 6: Regulation Confederate States Navy officer's sword and scabbard
7 and 8: Foot officer's sword and scabbard made by Agruider Dufilho of New Orleans

9: Side knife made by Boyle, Gamble and Company, Richmond, Virginia
10 : Gold, jeweler-made pin, with artillery insignia
11 and 12: Officer's light artillery saber and scabbard
13 and 14: Presentation naval dirk, with silver mounts inscribed to John T. Wood
16 and 17: Side knife with etched blade together with leather and brass scabbard, made by Boyle, Gamble and Company, Richmond, Virginia. Inscribed with owner's name on scabbard: Arthur Babcock, 43rd Battalion, Mosby's Command

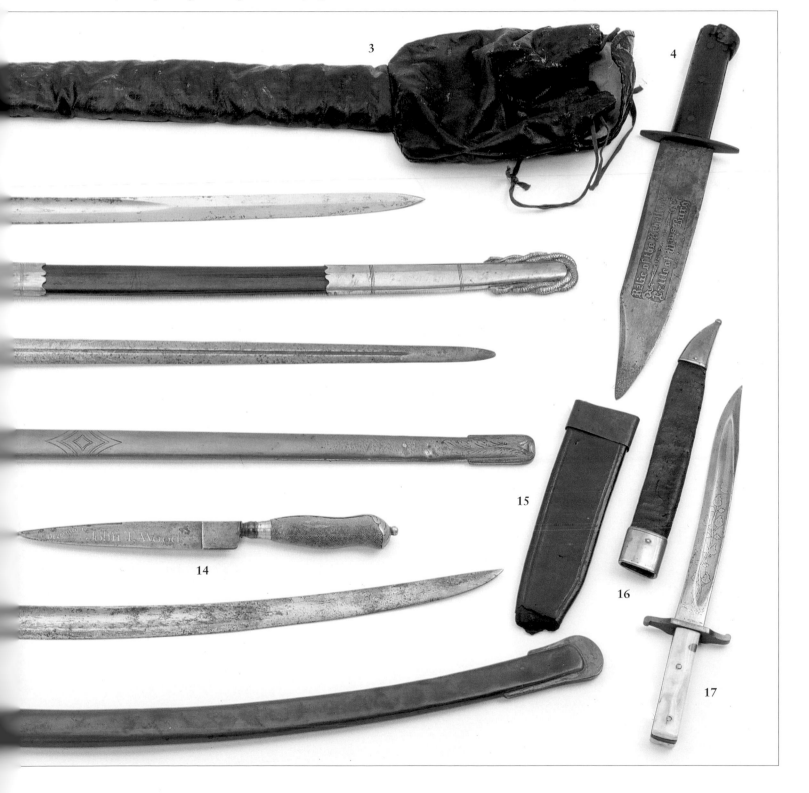

the battlefield or taking them from captured Yankees.

Dozens of varying patterns were manufactured by Confederate makers, but the basic design differed very little, almost all being sharp on the front edge, blunt on the back, with so-called "blood grooves" running down the sides, and "three-bar" brass grip guards. Officers carried the Model 1840 cavalry saber or the lighter Model 1841 light artillery saber, though many commanders, especially in the Confederacy, brought their own blades from home, or bought them from private makers like the Ames company of Chicopee, Massachusetts.

A significant number of English Pattern 1822 foot officers' sword, and Pattern 1853 troopers' sabers were imported through the blockade, as were an unknown number of Austrian sabers.

Edged weapons made within the Confederacy generally did not exhibit the quality of Federal counterparts. Most had sand cast hilts that were roughly finished in some cases, and forged blades that lacked a fine polish. Most Confederate enlisted men's sabers had sheet iron scabbards and some scabbards were even copper or wood.

Some of the officers' swords made by Thomas, Griswold and Company of New Orleans early in the war were as fine examples of the swordsmith's art as could be found. Bissomet of Mobile and A. H. Dufilho of New Orleans also made beautiful swords.

The Confederate States Armory in Kenansville, North Carolina, The Nashville Plow Works and College Hill Arsenal, both in Nashville, Tennessee, and Louis Haiman and Brother in Columbus,

Georgia, developed their own hilt design that featured the letters CS or CSA. These were quite striking.

Union officers' swords were more ornate and had become primarily a badge of rank by the mid-19th Century. The Model 1850 foot officers' sword was carried by Company grade officers, lieutenants, and captains; the Model 1850 staff and field officers' sword was authorized for majors, colonel, and general officers.

The Model 1860 staff and field officers' sword, much lighter, was also authorized and saw some service. Cavalry and

Below left: *First Lieutenant, 2nd Rhode Island Infantry. The sword being carried here is a Model 1850 foot officer's sword. Reflecting the tradition that still bound the army, an officer carried his pistol in a holster that required drawing it with the left hand, freeing the right for drawing the saber, despite the fact that bullets inflicted hundreds of wounds for every edged weapon wound. This first lieutenant shows the distinctive early war uniform of this state's first 90-days regiments. The pleated blouse with the full skirt, and the rolled collar, would be very little seen after 1861. Future Rhode Island uniforms followed more traditional Union designs.*

Below: *Union infantry officers, such as these with their regular-issue swords, carried their blades as an official badge of rank. As the Civil War progressed, it soon became apparent that the sword as a weapon had become obsolete. Many veterans of the Civil War sent swords home or else relegated them to the wagons, preferring instead a reliable revolver or a rifle-musket in some instances. After the Battle of Shiloh, for example, Rebels in Nathan Bedford Forrest's command were ordered to turn in their sabers as they were now considered obsolete. Instead the men often fought dismounted with pistols and carbines.*

artillery officers' sabers were more elaborate and of higher quality versions of the pattern carried by enlisted personnel. The Navy used the Model 1852 sword for all officers. Cutlasses of the 1841 or 1860 pattern were used, though rarely, and only occasionally actually worn by seamen.

Union sword makers included the Ames company, C. Roby and Co., and Sheble and Fisher. These made most of their swords under contract to the Ordnance Department. There were a considerable number of non-regulation officers' swords and sabers imported from Soligen, the

blade capital of Europe, and a lesser number from France and England.

Officers and enlisted men alike agreed upon one thing, whatever variety of sword they used, and wherever it came from, the thing was practically useless. Officers rarely put their to any better purpose than holding it over their heads for the men to see and rally around during an attack, or else as a tool to threaten wavering men back into the ranks.

For cavalrymen it was much the same. Indeed, most eventually acquired a disdain for their long blades, and many a trooper

either left it behind when going into action—trusting to his pistol and carbine—or else discarded it altogether. "The saber is of no use against gunpowder," declared the dashing Rebel raider John S. Mosby, while one of the troopers in Confederate General John Hunt Morgan's famous cavalry asserted that, after 1862, any man seen carrying a sword "would be forever after a laughing stock for the entire command."

The cavalrymen of the Civil War did far more damage to themselves and to their own horses than they ever inflicted upon

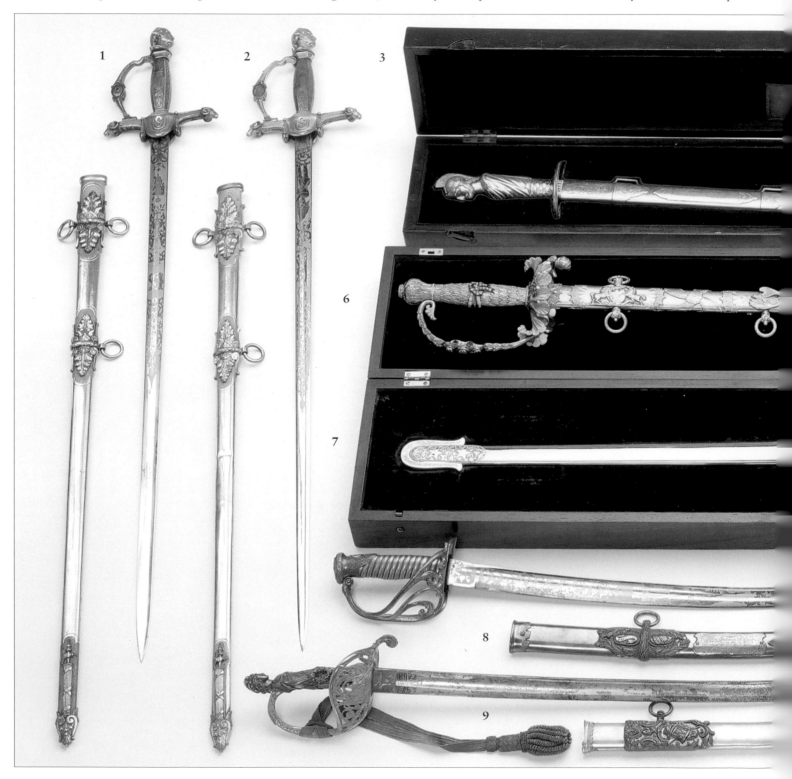

enemies with their blades. No wonder that almost all swords finally saw only the same limited service given to bayonets. As Mosby put it, "the only real use I ever heard of their being put to was to hold a piece of meat over the fire."

In the end there could be little more eloquent testimony to the obsolescence of edged weapons in warfare by the time of the Civil War than the fact that out of the millions of wounds inflicted between 1861 and 1865, only four-tenths of 1 per cent— four out of every 1,000—were inflicted by a sword or bayonet.

Union Officer's Presentation Swords.

1: Deluxe sword made by Tiffany, New York, and presented to Brig. General Godfrey Weitzel
2: Deluxe sword made by Tiffany, New York, and presented to Maj. General John M. Schofield
3: Cased deluxe sword given to Brig. General John Cook for gallantry at the capture of Fort Donelson, 1862
4: Eaglehead sword sold by Spies, New York, and owned by Colonel Sylvanus Thayer, "Father of the U.S. Military Academy"
5: Militia staff and field officer's sword presented

to Thayer by graduates of the West Point class of 1820
6: Deluxe sword made by George W. Simmons and Brother, Philadelphia, Pa, and presented to Brig. General Charles Ferguson Smith
7: Cavalry saber made by Ciauberg, Soligen, Germany, and given to Maj. I. Townsend Daniel
8: Cavalry saber made by Sauerbier, Newark, New Jersey, and given to Brig. General Judson Kilpatrick
9: High quality sword made by Frederick Horster, Soligen, Germany, retailed by Tomes Son and McLvain, New York, given to Colonel H. F. Clarke

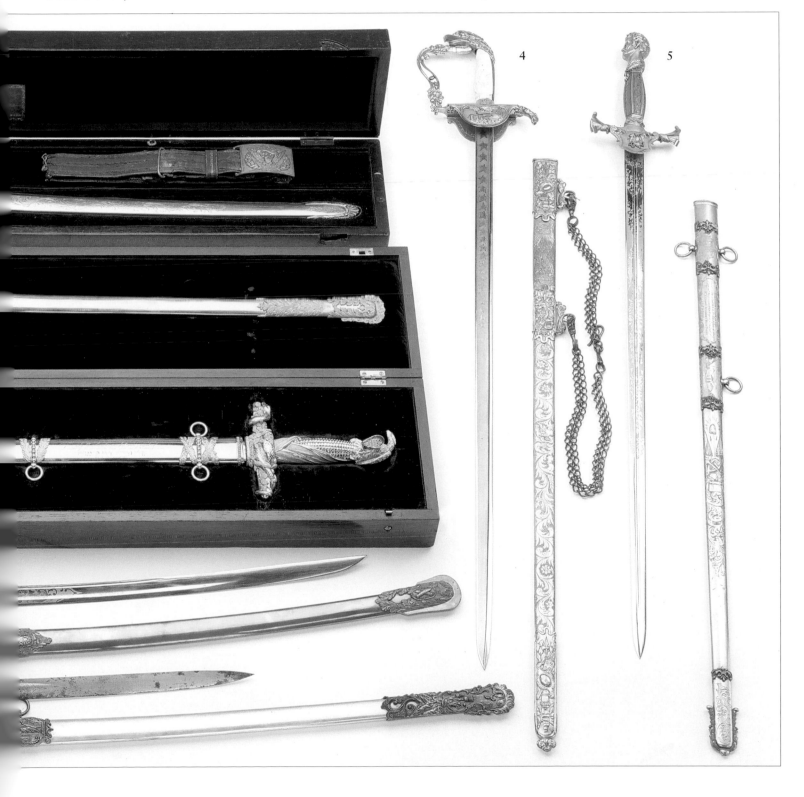

THE NAVAL WAR

❖❖❖

THE FEDERAL BLOCKADE AND THE WAR ON THE WATER WERE central to the North's demand for unconditional surrender. Yet war on land had always received much more than the lion's share of attention. Perhaps that state of affairs is the result of the fact that there were no epic naval struggles involving hundreds of thousands of men and countless casualties. Numerous apsects of the war on the water were significant but are often overlooked. Ponderous warships capable of belching immense quantities of iron have received more attention than have gunboats that operated on rivers. Yet these small craft were central to victories on land at Fort Donelson and many other points.

Above: A Union naval officer's octant.

Right: The USS Miami's pivot gun crew goes through a training exercise. They would have been under the watchful eye of an officer (out of picture). It required 10 men to jack the piece into position, fix it in place, load the charge, aim, and fire the gun.

The Rival Fleets

❖

THERE HAS ALWAYS BEEN A FORGOTTEN Civil War, a realm of endeavor in which the services of officers and men are little known and more often ignored. Perhaps it should not be much of a surprise, considering that the role of the navies, North and South alike, was very much a passive one through the bulk of the conflict. Only one or two so-called "fleet" engagements occurred in the entire war, all on the Mississippi River, and there were only a handful of individual ship-to-ship combats. Most of the hostile actions of Union and Confederate warships were against unarmed merchantmen or blockade runners. Certainly the blockade of the Southern coastline made a significant contribution to the eventual Rebel defeat, just as the activities of Confederate commerce raiders on the high seas distracted enemy vessels from the blockade while Rebel gunboats on the rivers and harbors of the South helped impede the advance of Lincoln's armies. Nevertheless, this was a war fought and won primarily on the land. As a result,

even in their own time, the men who served in the navies of the North and South found themselves often ignored or forgotten. To posterity and history they are, for the most part, all but lost.

Not surprisingly in a continent bounded by the seas, where there were not a few Americans North and South who chose another kind of service in the rush to arms. The old Union, to a large extent, had always been a maritime nation. Despite its reputation for gallantry in action and the high quality of its shops, it was not a large force compared with other major nations.

In 1861, out of a commissioned fleet of 90 vessels, some still uncompleted, the Union could count on just 35 modern vessels, with only three steamships readily at hand and not on some foreign station. That was not much of a force to cover some 3,500 miles of Confederate coastline, resupply isolated Federal outposts at Fort Pickens, Florida, and elsewhere, and maintain effectively the blockade of Southern ports proclaimed by Lincoln. Equally understrength was the manpower of the service, with just 7,600 seamen in uniform. Of course, the Confederacy had

Below left: *A lieutenant USN and first lieutenant US Marine Corps. The lieutenant at left wears the optional white trousers with his dark blue tunic, capped with a white service hat. The lieutenant of marines shows the similarity between marine and army uniforms. The differences exist chiefly in the insignia and gold lace around the collar.*

Below: *On July 9, 1862, officers pose before the turret of the USS Monitor. On December 30, 1861, the vessel foundered off Cape Hatteras. The ship took four officers and 12 men to the bottom.*

no navy whatsoever at the outset, whereas the existence of a host of local militia units did give it an impressive head start for its army. Thus for both North and South, there was a massive task ahead of the respective Navy Departments in acquiring ships and men to crew them.

Finding ships was, for both sides, a matter of building some, converting others to war purposes, and buying the rest. The South put into service perhaps as many as 500 vessels before the end of the war, though most were small, *ersatz* boats hardly equal to the demands made upon

them. A few Rebel ships, however, achieved well-deserved notoriety, most notably the commerce raiders *Florida*, *Alabama*, *Tallahassee*, and others, and the river and harbor ironclads like the *Virginia* (*Merrimack*), *Arkansas*, and *Albemarle*. As for the Union, by 1865 its Navy had seen service from 716 vessels, all but a few newly constructed specially for war.

Finding the men to run those ships remained a constant challenge. A big problem, ironically, was the army. In the first rush of enthusiasm, everyone hurried to take up a rifle. No one even thought of

the war lasting long enough for the navy to play a big role, nor did they really anticipate that there would be much need for naval engagement, even if the war did extend beyond the summer of 1861. Worse, the bounties offered to induce men to enlist in newly-forming regiments usually lured the few experienced seamen to try their hand at land service instead. So great did the shortage become that colonels of many regiments were urged to comb their ranks for men who had the skills to serve on boats, and to transfer them to the navy instead. Unfortunately,

many officers used the opportunity not to transfer good men, but to get rid of undesirables from their ranks.

Before long, Congress authorized the payment of bounties for naval enlistments, though they were never as effective as with army enrollments, and by 1864 some volunteers were being paid as much as $1,000 per man to sign on. Though it never became a flood, Union naval enlistments rose sufficiently to crew every ship put into service, and during the course of the war some 132,554 eventually wore the blue. Across the lines,

with far fewer ships of any size, and a fleet—such as it was—that was almost entirely confined to rivers and bays, the Confederate Navy had substantially smaller manpower needs. Even then, it was always hard-pressed for crewmen, and frequently had to borrow them from nearby army units when action approached. Probably not much over 5,000 men enlisted in the Southern navy during the war.

Even as a few warships began to return to home ports with the rising of the crisis, the Navy felt the same strains of loyalty

that tore apart the Old Army. There were naval bases all around the South, from Norfolk, Virginia, with its vital navy yard, down the Atlantic coast to Key West, and along the Gulf of Mexico at Mobile,

Below: *The Confederate blockade runner* Old Dominion *being fitted out in Bristol, England. More than three hundred steamers made over 1,300 attempts to run the blockade during the Civil War. Many of these were normal merchant vessels, but an ever-increasing number were purpose-built, with low silhouettes, light draft, and high speed.*

Alabama, Pensacola, Florida, and elsewhere. The security of all, when and if war came, would depend upon the loyalty of the officers in command, and of those loyalties the government in Washington could not be entirely sanguine.

While not as popular a vocation as the military, still a commission in the navy enjoyed considerable prestige in the old South, and a sizeable proportion of those 1,554 serving officers when secession commenced were natives of the seceding states. Which way they would "jump", as the Confederate army commander Pierre

Beauregard had put it, became a primarily concern of the Navy Department in Washington. It needed these trained and experienced men to command its ships; at the same time it recognized that, as with the army, the Federal navy would be regarded as a prime source of officers for any new Confederate naval force that might emerge.

In the end, the old navy would find itself particularly hard hit exactly where it hurt the most, among the younger mid-level officers who would be expected to take the bulk of the warship commands in the

coming war. While there were 93 serving captains—then the navy's highest rank—only 15 eventually left, and of them 12 joined the Confederate Navy. Certainly they were missed but most were elderly, and several too feeble ever to take shipboard commands. From the next level, however, 34 out of 127 commanders resigned, 29 of them taking Rebel commissions. Even worse, out of the 351 lieutenants then serving, 89 departed. Of the 123 commanders and lieutenants who turned in their commissions, only 15 did not don the Confederate gray, and it was

those who did that formed the overwhelming majority of those who would one day command their own ships for the Confederacy. For the Union, which would commission hundreds of ships before the war's end, the loss of this pool of potential captains was the biggest blow of all.

The only source for replenishing trained officers lost due to battle or resignation were the naval academies. The United States Naval Academy had been established in 1845 at Annapolis, Maryland, and there it continued until

May 1861, when the tenuous state of Maryland politics made a move judicious. That month the Navy Department moved the Academy to Fort Adams near Newport, Rhode Island. Five months later it moved again to quarters in the Atlantic House, a hotel, and there it remained until after the close of the war. All of their books, instruments, and other articles of learning went with them.

When the outbreak of war came and there was an initial need for more officers to replace those who had resigned, the class scheduled for graduation in 1862

Below: Confederate naval officers' uniforms and equipment. Material from the Confederate Navy is exceedingly rare. The dolphin head naval sword (three examples are shown at the bottom of the photograph) is one of the most desirable objects in the whole field of Civil War collectibles. The epaulettes in their box belonged to Cdre. French Forrest. As with their army, Confederates deliberately designed naval insignia that would be different form that of the old Union. Their shoulder straps particularly made their insignia more in keeping with that of officers of comparable rank in the Confederate States Army.

was detached from the Academy for special duty. They never returned and were never graduated, though always thereafter treated as a graduates just the same.

Those who stayed behind at the Academy studied seamanship, naval construction, tactics, practise exercises, signals, swimming, gymnastics, ordnance and gunnery of both field and naval variety, fencing, algebra, geometry, trigonometry and calculus, steam engineering, astronomy, navigation, surveying, physics and chemistry, mechanics and applied mathematics, English literature, history and law, French and Spanish, drawing, and chart-making.

It was, to say the least, a rigorous program of study. Because of the rigid system of promotion through vacancy only, none of the graduates of the wartime classes had an opportunity to achieve much in the way of distinction, and few rose above their graduated rank of passed midshipman by 1865.

The case was a little different to the South. On March 16, 1861, President Davis was authorized to appoint midshipman, and a month later the limit as set at 106.

By 1865 that limit had risen to 150, though through the course of the war a total of nearly 200 young men were so appointed. Many failed to pass the courses, or else left to join the army, accounting for the attrition. However, it was not until later in December 1861 that Congress mandated "some form of education" for midshipmen.

The following spring, Congress provided for the appointment of midshipmen cadets by representatives and senators, as well as the president, and in

May 1862, with no funds or location for a permanent Academy campus, the ship CSS *Patrick Henry* was officially designated as the Confederate Naval Academy, moored off Drewry's Bluff on the James River.

As there was insufficient space to house all the appointees extra cabins were built ashore at Drewry's Bluff and alterations were made to the sidewheel steamer *Patrick Henry* to accommodate more midshipmen. Still only half of the 106 appointed cadets could live aboard the ship. They were therefore rotated between ship and shore. The students had essentially the same program as the United States Naval Academy, only with the addition of political science. Sometimes cadets also laid mines, assisted in boarding parties to capture enemy vessels, and even took a hand in defending against Federal land movements.

In the end only two classes graduated, totaling in all a mere 48 midshipmen. Many more simply did not have enough time to complete their studies and examinations before the war closed.

For all the officers, whether midshipman or masters, commodores or captains, the life of a serving commissioned leader was governed by his branch of service and posting, and each had its distinctive features. Officers on blockade duty saw a different sort of war from those in the river flotillas and squadrons. Officers on ironclads had a more varied existence and

Below: *The USS* Santiago de Cuba, *a former packet ship once running between New York and Havana, was purchased by the Union and armed with 10 guns as a blockading vessel to chase runners creeping in southern ports. Such ships did see combat but casualties were very light.*

routine than those aboard conventional ships, while the men on the cruisers or the men on shore stations lived in yet other environments.

Most Confederate vessels of all types never fought in more than three engagements in the American Civil War, while most ships in Federal service chased unarmed blockade runners or bombarded shore positions that often did not return fire. For all the hellish nightmare quality in action, the navy, North and South, was not an inherently dangerous place—just extremely boring.

Left: *The gun deck of the USS Merrimac (CSS Virginia). The guns depicted in the engraving are 100-pounder Armstrong breech loading rifles. The USS Merrimack, however, carried no guns of this type.*

Below: *Union naval officers' uniforms and equipment. Naval artifacts in general are quite scarce, due primarily to the fact that the navy was small in comparison to the army. Much naval material was also quite functional, and postwar changes in regulations did not necessarily make uniforms obsolete; so they were used until worn out.*

The Sailor

THE COMMON SEAMAN'S DAY, NORTH and South, was much the same—one continuing routine, varied little except by the type of ship the man served, and the duty assignment of the vessel itself. Sometimes, if special duties like refueling or cleaning the ship were due prior to departure, the boatswain awakened the men well before dawn. More often, however, a bugler—a marine if the ship was large enough to carry a marine contingent—sounded reveille at 5 o'clock in the morning. While the bleary-eyed tried to clear their heads, the boatswain and others from the watch coming to an end ran along the berth deck shouting at the men and adding incentive by shaking or jarring their hammocks.

The first duty of the sailor was to stow his gear, wrap his blankets if any inside his hammock, roll it into a tight little ball, and stow it on the main deck in a special hammock netting behind the ship's bulwarks. There it served a dual purpose, for the netting and hammocks so placed could catch dangerous splinters sent flying

about the deck by enemy cannon fire, and at the same time provide an obstacle to boarders in a close action. A seaman was expected to take only seven minutes from the sounding of reveille to the placement of his bedding in the netting, but depending upon the punctiliousness of his captain, and how much long, monotonous duty may have loosened discipline, he more often than not took longer.

With his bedding stowed, the sailor had more chores ahead of him before he was served his morning meal. He had to scrub his berth deck with seawater, and then use holystones to clean the main deck. That done, there were the guns to clean, with all exposed iron to be burnished to keep off rust. A ship carried lots of brass—bells, fittings, even ornamental hardware—and all of it had to be polished.

Sails and rigging—if any—needed to be checked for mildew and wear, and the ship's ropes and tackle put in order. Only when his vessel glistened bright and clean in the morning sun did the sailor receive orders allowing him to have a wash and brighten himself. By 7.30, all this behind him, the seaman dressed and waited for

Below left: *The USS* Galena *on the James River, Virginia, June 1862.*

Below: *A US Navy petty officer from the USS New Hampshire. The petty officers were the men who, some said, really ran the ship. Petty officers wore much the same type of uniforms as the common seamen, blue wool or white duck trousers and frocks with blue striped cuffs and collar. An embroidered four anchor was to appear on the sleeve of their jackets as a mark of rank. The boatswains carried pipes or whistles, and all petty officers could carry weapons such as pistols and cutlass as sidearms.*

the sound of the boatswain's pipe calling them to breakfast. The men ate in "messes" of eight or more to a table, usually eating with others who shared their specific duty posts, such as gun crews, topmen on sailing ships, engineers, and the like.

What they actually ate varied with the season and the climate of their station, as well as what might be locally available, but in the main every seaman was supposed to have a pint of strong coffee and a sizeable piece of hard, salted beef, called "junk"—and not without reason.

Ordinarily the sailors took turns at acting as cook for their messes. As soon as the meal was finished, each sailor kept his cutlery and mug, while the mess orderly of the day stowed the cooking utensils and plates in the mess chest.

Happily, after a busy early morning, the sailor generally enjoyed a few hours of leisure after his breakfast, expecting perhaps a general call to quarters for inspection. Otherwise, he wrote his letters—if he could write—mended his clothing, played cards or backgammon with his mates, and tried any other means

available to escape what could be an endless round of tedium, especially for the Yankee sailors on blockade duty.

Noon brought yet another meal, this one more substantial with salt pork or beef, vegetables, coffee, and whatever local produce might be available, especially eggs or cheese. Victuals varied greatly, with Union sailors enjoying a much more standard bill of fare, while Rebels ate in much the same *ersatz* fashion as their compatriots in the armies. Only the men aboard the commerce raiders like the *Shenandoah* or *Florida* enjoyed really

ample tables, thanks to what they captured from the prizes they took. As the war wore on, many Confederate seamen received issues of meat rations only two or three times a week.

Training and drill occupied some of the afternoon, though there was little actual schedule or regularity about it. Indeed, one ship's boy on a Federal blockader in 1863 wrote that "The life of a sailor is not one of a real and regular work, his hours of rest may not be uniform but they are more or less regulated." The details of ship's routine might vary considerably

Confederate Naval Arms and Accoutrements

1: Typical Confederacy Second National Bunting Flag as displayed by warships adn other vessels of the South

2: British Pattern 1859 cutlass-type design of bayonet for use in conjunction with British Wilson breechloading naval rifle depicted below. Complete with protective scabbard.

3: Thomas, Griswold and Company design of naval cutlass with belt

4: British Wilson breechloading naval rifle complete with ramrod in stowed position

5: Short-barrelled type of pistol used for firing

warming flares or colors of the day

6: Typical design of canvas sea bag as used by sailors on Confederate warships

7: Naval cutlass complete with canvas waist belt and protective scabbard

8: Firing mechanism for ship-borne cannon armament embarked on Confederate ships of the line

During the Civil War the Confederate Navy used a combination of imported arms carried on ships constructed abroad and locally manufactured arms aboard craft constructed within the Confederate states.

from day to day, the ship's boy observed, "yet its original outlines are the same day after day."

The one immutable factor, other than reveille, and the early morning duties, was mealtime, and thus many sailors came to measure their days not by hours but by when they ate. Like all other meals, 4pm light supper came at the end of a four-hour watch, and here there could be a problem, for this was the final meal of the day, and it would be 16 hours before the next day's breakfast. Men with late night watches could be painfully hungry.

Following supper, the crewmen had one more call to quarters for inspection at 5.30pm before the ship was essentially finished with its active day—excepting, of course, vessels engaged in open sea steaming or on active blockade duty where most of the real action took place at dusk and after. Once the ship's inspection was done, the crewmen had the rest of the evening to themselves.

The sailors retrieved their hammocks and slung them on the berth deck. They crewmen then lounged, slept, read, and secretly engaged in a variety of forms of

gambling, though officially it was against regulations and offenders could be disciplined or fined. They threw dice, bet on dominoes and cards, tossed coins, and even bet on times and distances involved in their vessel's travels.

But much more was available for those who craved recreation and entertainment. Banjos, guitars, fiddles, and more, came out on deck in the evenings.

Obviously, because men would misbehave, there had to be means of punishment for offenders, though this presented special problems in the confines

of a ship at sea or on station in a river in enemy territory. Serious offenses like mutiny, disobeying orders, desertion, treason, and the like, were to be dealt with by courts martial. Even seemingly minor infractions like swearing, drunkenness, and gambling could be thus tried, as could duelling. A man could be demoted and his pay reduced accordingly. He could be confined to the brig with or without hand and leg irons. Offenders could also be denied shore leave or punished with extra duty. Serious crimes could be punished with the death penalty. Generally, the

seamen encountered less formalized punishments for their misbehavior, as officers suited the penalties to the crimes.

There was considerable variety in the conditions experienced by seamen, depending upon their postings. Yankees stuck on blockade service endured, arguably, the most tedious life of all, spending months at a time patrolling back and forth a few miles outside a harbor or river mouth, waiting to catch an occasional runner. If the seas were down and the winds were low, it could be hot and sticky. When the weather rose, the

churning seas battered ships and men alike, leaving the latter sea-sick and debilitated. It was somewhat better for the sea-going cruisers that piled the oceans in search of the Rebel commerce raiders. Though they spent months at a time on cruiser, at least they encountered unusual or exotic ports, and more shore leave when available. The same was true of the men aboard the ships they hunted.

Sailor-for-sailor there was far more real

Below: *Gunners from USS* Hunchback *loading a 12-pounder, field-mounted Dahlgren howitzer.*

action, and much more relief from tedium, for the men stationed aboard the river gunboats. Hundreds of these plied the Mississippi River and its tributaries, as well as the major navigable rivers along the eastern seacoast. Smaller, shallow-draft vessels, they usually operated out of bases in the interior, or else in a harbor, and returned frequently to refill their small coal bunkers. That meant many more opportunities for the men to get leave to go ashore. Additionally, water, wood, and foraging parties often left the vessel while on patrol, spending a few hours or even

days on the riverbank and in the interior. It was still hot service, and muggy along the Southern waterways, but foul weather presented much less of a hazard.

The tedium was further relieved by the very real hazard of action, for a river gunboat might frequently encounter enemy shore batteries, an attack from shore-based boarders, or even an occasional raid by cavalry. And now and then, especially on the Mississippi River, there could be a major fleet battle or attack upon some fortified city like New Orleans or Vicksburg. For every blockade

sailor who died of sea-sickness or scurvy, a river seamen died in action.

What fighting a seaman did engage in was usually ship-to-ship or ship-to-shore manning the cannon of his vessel. He worked a variety of guns almost as great as that of the artillerymen in the army, though generally the ship's guns came in more awesome sizes. There were the rifles that fired projectiles ranging from 12 to 150 pounds, most of them Parrots, though also a number of the newly designed Dahlgren rifles, often called "soda pop" guns thanks to their shape resembling that

of a bottle, aboard some of the bigger vessels, and especially on ironclads expected to combat forts or other ironclads, massive smoothbores firing projectiles weighing 440 pounds or more, were also served by the gun crews. And there were a lot of them. By the last year of the war, the Union Navy alone carried over 4,600 guns aboard its ships. Numbers for Confederate vessels are far less precise, but certainly more than 2,500 saw service. Regulations differed according to the gun and the availability of men, but in general it took 16 men to

Union Naval Arms and Accoutrements.

1: Typical National Bunting Flag as displayed by warships of the Union Navy during the Civil War

2: Type of pike used to facilitate the boarding of Confederate warships during close-order naval engagements

3: Parallel ruler of type used as an aid to navigation by Union naval personnel at sea

4: Presentation case containing 1862 design of Navy Medal of Honor as awarded to Union sailors for conspicuous gallantry in battle

5: US Navy Model 1842 muzzle-loading type of percussion pistol complete with integral ramrod

6: Typical design of box containing primer

7: Stand of grapeshot of type used in sea battles of the American Civil War

8: Dahlgren-manufactured example of bowie type of bayonet complete with protective scabbard.

9: Union officer's naval cutlass of Model 1860 design

10: Union officer's naval cutlass of Model 1841 design

operate one muzzle-loader, most of them performing functions that corresponded closely to the duties of the artillerymen with the army forces. In addition, the massive guns had to be manhandled forward by rope and tackle after every recoil, and that task alone could occupy nine seamen.

The experiences of sailors both North and South were quite apart from those of the soldiers, and distinct to the kinds of ships they manned. Rarely did any man ever have to face the ultimate test of a hand-to-hand, face-to-face encounter with an enemy. Most of the water-borne action of the war took place on the rivers and harbors of the South, between gunboats and ironclads, or such vessels and Confederate forts.

In either case, most of the time the gun crews enjoyed the protection of an iron casemate or turret in the case of the ironclads, and at least some kind of reinforced wood, or even cotton, bulwarks aboard the gunboats and converted river steamers. As a result, the seaman's view of the action was limited to what he glimpsed through his gun-port.

Fighting was for him a methodical repetitive performance of the functions necessary to load and fire. Unless his ship took a bad hit, the most common enemy was the smoke, choking heat, and deafening noise inside the gun deck.

The advancements in warfare had made fighting increasingly more dangerous for the footsolider. For the seaman, however, the Civil War was comparatively the safest conflict to date. Consequently, of more than 132,000 Yankee sailors, just 1,804 were killed in action or died as a result of wounds, and of them nearly one-fifth were

THE CONSCRIPT BILL!
HOW TO AVOID IT!!
U. S. NAVY.
1,000 MEN WANTED, FOR 12 MONTHS!

Seamen's Pay.	$18.00 per month.
Ordinary Seamen's Pay,	14.00 " "
Landsmen's Pay,	12.00 " "

$1.50 extra per month to all, Grog Money.

$50,000,000 PRIZES!

Already captured, a large share of which is awarded to Ships Crews. The laws for the distributing of Prize money carefully protects the rights of all the captors.

PETTY OFFICERS.— PROMOTION. Seamen have a chance for promotion to the offices of Master at Arms, Boatswain's Mates, Quarter Gunners, Captain of Tops, Forecastle, Holds, After-Guard, &c.
Landsmen may be advanced to Armorers, Armorers' Mates, Carpenter's Mates, Sailmakers' Mates, Painters, Coopers, &c.
PAY OF PETTY OFFICERS.—From $20.00 to $45.00 per month.
CHANCES FOR WARRANTS, BOUNTIES AND MEDALS OF HONOR. All those who distinguish themselves in battle or by extraordinary heroism, may be promoted to forward Warrant Officers or Acting Masters' Mates,—and upon their promotion receive a guaranty of $100, with a medal of honor from their country.
All who wish may leave HALF PAY with their families, to commence from date of enlistment.
Minors must have a written consent, sworn to before a Justice of the Peace.

For further information apply to U. S. NAVAL RENDEZVOUS,
E. Y. BUTLER, U. S. N. Recruiting Officer.
No. 11 FRONT STREET, SALEM, MASS.

scalded to death by burst boilers. Perhaps another 3,000 died of other causes, but total Confederate naval casualties are difficult to ascertain, though their overall percentage was likely greater, since Southern protective armor was less effective than that of the North, and considerably more Rebel vessels were battered into submission. Still, when compared to a better than one-in-five chance of meeting death in some form or another for the soldiers, the sailors' hopes of survival were immeasurably greater. As for the seamen aboard Confederate commerce raiders, the few naval blockade runners, or the Yankee ships that chased both, injuries in action from enemy fire were almost non-existent. The commerce raiders took on only unarmed merchant vessels, and the blockaders the same. And when these vessels did fire, often as not their target was only a dim smudge of sail or a column of smoke on the horizon.

Indeed, for most sailors the real action of the American Civil War was invariably a dot on the horizon. That they did their part cannot be denied, nor is it arguable that the control of the rivers, harbors, and coastlines for which they vied, was not ultimately crucial to success or failure. Yet for the sailors, both North and South, who often endured a year of inaction for every day of battle in those ships and boats, theirs was a war on the margins of the great conflict.

Below left: *Prize money attracted thousands of recruits to the Union's navy while the army struggled to fill its ranks by offering bonuses.*

Below: *A deck scene from the USS* Monitor *on the James River, Virginia, in July 1862.*

EPILOGUE

❖

WHEN THE END CAME, IT CAME ALMOST ALL AT ONCE. On April 9, 1865, Grant forced Lee out of the defenses of Petersburg and Richmond, and his tattered army out in the open. Grant speedily surrounded his old foe near Appomattox Court House, Virginia. Lee had to capitulate. The Army of Northern Virginia would fight no more. A few days later the Army of Tennessee surrendered to Sherman. A week and a day later, remaining Rebel troops in Mississippi, Alabama, and part of Louisiana, surrendered. Finally on May 26 the Army of Trans-Mississippi gave up as well. All organized resistance had finally ceased.

Above: Colonel Yorke's 5th Corps badge.

Right: Names inscribed on to the Illinois Monument at Vicksburg. The monument has 60 unique bronze tablets lining the interior walls and name all 36,325 Illinois soldiers who participated in the Vicksburg Campaign.

NTZER
ROLL
ES

BULL
ED
MILLER

CIAN
MER
NER

PRIVATES

BELL, GREEN
BERRARDY, WILLIAM
BOSWELL, JOHN
BOWLIN, WILLIAM
BUDDENBURG, M.
BULL, JARRARD
BULL, NATHANIEL
CASSELTON, WM.
CLARK, ABRAHAM C.
CLARK, ANDREW J.
DELOUNEY, JOHN
DIVINE, JAMES

EAST, EDWARD
EBERLIN, BLASE
EDSON, WILLIAM
ENNO, TEOPHILE
GARDNER, ALEX.
GROOVES, BENJ.
HARRELL, S. W.
HASSEN, JOHN
HAYES, ISAAC
HOMER, MATTHEV
JORDON, ALFRED
KLEMME, ERNST
KNOWLTON, EDW
MACKER, GEORGE

NER
US

CORNELL
RT
LIAMS
POORE
RREN
IAN
K

WAGONER

JACOB ARBOGAST

PRIVATES

ADKINS, GEORGE
ADKINS, HENRY
BAKER, WILLIAM
BARRETT, ANDREW J.
BROCK, HOLLEN S.
CANFIELD, DAVID
CHAPMAN, ISAAC
CROSS, THOMAS Q.

DUNBAR, DAVID
DUNBAR, JASPER
ELDER, JOSEPH
ELLIOTT, JOSIAH
FAIRBANKS, JAS.
FLOOD, MICHAEL
GLIESENER, JOHN
GRANT, WILLIAM
INGRIM, JOHN
KINGRY, JOHN
LEE, JAMES W.
LYDA, MICHAEL
MARTIN, SAMUEL
MC COLLUM, ASA

The Veterans

❖

FOR THE WINNERS, VICTORY WAS A HEADY feeling indeed. When the news of Lee's surrender reached the camps of the Army of the Potomac, a few men cheered, and at least one black regiment fired rifle shots in celebration. Yet most men met the news with quiet, and a surprising measure of compassion for the feelings of their defeated foes. The victors were simply glad that they had won, and more pleased that at last it was all over. While some Union veterans would retain hard feelings for their old foes for the rest of their days, the great majority seemed surprised at how quickly all the hostility evaporated after the war officially finished. They had never wanted to fight their own kind. Now it was done, they could not wait to put it all behind them.

It was not so easy across the lines. No Americans had ever been defeated in a war. Worse, Southerners had always entertained a substantial martial tradition. Now they were beaten. It was almost more than some could bear. After the first shock, though, most of these men's

feelings subsided to match those of the overwhelming number of their comrades.

Of those who could not face defeat, a few hundred simply melted into the countryside rather than face the inevitable formal surrender ceremony. A handful even committed suicide. For most, the extent of final resistance came when they buried their flags or tore them to shreds rather than give them up.

However the end came, and wherever, there was one question that had to be faced by every commander, Union or Confederate: How were all these men who had been soldiers for so long to be returned to civilian life? No one in the reunited nation had ever overseen disbanding armies of such proportions. Ironically, it proved to be a greater problem for the victors than for the vanquished side.

At the time of the surrenders in April and May of 1865, the Union Army had at least 1,034,000 men in uniform, spread from the Atlantic to the Pacific, and from the Gulf of Mexico to the Ohio River and beyond. Worse, units from any one state might be found in several armies hundreds of miles apart. An army could not simply return to its region and disband there. Instead each army corps had to be broken regiment by regiment, and the men sent home in that fashion. An even greater challenge faced the Union War Department. For potential pension purposes, Washington needed to be sure

Below: *Years after the war came to an end, the pride in what they had done lingered on. Johnny Rebs like these veterans at the Kentucky Confederate Home could refight all their old battles, with truth now the only casualty.*

that it had a service record of each man.

To achieve all this the authorities reversed the means by which men had been brought into the army, employing the very same apparatus. Without altering individual army organization, the men were to be gathered at rendezvous points where muster and pay rolls would be created. Then the same rail and shipping lines which had brought them to the war would be used to return the individual regiments to their home states. There they would be given their final discharges and their last pay issue.

How different it was for their one-time foes. Once a Confederate soldier turned in his weapons and signed his parole, he was no one's responsibility. He had no government of his own any longer, and the government to which he had surrendered certainly felt no obligation to help him out. When and how the Confederate soldier returned home was exclusively his own concern. Within a few weeks of the surrender, the roads of the South were crammed with former Confederates moving singly and in groups, walking and working their way home.

Their journey was made worse by having to pass through a ravaged South whose every miles reinforced again and a again the depth of their defeat. Reaching home could be even worse, as men found homesteads either destroyed by the armies, or else run down from neglect.

Some, too proud to concede defeat, headed toward the Rio Grande where they joined with a few generals who led their commands across the river into Mexico. As many as 5,000 Confederate veterans crossed the border, offering their services to both sides involved in the civil war

going on there, and settling down to start small colonies. Others went even farther, to Central and South America, to Europe, the United Kingdom, the Far East, and Canada. In all, about 10,000 Southerners took part in what became the largest expatriation movement in American history. Most eventually returned within a few years, disillusioned with their new homes, and longing for their old ones.

Due to continued resistance in some more isolated areas, especially Texas and Missouri, Washington did not declare an official termination of the "insurrection"

until August 20, 1866. Scores of small bands of Confederate veterans, mingled with the renegade Federals, and men who had never worn any uniform, operated simply as outlaws. Many were hunted down, and more simply disbanded, some to make careers putting the "wild" in the so-called Wild West.

Confederate leaders like Lee counseled all who asked, to accept the verdict of the war, go home, and start building the South anew. From the first, too, these leaders tried to instill in the men who had followed them a strong sense of pride in

Below left: *A captain in the US Veteran Reserve Corps. As the war progressed, both sides faced the growing problems of reduced manpower and the growing number of convalescent men able to perform light duties but not return to the front. Thus was born the Veteran Reserve Corps for men who could undertake light duties. They served as guards, recruitment officers and freed able-bodied men for service in the field. The Confederacy never successfully created a counterpart organization.*

Below: *A Civil War memorial at the Tupelo National Battlefield site in Mississippi.*

what they had stood and fought, and died, for. That their cause failed somehow only more ennobled their sacrifice, with the result that it was a rare Confederate indeed who held his head low in later years. Defeat did not mean dishonor, and with that soldier wit which even the hardest of circumstances could not dampen, some former Rebels even took to denying that they were in fact defeated at all. For many, humor was all they had with which to face a hard future.

For all the Johnny Rebs and Billy Yanks who went home after the end of the war,

there lay ahead a new life unlike that known by their forefathers, and which would not have come about had it not been for the war. The conflict had made the United States a power on the world stage, and for the first time even simple farm boys became in some degree aware of the interrelationship of nations, since every one of them came to know that foreign intervention in their war was a theoretical possibility. They knew that just across their border France was adventuring in Mexico, and many regiments that might otherwise have gone

to the victor's Grand Review parade in Washington were instead rushed to the Mexican border to prepare to meet the Emperor Maximilian's French forces if need be.

More immediately apparent to the men who served was what they had seen and learned of their own country. Boys who ordinarily might never have set foot outside their home counties had seen more than "the elephant" or the "monkey show" as they called the war. They had seen America, some travelling thousands of miles, exploring cities undreamed of in

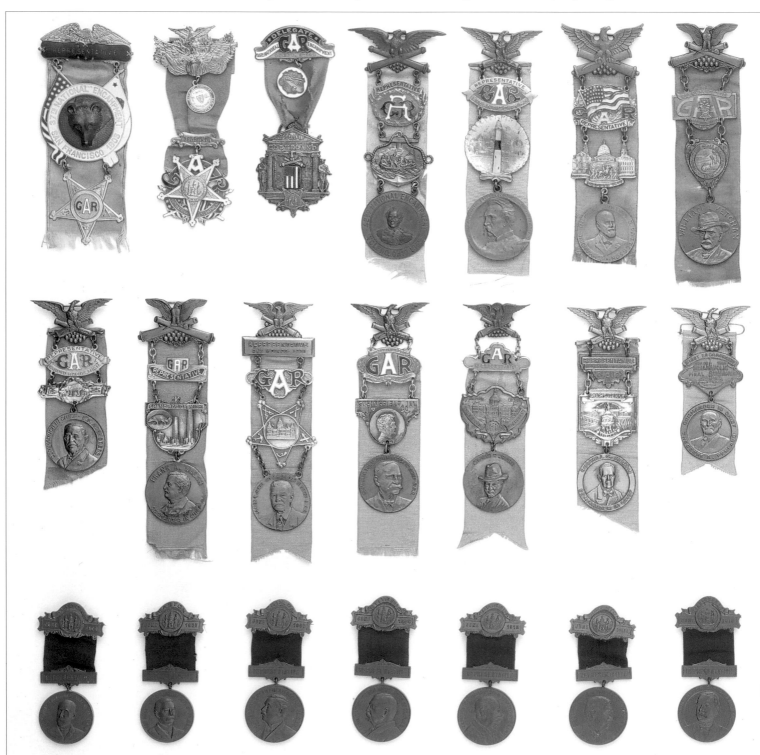

their youth, and other literally saw the world aboard ships that called at every major foreign port. Moreover, these men had seen deeper within themselves than most men are called upon to delve, tested by trial and fire, and most were not found wanting. They were in a degree changed men, a generation who had paid with their blood and received in exchange a greater awareness, self-confidence, and assertion. For the next half-century, the course of the growing American nation, the conquest of the West by gun and rail and plow, and the beginnings of empire outside its borders,

lay in the hands of the generation of battle-tested young men. and not just men who had worn the blue, either, for former Confederates as well took part. A host of these veterans settled the new lands west of the Arkansas. Not a few donned the blue to serve in the United States Army out west. Some even fought in the war with Spain in 1898. Both Joseph Wheeler and Fitzhugh Lee, major generals in the Confederacy, became major generals of volunteers in 1898, and were retired respectively, in 1900 and 1901, as brigadiers in the Regular Army. Ironically,

this made them and all the other veterans who returned to the military eligible to

Below: *Veteran's medals and Medals of Honor. At the start of the war, neither side had recognized awards for valor. To remedy this oversight, President Lincoln instituted the Medal of Honor (far right). Confederate efforts along these lines were unsuccessful due to wartime pressures. After the close of the conflict, veterans' organizations, even at regimental level, flourished in the North. Veterans from the impoverished South did not organize until the latter part of the 19th Century.*

receive a pension from the government they had once fought to overthrow. Only in America.

Veterans from both sides sat in Congress halls and legislatures, began industries and corporations. Within two decades after Appomattox, almost all of the once-Confederate states were again firmly under the control of the men who had been captains and colonels and generals in the armies of the gray. Major General John Gordon would become a United States' Senator and later governor of Georgia. General Francis T. Nichols became

governor of Louisiana, and Major General John S. Marmaduke won the governorship of Missouri. No-one has counted the total number of former Rebel officers who became governors, senators, and congressmen, or elected and appointed state officials, but surely it runs into the thousands. Several even became Republicans, like Lieutenant General James Longstreet and Major General William Mahone, earning no little criticism from their old comrades in arms. And one, the often-imposed-upon Lieutenant General Simon B. Buckner,

finally had a measure of repayment for the surrenders forced upon him during the war by being nominated for the vice presidency in 1896. His running-mate was one-time Union Major General John M. Palmer, and though they lost, still their candidacy truly represented the unity of the reunited states. Buckner's own son and namesake would become a lieutenant general in the United States' Army, dying on Okinawa in 1945.

In the years following the war, service in that conflict became almost a prerequisite for winning political office. Only two of

the presidents ever elected during the remainder of the century were not veterans. Andrew Johnson, Ulysses Grant, Rutherford B. Hayes, James A. Garfield, and Benjamin Harrison, had all been generals. William McKinley, who took office in 1897 and served until his death in 1901, had been a lieutenant in Rutherford B. Hayes' regiment. The United States as a whole was in the firm grip of men who had led its companies and regiments and armies in the great war for the Union.

In time the veterans came to stand side-by-side with their old foes—even in commemorating the war they had fought together. In the end, for many of the Civil War veterans, the old fraternal bonds of common blood and language made it impossible for the animosities of the war to last long. Indeed, many never felt real hatred of the enemy even as the conflict raged, as evidenced by the innumerable episodes of camaraderie and charity between the opposing sides. With the war done, only a few could preserve their anger. Men of both sides formed veterans' organizations, both to gather for fraternal reasons, and to lobby for pensions.

Washington granted increasingly attractive benefits to Union veterans, including land grants in the western territories for many, and the Grand Army of the Republic, as Union veterans styled their organization, became the most powerful political and social lobbying force of the era. Confederates, having no surviving government, could look only to their

Below: *Veterans of the 23rd Ohio meet together some 20 years after the guns fell silent. Beneath their battered banners they reminisce of days and comrades long gone.*

impoverished states for any sort of service pensions. A few were forthcoming from Virginia and other states, and in the end, ironically, Washington even began paying pensions to Confederate veterans and also to widows.

Immediately after President Lincoln's assassination, a group of Union officers formed the Military Order of the Loyal Legion of the United States, generally known by its much less cumbersome acronym "MOLLUS". Originally intended as a sort of guard to protect against chaos in the wake of Lincoln's murder, it quickly

turned to more peaceful pursuits. State commanderies were established in every Union state, and not many years passed before they began a systematic program of publishing papers by officers recounting their Civil War experiences. While many officers also belonged to the much larger Grand Army of the Republic, only officers were allowed MOLLUS membership, and the contribution of their collection and publication of memoirs and reminiscences of the war would prove to be a major boon to historians, just as the museums they established in their commanderies

kept alive for visitors the exciting years they had shared.

A flood of memoirs and histories began to emerge from the Northern and Southern officers alike almost as soon as the war ended. Captain Ed Porter Thompson of the old 1st Kentucky Brigade actually started writing his unit history in 1864, before the war was over, and hundreds more would follow. Having lost the contest by the sword, the old Rebels quickly won it with the pen. In 1876 former officers who had formed the Southern Historical Society began

publishing an annual series of "Papers" that would eventually run to more than 50 volumes, providing one of the most reliable sources of first-person accounts of the Confederate side. The *Confederate Veteran*, launched in 1892, published articles about the war and veterans' affairs for 40 years. Federal officers also wrote important books. McClellan, Custer, Sheridan, and dozens of others left behind important books telling their sides of the war. Sherman and Grant, wrote particularly fine memoirs. Some 50,000 books and articles would be published on

the war, perhaps a fifth of them by veterans from both sides.

As the years went on, the aging veterans' ranks grew thinner. Still there were thousands of them able to attend the 50th anniversary reunion held in Gettysburg in 1913, and a few thousand still remained to come to Pennsylvania again in 1938 for the 75th anniversary. But from then on their numbers dwindled fast, and the last of them died in the 1950s, just as America prepared for the centennial of the war they had fought. All are gone now—but they are remembered for what they did.

Far left: *The future could look bleak for some veterans who lost arms and legs. Artificial limbs like these were in some use by this period.*

Middle: *A detail from a Ohio monument at Vicksburg. Rather than construct a single state memorial, Ohio choose to erect a memorial for each of thirty-nine units that participated in the Vicksburg Campaign.*

Below right: *A disabled veteran from the war. For all too many the amputation of a limb was the only way to deal with shattered bones. In the 1860s his future was grim.*

The Reenactor

Taking up the hobby of what is known as War Between the States' Reenacting is not a decision to take lightly. It is demanding of your time, money, and physical and mental capabilities. While age is not an important factor, one needs to be reasonably fit. Reenactment events occur during all kinds of weather and temperatures. To fully experience them fully you must be willing to live in a tent or in the open at an event, march endlessly, drill often, wear wool when it is 100 degrees, and eat like soldiers did at the time. You cannot expect to stay in a hotel and live out of a cooler and experience the life of the 1860s soldier. Many who ascribe to the hobby try to include these modern conveniences and most of them just look forward to the battle reenactments as an opportunity to burn powder and shoot at Rebels or Yankees. But if you really want to relive history, to relive truly the period you are trying to portray, that is not the direction in the hobby that you should take.

Reenacting is an expensive hobby. Like

everything else in life you only get out of it what you are willing to put into it. Yes, you can save money by making some of your accoutrements, and by buying used uniforms and equipment, but you still must make that initial investment required just to set foot on the field, not to mention travel expenses to get to events. If you want to try it out first to see if you like the hobby, most reenactment units you may join can provide your basic needs to attend an event. Do not expect them, however, to keep you outfitted on "loaners" for a long period of time. They will expect you to

abide by the uniform and equipment guidelines of the group and to contribute to the organization with an accurate portrayal of what the members of the group represent.

Reenacting can also be very time consuming. Do not let the hobby consume all of your time; if you allow it to it will. Remember, it is just a hobby, not a lifestyle. With that in mind, however, bear in mind that the group you may belong to will have some expectations of your time contribution to the group's efforts.

You may ask, "Why even join a group?"

While it is not as demanding on your time to freelance as a reenactor, it is difficult to just show up at an event and fall in with a group. You must obtain members' permission and meet their expectations in your appearance and drill. This type of participation in the hobby could be more expensive, since you would have to have a wide range of equipment to maintain several historical impressions so as to be able to fit in at a moment's notice. As a

Below: *A national military park ranger gives a "living history" talk to a group of visitors.*

freelance it would be best to establish a relationship with several groups and try to be included in the ranks of one of them prior to an event you wish to attend, rather than just showing up. This could save you much time and effort at the event. Indeed, in many reenactments it is a requirement that reenactors be officially associated with a specific group if they wish to take part.

No one should be allowed on the field of a reenactment without the proper training. Every unit should have an officer devoted to monitoring safety at every event.

Accidents will occur but reenactments must take steps right down to the individual soldier to make it a safe hobby. Everyone on the field must remember that deaths have occurred, limbs have been lost, and lives have been changed due to some simple careless act in pursuit of the hobby. Alcohol, drugs, and gunpowder do not mix. There are many publications available on black powder safety. Check with your local gun dealer who sells black powder and caps for information. There are strict government regulations involving black powder and caps

It is recommended that you attach yourself to a group as a new member of the hobby. This will give you the training and drill instruction necessary to get your feet on the ground. To find the right group ask yourself what you want to portray, Union, Confederate, or both; infantry, cavalry, artillery, navy, marine, civilian; or a member of specific unit. Rank is earned in the hobby just like it is in the military of the day, so do not expect to be anything but a private when you start.

Once you have decided on what you want to portray you can check with

museums and historical societies for contact details of the local groups. You can also attend a reenactment event and scout the participating groups. One of the best places to search for a unit today is on the internet since many reenactment groups now have their own websites.

When you have made contact, ask a lot of questions. Check them out for the authenticity level and compare it to the standard you wish to achieve in your impression. All groups tend to vary in authenticity, from mainstream reenactors to hardcore living historians.

Within the hobby, those who achieve the hardcore title are often called "stitch counters," while those who achieve less than what is required in the mainstream reenacting community are called "farbs" ("far be it from me to question his impression"). Make sure the group you choose is comfortable for you or you can become frustrated by the group's inability to meet your expectations.

Now begins the search for the right clothing and equipment. During the war the troops were serviced by traders called sutlers, who sold all sorts of items from the backs of their wagons. It is much the same today, as sutlers follow reenactors and reenactments as well. They set up and sell their wares at all the reenactment events on what is called "sutlers' row," a sort of an outdoor reenactors' retail mall. Today's sutlers also sell their wares by mail order and on the internet.

When considering clothes its best to start from the feet up, because when your feet are unhappy so will you be unhappy.

Below: *Union general Ulysses Grant and some of his officers.*

The basic footwear of the War Between the States soldier was the brogan. The Federal Government issue brogan was a black ankle-high boot with the rough side of the leather turned out, wooden heels, thick leather soles fixed with wooden pegs, and leather shoelaces without metal eyelets. These boots have a left and right foot and should include a metal heel plate and toe plate so as to extend the life and wear of the brogan.

Confederate brogans vary in quality and style from the US-issue boot. One type of Confederate brogan has no left or right foot and is made with the smooth side of the leather out. It has pegged wooden heels and a stitched heavy leather sole. The fact that it doesn't have a defined left and right foot sounds a little uncomfortable, but it is not. In time the shoes will conform to the shape of your feet if you consistently wear them on the same feet. It is advisable to wear heel plates with any Confederate brogan, to extend the life of the boot. There is an advantage to wearing the smooth-side-out boot in a Confederate style as opposed to the US-issue rough-side-out brogan: the smooth-side-out boot repels water better and thereby could last longer than the rough-side-outs.

In the Confederate Army and in some Union regiments, such as the Garibaldi Guard, a battle shirt was worn when proper uniform coats were not available or when the unit's uniform required it. Battle shirts were large-fitting flannel shirts with voluminous ballooned sleeves. They often had some sort of piping and large pockets. In the Confederate Army the battle shirt was seen most often in the western theater of war.

Military trousers of the time were made

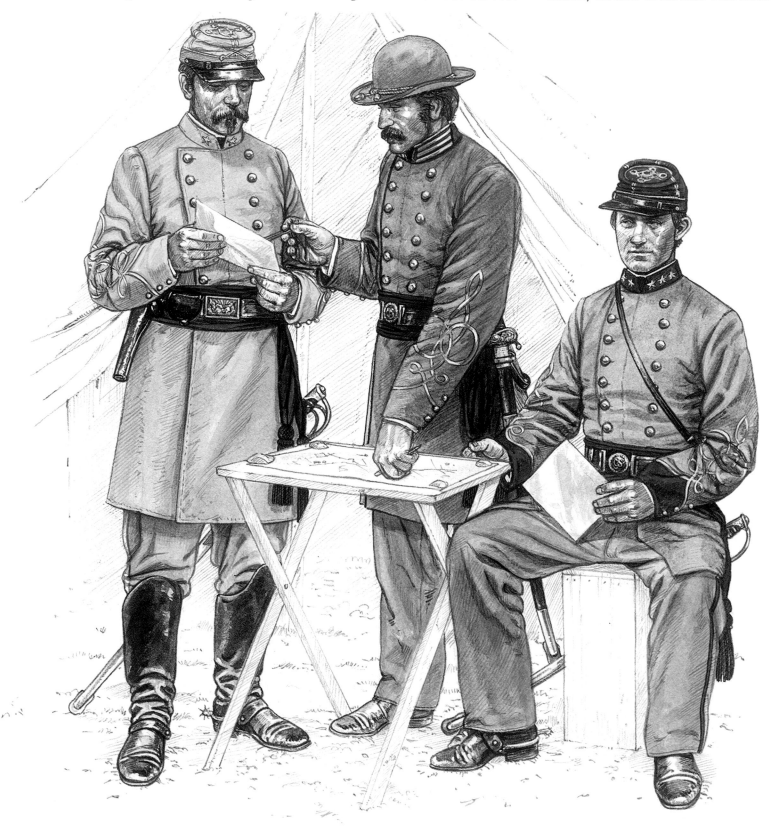

of wool, which had a very loose weave to the fabric. Three- and four-hole metal buttons were used on the fly and as suspender buttons. There were no hip pockets, only side pockets and on occasion a watch pocket. The waist of the pants was open in the back and tied or buckled. Other types of material used in trousers were a form of heavy jean material and a combination of wool and cotton called "linsey woolsey."

The reenactor will need to break in new trousers. Wool shrinks, but if carefully hand-washed in cold water and air-dried in a cool place, new trousers will soon acquire a used and comfortable look and feel to them. Never heat-dry, iron or crease your trousers.

Most War Between the States coats were made of the same fabrics as the trousers and, with the exception of the Federal-issue sack coat, were lined with various materials. As during the war, this lining could be to the reenactor's advantage in hot weather. As you perspire into the lining the dampness can serve to reverse the heat and cool your body.

Hats of the period varied but the soldier of the 1860s, for the most part, wore the forage cap in the Federal Army of the eastern theater, while the broad brim slouch hat was worn by Federal troops in the western theater and by the Confederate Army. The slouch hat, while

Far left: *Confederate officers of cavalry, infantry, and artillery.*

Middle: *Confederate quartermaster's uniform coat, front and rear.*

Below right: *Confederate artillery officer's coat.*

looking less military than the forage cap, was better suited to protect its wearer from the elements.

It is for the most part a far simpler task to research the uniforms worn by Federal forces during the war than those worn by Confederate soldiers. With the exception of many early war state units, most Federal regiments were supplied with government-issue uniforms. Even the non-conventional uniforms worn by early Federal troops are well documented, however, and many examples still exist in museums for study. The Smithsonian Institution has created a video tape (*Enlisted Uniforms of the Civil War*) with graphic detail on the styles, cut, and colors of the issue uniforms of the Federal government during the war. In addition there are numerous resources for viewing original photographs of Union soldiers.

The Confederate soldier, on the other hand, used an endless variety of "uniforms," including civilian dress. There was very little commonality, even among regiments. Uniform cloth was made locally and in Britain by a multitude of suppliers. Dyes varied from a greenish gray, cadet gray, and brownish gray to many shades of brown called "butternut." The styles of the coats varied by state issue, prewar militia, and issuing government depots.

Reenactors rarely use authentic items. Almost anything you need for your impression has been reproduced and is available from sutlers. An authentic weapon may be seen on occasion or an authentic item may be used in a living history presentation, but no reenactor in his right mind would risk endangering an historical and valuable artifact.

The best approach to researching what

would be appropriate for your impression is to seek out examples worn by the men in the unit you represent at museums and historic societies. Examine photographs of men who served in the unit you are portraying. There are several published sources for Confederate images, including William Albaugh's *Confederate Faces* series of books, William Turner's *Even More Confederate Faces*, and D. A. Serizano's *Still More Confederate Faces*. More resources for photographs include the series *Portraits of Conflict* and, for North Carolina troops, *State Troops and Volunteers* by Greg Mast. Extremely fine books describing and portraying the equipment, conditions, and battles of the Civil War forces have been written by William C. Davis and published as a trilogy by Salamander Books (*Fighting Men*, *Commanders*, and *Battlefields of the Civil War*).

Another excellent source for color photographs of original Union and Confederate uniforms is *Army Blue* by John Langellier and the Time Life Books, *Echoes of Glory*. The Union and Confederate uniform system is well explained and illustrated in *American Civil War Confederate Army* by Ron Field and *Civil War Uniforms* by Smith and Field. Manuals such as *Hardee's Tactics* and the *US Army Regulations* of 1861 have even been published in simpler versions that even modern man can understand. Authentic sutlers have already done a great deal of research on uniforms and can be of help during your search for the right impression.

Below: *Mounted officers at a reenactment of McPherson's Ridge, Gettysburg.*

The types of leather accoutrements and equipment available vary only in authentic quality. For example most sutlers who provide leather goods can come up with an adequately functioning cartridge box, but there are some sutlers who deal in reproduction cartridge boxes that are authentic in every detail.

The sutlers study authentic examples in private collections and museums and through practice and trial and error reproduce the original for use by the reenacting community. Naturally, the more authentic the piece the more you will have to pay for it. Quality costs. This adage applies to all uniforms and equipment offered by sutlers. You must study the requirements of your group.

Federal-issue leather accoutrements are fairly standard and vary only by model. Confederate leather accoutrements, however, can vary a great deal. Waist belts are a good example. Confederate waist belts were not made to any government standard. They were made and sold to the government or state by a multitude of manufacturers, including back-yard leather works. Belts varied in width, color, belt plate or buckle and material. When leather was in short supply some "leather" accoutrements were even made of heavy canvas material. At the other end of the scale, the finest in Confederate-used leather accoutrements were imported from suppliers in Britain.

Of special interest in the area of equipment for every reenactor will be a canteen. An study of canteens can be found in the book *Civil War Canteens* by Steve Sylvia and Michael O'Donnell.

The Civil War-style bedroll is made up of a wool blanket and a rubberized canvas

blanket, which serves several purposes. At night it is to be placed on the ground under you, rubberized side down, to separate you from the damp ground. It can also be used to wrap your wool blanket in when on the march to prevent rain getting onto it.

All manner of swords, sabers, and bayonets are available from sutlers, as are firearms for reenacting. There is a very wide range of reproduction weapons available today. Infantry arms include the Model 1842 Springfield, Model 1855 Springfield, Model 1861 Springfield, and

Model 1863 Springfield. Others, for Confederate use, include the Mississippi Rifle, Richmond Musket and Model 1853 Enfield. Sharps, Henry, and Spencer carbines are available for the cavalry trooper, along with the Colt Army, Colt Navy and Remington handguns.

Remember to purchase a weapon that fits your impression. If you are creating the impression of a Civil War infantryman you cannot go wrong with a Model 1861 Springfield rifle for a Union impression and a Model 1853 Enfield for a Confederate impression.

An authentic reenactor does not only aspire to perfection of his impression on the field but also to the public in what the hobby calls "first person." The reenactor now becomes a living historian by taking on the identity of a soldier. Create a person, never stray from the 1860s as your time. Become that person, talk and act like him. As you become completely absorbed in the character the viewing public loves it and you both learn from it.

Below: *Troops posing with their weapons at Harper's Ferry, Virginia.*

Brady's Images

❖

WHEN, LATE IN 1862, MATHEW BRADY posted a notice on the door of his New York studio reading, "The Dead of Antietam," it caused a sensation. It proclaimed an exhibition of photographs taken by him and his assistants of the aftermath of the bloodiest day in American history. It was the first time that most people witnessed the carnage of the American Civil War, bringing home to them the terrible reality and earnestness of the conflict.

In fact, the Civil War was the first to be covered in detail in photographs, and literally thousands of them were taken by Brady and his assistants operating out of New York and Washington, D.C. Before the war, photography itself was still in its infancy, but Brady forged a name for himself as a portrait photographer, choosing as his subjects the country's civilian and military leaders, and foreign dignitaries, and chronicling the nation's history as painters had done before him. As war loomed, Brady planned to document the war on a grand scale and

organized a corps of photographers to follow the troops in the field. Spurning the advice of friends who warned him of the battlefield dangers and financial risks, Brady proved with his war scenes that photographs could be more than posed portraits. He established the craft as an art form, such that photographs credited to his studios have inspired countless photographers ever since.

Brady's studio teams carried their cameras and darkroom equipment in horse-drawn carts around the camps and the battlefields, recording for posterity the commanders and soldiers, the weapons, the pageantry, the triumphs and the suffering of the sick and wounded, and sadly the death and sheer destruction in the cities and cornfields during the war.

For Brady himself, the war proved a financial disaster, and even the sale of his archive some years later could not save him from bankruptcy. In his final years, he said, "No one will ever know what I went through to secure those negatives." He died in 1896, penniless and largely unappreciated. It was not until decades later that his skill and artistry with the camera were acknowledged. Fortunately, many of his images survive. Mathew Brady is now considered to be the first person to take a camera on to the battlefield to create a comprehensive photo-documentation of war.

Below: Near Brandy Station, Virginia, Brady or one of his operatives caught sight of an unusually colorful group of men who belonged to a horse artillery brigade. Excessive light bounded off the canvas tent at the right rear, but a fellow standing just to the left of the tent did not get enough light.

Left: *William T. Sherman, who rarely wore gloves, posed some time after April 15, 1865. That is proved by the distinct white arm band visible at the end of his left sleeve. All Union officers were required to wear it during the six-month period following Lincoln's death.*

Right: *A group of marines with muskets and bayonets at the Washington Naval Yard, 1864.*

Below: *Brigadier General Joseph Hooker astride his horse. In February 1863 if you compare the careers of Generals Hooker and Grant, there were remarkable similarities. Both were accused of alcoholisma and both had established reputations as fighting generals. However, the bombastic Hooker was overwhelmed by the responsibilities of independent command whereas the modest Grant proved his there.*

Below: *Able-bodied seamen had none of the luxuries enjoyed by officers. The size of the crew of the Union gunboat Hunchback is proof that the men were crowded into the vessel. The banjo-strumming contraband and the newspaper reader close to the left may have been showing off. It is equally possible, however, that they were carefully guided as to their pose.*

Right: *Behind the makeshift flagstaff can be seen the effects of Fort Moultrie's fire on the officers' quarters and sally-port of Charleston's Fort Sumter. Since the fort had not been designed to fire at "home territory" almost all of its guns and embrasures faced out to sea.*

Left: *Four general officers. Harvard graduate Francis Barlow (left) enlisted as a private and became a brigadier. Winfield Scott Hancock (seated) became a general officer in 1861. John Gibbon (standing behind him) was a brigadier who had three brothers in gray. David B. Barney (right) became a major general in 1863.*

Right: *Major General Edward Ord with his wife and daughter. Ord was seriously wounded at Corinth and near Richmond.*

Below: *This big Dahlgren gun reveals details that were seldom clearly photographed. A colonel's left arm, resting on the elevating screw, gives a clear idea of the size of this device. Few photographs match this one in giving the viewer an instant appreciation of the role that hemp played in the war.*

INDEX

CREDITS AND ACKNOWLEDGEMENTS

The editor would like to thank William C. Davis, Russ A. Pritchard, David E. Roth, and W. C. Smith III, for their contributions to this book.

The publishers are grateful to the following individuals and organizations that have provided illustrations and/or artifacts for use in this book, including:

INSTITUTIONAL COLLECTIONS:

The Civil War Library and Museum, Philadelphia, Pa.; The Museum of the Confederacy, Richmond, Va.; the Virginia Historical Society, Richmond, Va.; Virginia Military Institute, Lexington, Va.; West Point Museum, West Point, N.Y.; Chester County Historical Society, West Chester, Pa.; Gettysburg Museum of The Civil War, Gettysburg, Pa.; Milwaukee Public Museum, Milwaukee WI.; The Union League of Philadelphia, Pa.; U.S. Army Ordnance Museum, Aberdeen Proving Ground, Md.; U.S. Army Quartermaster Museum, Fort Lee, Va.

PRIVATE COLLECTIONS:

Guy Leister, Sunbury, Pa.; William LePard, Ardmore, Pa.; Russ A. Pritchard, Mississippi; Mort Sork, Gladwyne, Pa., David Stewart, New Hope, Va.; Donald R. Tharpe, Midland, Va.; Don Troiani, Couthbury CT.; Bob Walter, Arlington Heights, Ill.; John G. Griffiths, Fredericksburg, Pa.; William L. Leugh, III, Chantilly, Va.; Wendell Lang, Tarrytown, NY.; William Smith, Boonsboro, Md.; J. Craig Nannos, Ardmore, Pa.; Benjamin P. Michel, Millburn, N.J.; George Lomas, Hatboro, Pa.; Michael J. McAfee, West Point, N.Y.; CDR James C. Reurmund, USN (Ret), F.R.N.S, Richmond, Va.

PHOTOGRAPHERS AND PHOTOGRAPH LIBRARIES:

Don Eiler of Don Eiler's Custom Photography, Richmond, Va., for the vast majority of excellent artifact photographs in this book; Anne and Rolf Lang, of Arlington, Va.; and the National Archives and Library of Congress for the many contemporary photographs reproduced here.